Philadelphia's Wissahickon Valley 1620-2020

METROPOLITAN
paradise

THE STRUGGLE FOR NATURE IN THE CITY

Volume 3 | Valley

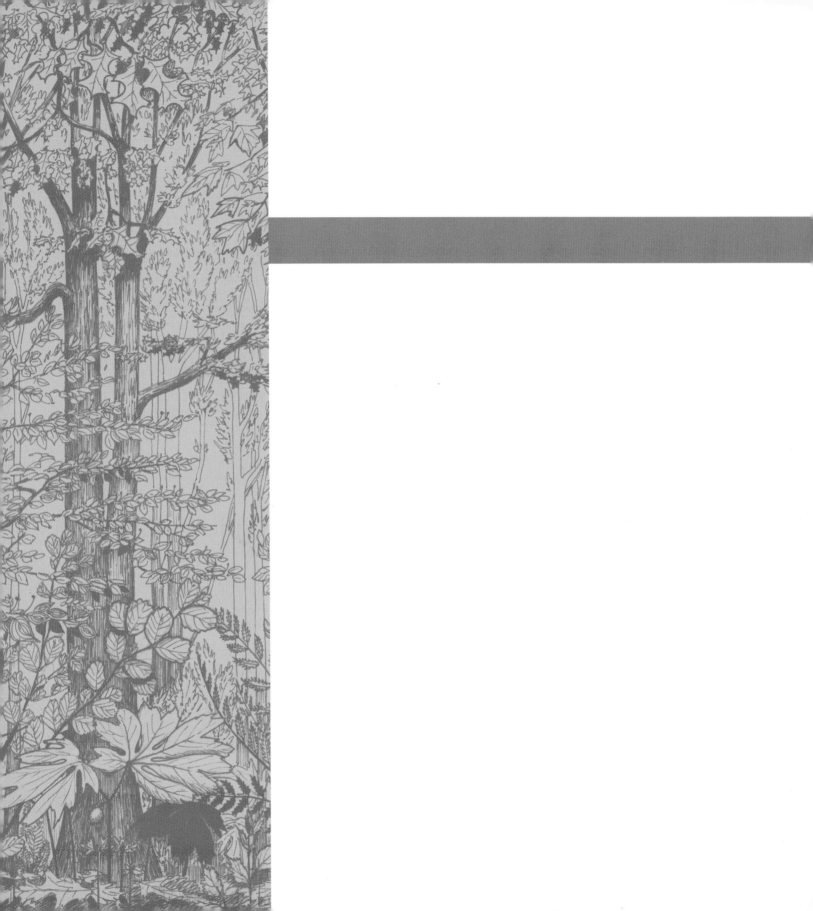

Philadelphia's Wissahickon Valley 1620-2020

METROPOLITAN
paradise
THE STRUGGLE FOR NATURE IN THE CITY

Volume 3 | Valley

David Contosta | Carol Franklin

SAINT JOSEPH'S UNIVERSITY PRESS

PHILADELPHIA

This publication was supported by the following foundations:

Drumcliff Foundation
Foundation for Landscape Studies, New York: David R. Coffin Grant
Levittees Foundation
Morris Arboretum of the University of Pennsylvania
Preservation Alliance for Greater Philadelphia
Whitemarsh Foundation

Library of Congress Cataloging-in-Publication Data
Contosta, David R.
Philadelphia's Wissahickon Valley, 1620-2020: metropolitan paradise, the struggle for nature in the city / David Contosta,
Carol Franklin. – 1st ed.
        p. cm.
Includes bibliographical references and index.
ISBN 978-0-916101-66-4
1. Wissahickon Creek Valley (Pa.)–History. 2. Wissahickon Creek Valley (Pa.)–Historical geography.
3. Wissahickon Valley Park (Philadelphia, Pa.)–History. 4. Environmentalism–Pennsylvania–Philadelphia Region–History.
5. Environmental policy–Pennsylvania–Philadelphia Region–History. 6. Nature–Effect of human beings on–Pennsylvania–Philadelphia
Region. I. Franklin, Carol, 1941- II. Title.
F157.W62C66 2010
974.8'11–dc22
                            2010024792

Cover photo, Volume 3: Graffiti on rocks at Devil's Pool. Source: Photograph by David Soffa

This volume was designed and typeset at Saint Joseph's University Press, Philadelphia.
Book design: Jonathan Dart and Kori Klyman
Slipcase and cover designs: Jonathan Dart
Image editing: James Brack and Patricia West and Hannah Coale
Index: Joseph Lea
Typeset in Optima, Stone Sans, and Skia
The paper meets the guidelines for permanence and durability of the
Committee on Production Guidelines for Book Longevity of the Council on Library Resources.
Printer: Courier-Kendallville, Kendallville Indiana

Published by
Saint Joseph's University Press
5600 City Avenue, Philadelphia, Pennsylvania 19131-1395
www.sju.edu/sjupress/

Saint Joseph's University Press is a member of the Association of Jesuit University Presses

Table of Contents

Metropolitan Paradise

Preface

Sacred to the Lenni-Lenape and to many early Europeans who settled in the area, the Wissahickon Valley has all the elements of "paradise" recognized in many cultures—the dramatic gorge with high cliffs, twisted rocks, dark hemlocks, sparkling water and the bountiful, rolling terrain directly to the north. Ironically, this paradise is part of a large, old North American city and its adjacent suburbs, and suffers from all the troubles of a modern urban area.

In this present era, we are seeing the explosion of cities and their metamorphosis into complex, densely packed, multi-dimensional regional organisms. With six billion people on the planet and a projected nine billion within 50 years, almost everyone will be living in a megalopolis. The 19th century division between nature and the city must be dissolved to make these new conurbations livable. Current scientific insights and technological advances can make a new fusion possible and bring natural systems back into the life of the city.

Philadelphia's Wissahickon Valley provides an unfolding narrative of this struggle to establish and maintain connected natural systems of adequate size, within a densely developed region. The preservation and restoration of this valley is offered as a model for metropolitan regions around the world. As Jaime Lerner, former mayor of the city of Curitiba in Brazil, has said, "The city is not the problem; the city is the solution."[1]

Because we believe, like Salman Rushdie, in the important payoffs of "mongrelism," the authors have combined insights from two different perspectives to create this book.[2] David is a cultural and intellectual historian, and Carol is a landscape architect with a foot in the camps of ecological design and ecological and cultural landscape restoration.

Both of us have a dogged and perverse devotion to Philadelphia, and like so many Philadelphians, we are hopelessly in love with Wissahickon Park and with the rural landscape of the middle valley above it. We have come to see this valley as a microcosm of changes in the American landscape over the past 400 years and believe that the lessons of its history, present treatment and creative future, are both universal and unique. This book is a journey into where we live locally, and by extension, into what we can do to resolve the crises of a natural world that is collapsing all around us.

Left Side
Suggesting that Philadelphia's rivers are vital to the life of the city, the Swann Memorial Fountain is the centerpiece of Logan Square on the Benjamin Franklin Parkway. The fountain looks both towards City Hall and the Philadelphia Museum of Art and to the beginning of the scenic drive along the Schuylkill River that leads to Wissahickon Park. The fountain was designed in 1924 by sculptor Alexander Stirling Calder and architect Wilson Eyre.

Adapting the tradition of "river god" sculpture, Calder created three large Native American figures to symbolize Philadelphia's major waterways: the Delaware River (a man), the Schuylkill River (a woman) and Wissahickon Creek (a girl).
Source: Photograph by Kori Klyman

Sustaining natural lands within the matrix of an increasingly pervasive urban landscape is crucial. These places are our "canary in the mine"—if they cannot succeed, all wildness is imperiled, impoverishing our lives and ultimately threatening our survival. If these wildlands are not connected systems, suffused throughout the fabric of our lives, they will not survive. There is a Quaker saying, "better to light a candle than to curse the darkness." This book is our personal candle in a remarkable and widespread effort to restore the Wissahickon Valley to some semblance of its former glory and to envision a future of bold, imaginative potentials.

How to Read this Book

In this book, the landscape of the Wissahickon Valley is viewed through many lenses— history, ecology, planning, architecture and landscape architecture. It is our hope that by intermingling these different areas of concern, until they fuse and create something new, like the flavors of separate ingredients in a stew, the reader will come away with a better appreciation of the complex and dynamic interaction between people and place.

This study of the Wissahickon Valley is undertaken in the tradition of two classic works: *The Making of the English Landscape* by W. G. Hoskins and *Design with Nature* by Ian L. McHarg. By examining changes in the English landscape over time, and the forces that shaped these changes at certain crucial periods, Hoskins pioneered the idea of the cultural landscape as an evolving entity. He demonstrated that landscapes are the product of the continuous laying down of later patterns of land use over earlier ones, with a surprising amount of the earlier fabric, still present and still germane. Following Hoskins example, each chapter concentrates on a significant period of transformation, highlighting key decisions, fulcrums of change and the physical patterns modified by these changes.[3]

Ian McHarg's *Design with Nature* laid the foundations for design decisions based on a scientific understanding of the natural and social processes that shaped, and continue to shape, each place. This understanding was to be rooted in the latest, best science from ecology to anthropology. Following the McHargian method, the Wissahickon Valley is analyzed and diagnosed. The constraints and opportunities are highlighted, and solutions are suggested that grow from its fundamental qualities. Out of the welter of the rich details of human interaction with the lower and middle valley, during so many generations, instructive patterns should emerge that can lead to better planning and policy decisions.[4]

One of the premises of this book is that complicated places are best understood by exploring the forces that shape them—natural, social, cultural and economic. Following Hoskins and McHarg, changes over time are presented as a series of layers. These overlays have often been compared to a "palimpsest"—sheepskin book pages from the Middle Ages that had been written on and then erased by scraping off the ink. The pages would then be reused, but the old texts were often still faintly visible. All landscapes are palimpsests, whether they are simply an accretion of geological strata and plant and animal life, or have had a long human history.

One of the often-overlooked forces that structure the landscape is human perception of the world (once called "worldviews," and now called "paradigms"). Preserved by a series of decisions, both intentional and accidental, the lower and middle Wissahickon Valley has been shaped and reshaped by the central paradigms of succeeding eras. Recognizing, analyzing and incorporating each accreted layer is the first step in creating solutions that grow out of the best of the past and build new value for a future that is increasingly fluid and refocused on new and different lifestyles.

This book has been written with several audiences in mind. The authors, who live in the valley and are very much part of its larger community, were torn between the desire to explore every detail of interest to local loyalists, and the hope that we will be generic enough to provide insights for other communities with parallel issues. To satisfy both these ends, the more esoteric details of this particular place—vegetation and wildlife, buildings and artifacts and individual movers and shakers—have often been separated from the main narrative and put on individual pages. Accordingly, it is not necessary to read this book straight through, and the reader should feel free to delve into it at any point, moving backwards and forwards to flesh out particular interests.

Wilderness—Park—Valley—Corridor

The Wissahickon Valley is the result of a unique blend of landscape, social and political realities, land management and lifestyle and the consequence of a number of very different proprietors over time. To reflect these proprietors, their choices and the impact of these choices on the landscape, this book is divided into four volumes: Wilderness—Park—Valley—Corridor.

Valley

The third volume is called "Valley" because it covers the period when people began to see the open space network as belonging not only to the park but also to a larger environmental system that encompassed the entire Wissahickon watershed. World War II brought technological advances, population growth and an explosion of knowledge that changed both attitudes and demographics. Standing as a colossus astride a ruined world, America saw its science and technology as the tools that would fashion a new world. With attitudes captured in the mottos of big business—"progress is our most import product" and "better living through chemistry"—the natural world seemed irrelevant and park and conservation movements lost their energy.

An earlier push to extend a protected Wissahickon corridor into Montgomery County stalled when suburban politicians raised fears of city control. The farmland of the middle valley began to disappear and several of the institutions that had been protecting open space lost their purpose and energy, and faced the prospect of moving or disappearing. Individuals and organizations that had struggled to enlarge Wissahickon Park boundaries and to conserve park quality had died or were no longer active.

In Philadelphia, after generations of political corruption, political and urban renewal came together as parts of the same reforming impulse. New expressways and major arterials, which were a part of this reform, accelerated the movement of people and businesses to the suburbs. Not only was a large strip of West Park surrendered to the Schuylkill Expressway but also a set of exit ramps, located at the juncture of Ridge Avenue and East River Drive, destroyed the entrance to Wissahickon Park from the city.

As energy flowed into a civic renaissance in center city, almost simultaneously, there were efforts to revitalize neighborhoods adjacent to Wissahickon Park—Germantown,

Mt. Airy and Chestnut Hill. While Germantown's efforts foundered, Mt. Airy established a racially integrated community and Chestnut Hill put in place an organizational reform tied to physical renewal. Reforms in the city as a whole, and in the neighborhoods of Northwest Philadelphia, radically changed governance and physical appearances but left the park largely untouched. Roxborough, on the west side of the creek, had been undeveloped and left largely in farmland. With the postwar building boom, this community was subject to rapid development that cut it off from Wissahickon Park and seriously damaged the drainage network.

In both the lower and middle valley, this postwar building boom threatened the natural systems at every level. The synergistic effects of many physical assaults—from global warming and acid rain to mismanaged storm water runoff, water pollution, soil loss and invasive exotic plants and animals—radically simplified the organization, structure, species composition and productivity of the forest ecosystem.

Perhaps the greatest threat to the integrity of Wissahickon Valley has been political. In spite of the urgent need to re-animate the city and to value and refurbish its assets, the Fairmount Park system was largely unacknowledged by Philadelphia governments.

By the 1960s, attitudes were changing. A growing sense that postwar answers had led to destructive consequences sparked a great moral revolution. Widespread redefinitions of civil, sexual and environmental rights were at the center of this new sensitivity. For both the middle and lower valley, these changes in national attitudes were reflected locally in a radical shift in perception—from the earlier idea of a scenic wilderness to an embattled ecosystem. Gradually, existing civic organizations were revitalized and new organizations formed to tackle these problems with more holistic solutions. In the mid-1950s, in response to a series of severe floods, residents of the middle valley founded the Wissahickon Valley Watershed Association (WVWA).

Over time, these organizations professionalized, expanded their membership base and moved into new areas of expertise. They brokered agreements with developers, obtained and held preservation easements, formed partnerships and spearheaded political action.

In Montgomery County, there was no cohesive park system and piecemeal development devoured large tracts of farmland. The only portion of the middle valley that escaped suburbanization was a strip of varying width along the creek, a continuing combination of public parkland, semi-public institutions and large private properties.

In the lower valley, the FOW broadened their interests to a watershed focus, paralleling the interests of the WVWA in the middle valley. With a wider, public ecological sensibility, citizen groups in the 1970s made far-sighted regional plans to include environmental regulations for the Wisssahickon Watershed in the Philadelphia Zoning Code. In the middle valley, plans were made for a major open space system. A local recognition of the deteriorating planet re-energized environmental consciousness nation-wide. This consciousness was reflected in a renewed FOW. The organization expanded it's focus, and through a number of very active and effective committees, became increasingly involved in sophisticated projects to control deer, repair and redesign park trails, rehabilitate park features and reestablish park vegetation.

Institutions bordering the creek began to acknowledge their relationship and their responsibilities to the corridor. Along with the involvement of civic groups and local institutions, grants from foundations and governmental agencies made large-scale studies and projects possible. The most significant and effective of these has been the Natural Lands Restoration and Environmental Education Program (NLREEP), which began in 1996 with a 26.6 million dollar grant from the William Penn Foundation to the Fairmount Park Commission. This grant was the impetus for important changes in the lower valley and within the administrative structure of the Fairmount Park system, driving the establishment of a Fairmount Park department devoted to managing natural areas.

During the 1980s and 1990s, Fairmount Park commissioned a master plan, and the a then a strategic plan. During this time the park system also received a large infusion of money from the William Penn Foundation, which led to a reorganization of park operations. Philadelphia's politics have continued to cripple the Fairmount Park system. The city's budget for the park has been disgracefully inadequate. Recent ordinances passed by city council, and ratified by voters in 2008, abolished the Fairmount Park Commission as an independent governing body and put the park system under in a new city agency. Despite mayor Nutter's committment to the Fairmount Park system, and his appointment of a strong Commissioner of a new Parks and Recreation Department, a nation-wide economic crisis has undermined hope of immediate reform and the chance to create sustainable financial support for this extraordinary resource.

In the course of examining the current problems of the park administration, the book proposes a new administrative entity. This regional entity would fund, coordinate and manage the corridor in both city and suburbs. However, bringing together the various stakeholders to support this new governance will require far greater cooperation among political entities, conservation groups, local institutions, governmental agencies, residents and businesses throughout the region. A Wissahickon Institute is also proposed as the "brains" of the Wissahickon Conservancy—under the umbrella of one of the region's educational institutions, which would spearhead research, and public information and be the physical archive of the valley—past, present and future.

12

Prosperity and Pressures

1945-1960s

Valley

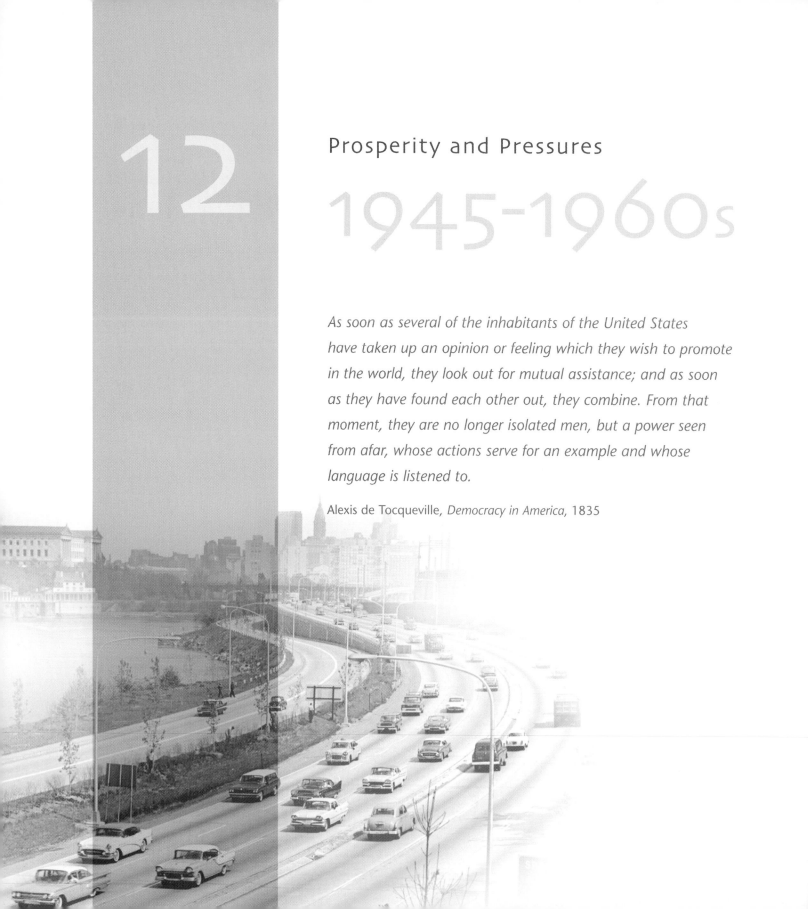

12

Prosperity and Pressures

1945-1960s

*As soon as several of the inhabitants of the United States
have taken up an opinion or feeling which they wish to promote
in the world, they look out for mutual assistance; and as soon
as they have found each other out, they combine. From that
moment, they are no longer isolated men, but a power seen
from afar, whose actions serve for an example and whose
language is listened to.*

Alexis de Tocqueville, *Democracy in America*, 1835

By the war's end, in the late summer of 1945, Philadelphia was contentedly corrupt and suffering from a number of physical constraints. Non-profit civic groups, such as the Citizen's Council on City Planning, had been preparing for several decades to take on the task of reform and renewal. The emphasis was almost entirely on cleaning up city politics and reinventing an ugly and moribund downtown.

Southeastern Pennsylvania, like many other parts of the country, experienced a postwar boom, but this prosperity drained jobs, people and wealth to the suburbs. These changes affected the communities of the lower Wissahickon Valley in different ways. As the factories in Germantown closed, these communities decayed further. The residential areas in Mt. Airy and Chestnut Hill were not as affected by these demographic changes, but lost a number of their wealthiest residents. Their commercial districts also suffered, unable to compete with the suburban shopping centers growing up just outside the city. The old estates along School House Lane in East Falls remaining largely unchanged for a decade or two after the war. Lower Roxborough stayed relatively static and working class. Upper Roxborough, flat and abutting Montgomery County, was still in open farmland. The far northwestern end of the city, like the immediate suburbs beyond, became a prime target for new residential and commercial development. In Upper Roxborough, although within city boundaries, development patterns of the emerging automobile suburbs would shape the new roads, houses and shopping centers.

Of all the Wissahickon neighborhoods in the city, Chestnut Hill was most successful in confronting the threats of the postwar period. A reawakening in Chestnut Hill directly paralleled postwar reforms that focused on the renewal of center city Philadelphia. Both the Philadelphia and the Chestnut Hill Renaissances were based on the understanding that physical revitalization was not possible without important changes in governance.

In Chestnut Hill, a resourceful group of leaders organized an innovative local government that allowed them to transform the deteriorating main street commercial district into a lively, functional and physically attractive community core. Unfortunately, neither renaissance tackled the issue of the renewal of Fairmount Park and the urgent need to continue to interweave Philadelphia's extraordinary stream corridor parks into the fabric of city life.

The Philadelphia Renaissance

DOWNTOWN PHILADELPHIA

The model (33 feet long by 14 feet wide) was made for the Better Philadelphia Exhibit by the Philadelphia City Planning Commission. Exhibited in September through October of 1947 on the fifth floor of Gimbel's Department Store, it showed what city planning was, how it works and how it could change the face of the city. The model was made in 13 sections. At rest it showed Philadelphia as it was in 1947. Each section would flip over to reveal the proposed transformation as a recorded speaker explained the vision for the future. Photograph by Ezra Stoller.
Source: Esto

During and after World War II, Philadelphia leaders created a series of civic groups whose goal was to initiate urban renewal through political reform. They understood that postwar urban renewal could not take place without major structural changes in administration. They also realized that exciting urban renewal projects could galvanize widespread support for political housecleaning.

In 1940, Walter Phillips, a Philadelphia lawyer and civic activist, organized young reformers in a group called the City Policy Committee. The purpose of this group was to focus on the city's future. Phillips was involved in an earlier charter reform effort that failed, and he saw this new committee as a longer-term solution to civic and political reform. Phillips had met and been greatly impressed by a young Michigan planner, Edmund Bacon. He helped Bacon get a job in Philadelphia, as the Director of an independent advocacy organization called the Philadelphia Housing Association, and invited him to join his newly formed City Policy Committee. Bacon led the group to concentrate on city planning, and in 1941 he persuaded the National Planning Conference to hold its meeting in Philadelphia.

Following this conference, the Mayor, Robert Lamberton, supported reform efforts to reinvigorate the city planning commission (originally established in 1929) with professional staff. A major element pushing the city towards an effective planning commission was the massive federal funds available to cities that had an effective planning commission and had adopted a city plan. Before the group had a chance to move the issue forward, Lamberton died in office and was replaced by City Council President Bernard Samuel, who (with most Republicans) opposed planning efforts. In 1942, despite Samuel's corrupt, inefficient and disinterested government, the planning commission was re-configured by an act of city council. Robert Mitchell was made its director.

In 1943, the Citizens Council on City Planning was formed to convince voters and government alike to support the reorganized planning commission and to act as a "watchdog...to preserve the integrity of the plan through different administrations in city government."[1] The citizens council led by Phillips and Bacon sponsored studies by architects Oskar Stonorov and Louis I. Kahn to replan Philadelphia's residential neighborhoods. This work, combined with the archive of earlier planning proposals, brought together by Robert Mitchell, led to the "Better Philadelphia Exhibition."

This 1947 exhibition showed the decayed city with all its problems. Various sections of the model could be flipped over to illustrate proposed projects and a vision for Philadelphia in 25 years. These projects included the removal of the "Chinese Wall" around the city, renewal of Center City and Society Hill and the construction of the Schuylkill Expressway. During the Christmas season that year, the model was shown to the public in Gimbel's Department Store, and over 385,000 visitors came to see it. Visually compelling, it engaged Philadelphians in critical municipal issues and helped lay the groundwork for political reform that included city planning as a key ingredient.[2]

Mitchell hired Bacon to work for the planning commission on this exhibtion. After its close, Bacon stayed on as staff and when Mitchell left the Commission in 1948 and Raymond Leonard, the next director died of Leukemia. Bacon become the executive director. Bacon was a powerful force in the city, able to reach a broad spectrum of movers and shakers and realize a range of key projects to revitalize the city.

A new city charter reinforced these planning efforts. In 1947, a bipartisan group of business and civic leaders established the Greater Philadelphia Movement to lobby for state legislation to establish a Philadelphia Home Rule City Charter Commission, with power to reorganize the city government.[3] Three Philadelphia lawyers, Robert T. McCracken, Abraham Freedman and William Schnader, drafted a new city charter. The reformers lost their first bid to take over City Hall, but the campaign pushed newspapers and local businessmen into investigating municipal corruption. The revelation of serious graft, kickbacks, favoritism and outright theft of city funds contributed to approval of the new city charter and to the triumph of the reform slate in 1951, breaking the hold of the Republican political machine, in office for nearly 80 years.

The new city charter created a "strong mayor" system, which gave the mayor broad appointive powers without the need for confirmation by city council. These appointees reported directly to the mayor and his staff. The council was reduced in size from 21 to 17 members, and the office of managing director was created to oversee all municipal departments. The civil service was overhauled to lay the foundations for a genuine merit system. The charter also called for a number of new boards and commissions, and for the strengthening of others that already existed. The city planning commission, with the redevelopment authority, became important forces within the reformed city government.[4]

Efforts to renew declining communities adjacent to Wissahickon Park grew out of the same forces and the same beliefs that produced the Philadelphia Renaissance and involved a number of the same people. This movement bound urban revitalization and physical change to political reorganization—integrating infrastructure and new facilities into both the appearance and the economic health of the city.

Joseph S. Clark (middle) and Richardson Dilworth (right) "sweeping out" corruption from City Hall, in a 1947 campaign photograph.
Source: Urban Archives, Temple University Libraries, Philadelphia, Pa.

12:1

The Schuylkill Expressway

"The Pennsylvania Department of Highways contemplates the early construction of a controlled-access highway from the eastern terminus of the Pennsylvania Turnpike at the intersection of US 202 and PA 23 at King of Prussia, to the Montgomery-Philadelphia county line near the Schuylkill River Bridge on City Avenue. This will justify a new artery within the City of Philadelphia to handle the traffic, as the existing highway facilities in the vicinity of City Avenue are inadequate even for present traffic. The Commonwealth has recognized that inter-regional highways connecting industrial and consumer centers can be fully effective in building up the economic vitality of the state only if adequate and efficient links are developed to the major destinations in the cities. Therefore, it has included in its program the construction of the Schuylkill Expressway, Vine Street Expressway and Roosevelt Expressway, which would carry traffic from other parts of the state highway system and the Pennsylvania Turnpike to the city center, to the industry of Northeast Philadelphia and South Philadelphia, and to the Port of Philadelphia."[1]

In 1932, the Regional Planning Federation, the predecessor agency to the Delaware Valley Regional Planning Commission (DVRPC), proposed a parkway system around Philadelphia. These parkways would be similar to those built by Robert Moses around New York City—four lanes with

Schuylkill Expressway soon after completion, shown here going through West Park adjacent to the Schuylkill River. The park drive (once West River Drive, now Martin Luther King Drive) can be seen directly beside the river. Source: Urban Archives, Temple University Libraries, Philadelphia, Pa.

controlled access, stone bridges and natural vegetation in the median strip and along the edges of the roadway. The proposed route, to be called the "Valley Forge Parkway" would run along the west bank of the Schuylkill River and connect Fairmount Park with Valley Forge National Historic Park. "Without a 'power broker' like Moses to coordinate efforts, the parkway system never came to fruition."[2]

After World War II, the Philadelphia City Planning Commission returned to a river route to Valley Forge. Instead of a parkway, the new road would be an all-vehicle expressway. In 1948, when the Pennsylvania Turnpike (I-76) was extended east from Harrisburg to Valley Forge, officials at the

Pennsylvania Department of Highways and the Pennsylvania Turnpike Commission planned an extension of this road southeast into center city Philadelphia, 20 miles away.

This proposed road was designed by the engineering firm of Clarke and Rapuano and became the Schuylkill Expressway. It followed the river corridor to Valley Forge, the same route taken by railroads a century earlier. The expressway, constructed between 1949 and 1959, ran through the edge of West Park and paralleled West River Drive, one of the historic carriage roads that linked East and West Park to Wissahickon Park.

While construction of a major arterial out of the city was central to plans for Philadelphia's revitalization, the route chosen has had a terrible impact on parkland in the city and on the entrance to Wissahickon Park. Failure to find a route that would not preempt the river and the failure to route the expressway away from West Park and the mouth of Wissahickon Creek illuminates the political weakness of the Fairmount Park Commission in the debate.

Even the engineers who designed the road struggled to avoid damage to West Park. "[Micheal] Rapuano spent two years trudging through Fairmount Park, trying to find a way to bring the expressway through the park without ruining this urban retreat. One of his solutions was to elevate the proposed expressway on a 100-foot-high platform through one mile of the park…. Meanwhile, Bill Allen, [chief engineer for Clarke and Rapuano]… charted a more pragmatic course in his design of the Schuylkill Expressway. Since resistance came from all fronts— from the communities through which it would be built, from the environ-mentalists who feared that Fairmount Park would be ruined (and that access to the Schuylkill River would be cut off), from the railroads whose tracks paralleled the route of the expressway, and from the University of Pennsylvania whose athletic fields would have to be sacrificed—Allen followed the path of least resistance by designing a riverside route [and] trying to squeeze in lanes wherever he could. This legacy lives on today in the form of underpowered inter-changes… and the absence of acceleration-deceleration lanes."[3]

Members of the Save the Park Committee, like Hannah Sweeton, felt strongly that the new Schuylkill Expressway would "gouge out the natural beauty of our state . . . because it is necessary for progress!

Where there is no vision, the people perish: Money comes and goes, but great treasures like our Fairmount Park… should not be left to the ruthless [few] who are for nothing but what they can get out of it."[4]

John B. Kelly (park commission member, leading Democrat, high-profile civic leader, rower and father of Princess Grace of Monaco) fought hard to persuade the city and state to build the expressway west of park boundaries. In hindsight it appears that avoiding West Park was never a real option. It eliminated the need to purchase land and demolish buildings and would have complicated a simple river corridor solution.

Most other Philadelphians—the Philadelphia Chamber of Commerce, the newspapers, and the general public—saw objections to the park route as snobbish and elitist, and elected officials had little impetus to listen to demands for alternatives. Richardson Dilworth, mayor of Philadelphia at the time of the construction, later confessed that allowing the Schuylkill Expressway to go through the park had been one of his worst decisions as mayor.

---

1. Philadelphia City Planning Report, 1950.

3. Schuylkill Expressway Historic Overview Website: phillyroads.com/roads/schuylkill/

2. Ibid.

3. Joseph S. Clark, Jr., and Dennis J. Clark, "Rally and Relapse," *Philadelphia: A 300-Year History* (New York, 1982), 696-98.

4. Hannah Sweeton, member of "Save the Park," c. 1955

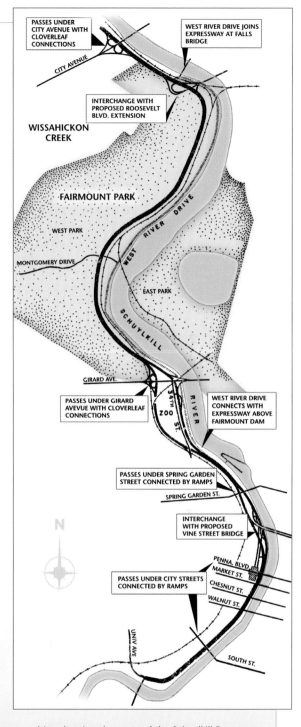

Map showing the route of the Schuylkill Expressway from south of Center City to East Falls, just below the mouth of Wissahickon Creek. The map shows this expressway cutting a long corridor (400 acres) through West Park.
Source: Urban Archives, Temple University Libraries, Philadelphia, Pa.

The Post-Reform Fairmount Park Commission

Philadelphia's 1951 home-rule charter restructured city government and changed the relationship of the Fairmount Park Commission to the city administration. The new strong mayor system weakened the authority of the park commission, even though it continued to operate as a separate entity under its 1867 state charter. With the adoption of the Philadelphia Home Rule Charter, the Fairmount Park Commission was incorporated as part of the Philadelphia City government and designated a "departmental commission" under the Department of Recreation. As city employees, the park staff was now part of a more stringent, structured civil service, and were hired, fired and paid by the city. These changes failed to solve many of the old problems of park governance and funding. Lack of competent, professional management still plagued the park system.

The Fairmount Park Commission had 16 members. Six of these commission members were ex-officio. They included the mayor, the president of city council, the commissioner of public property, the recreation commissioner, the water commissioner and the chief engineer and the surveyor of the department of streets. There were also 10 citizen members, appointed for five-year terms by the Board of Judges of the First Judicial District of the Pennsylvania Court. Individuals were nominated, either by themselves or others. A panel of judges interviewed the nominees and selected names to be sent to the Board of judges. In an "unofficial" selection process, the Board of Judges was frequently pressured by the major's office to appoint purely political candidates. These political appointees often knew little about the park system or the individual parks within it and still less about appropriate, modern park management.[5] Some of the citizen park commissioners continued to come from old Philadelphia families. Members of the Price, Ballard and Widener/Dixon families have been notable examples. Over the years, these individuals have made exceptional contributions as strong park advocates. With deep roots in the community, they felt a sense of "ownership" and responsibility for the park.[6] These members frequently contributed considerable amounts of their own money for park projects. They also took leadership on difficult and controversial issues.

Ironically, the reform of city government left a legacy of administrative confusion for the Fairmount Park system. The park commission now submitted budget requests to the city's managing director, who (in theory) passed these requests, along with park concerns, to the mayor. By this time, about 80 percent of the park commission's annual budget came from the city's general funds, derived from tax revenues. The remainder came from grants and earmarked trust funds. However, even when the park system raised its own money, these revenues went into the general fund and were not necessarily spent on park maintenance and capital improvements. This situation led to serious deficits in the park budget, which would worsen over time.[7]

In its original charter from the state, the Fairmount Park Commission had been granted the power of eminent domain, which had allowed it to condemn and take private property for park purposes. With the reorganization of city departments, it was no longer clear whether the commission still had this authority. The resulting confusion, coupled with a lack of political will to use eminent domain on behalf of the park and the fear of offending political constituencies, meant the park commission largely abandoned this tool to acquire land.

In addition, the head of the recreation department (appointed by the mayor) was a member of the mayor's cabinet, but the director of the Fairmount Park Commission was not. The commission thus had no direct advocate at City Hall, with the result that money allocations to the Recreation Department have been as much as six times higher than appropriations for Fairmount Park. In the postwar period, Philadelphia leadership clearly did not see the park system as an engine of urban renewal. As the reform movement lost steam and the city faced increasing budgetary constraints, few in city government had the vision or motivation to support Fairmount Park.[8]

Germantown Failure and Chestnut Hill Success

By the late 1880s, Germantown was densely built up and industrialized. As it lost the last of its rural qualities, prosperous residents left for Mt. Airy, Chestnut Hill and elsewhere. Once a manufacturing hub, during the Depression and World War II, Germantown gradually declined, as heavy industry shifted to other regions of the country. The postwar period exacerbated this decline, bringing unemployment, poverty and all the attendant social problems, including soaring crime rates.

The post-World War II boom in modestly priced suburban housing was another factor in Germantown's decline, providing an alternative to city living for the white middle class. New shopping centers—and later enclosed malls in these outlying communities—drained customers from Germantown's commercial spine along Germantown Avenue—the old Ridge Road.[9]

The movement of the white middle class out of Germantown accelerated when the pernicious practice of "redlining" was successfully challenged in the courts. Redlining is "the practice of denying or increasing the cost of services, such as banking, insurance, access to jobs, access to health care, or even supermarkets to residents in certain, often racially determined, areas. The most devastating form of redlining, and the most common use of the term, refers to mortgage discrimination."[10] Activists in Chicago apparently coined the term in the late 1960s. A red line circled districts on a map where lending institutions would not invest because they believed they would lose money. These areas were almost entirely poor, minority neighborhoods.[11]

Philadelphia Quakers saw redlining as a social justice issue. The effort to end these exclusionary policies was spearheaded by the Chestnut Hill Monthly Meeting's Germantown and Chestnut Hill Housing Committee, under the direction of Margaret Levy and William Coale. With the end of redlining in the early 1950s, African Americans confined to the blighted, low-income areas of North Philadelphia were finally able to borrow money to buy houses in adjoining Germantown. In the racially charged atmosphere of the time, this influx of people from North Philadelphia increased the movement of residents out of the city—an unintended consequence of good intentions. These pressures on the neighborhoods of Northwest Philadelphia also led to the formation of Mt. Airy's civic organization, the West Mt. Airy Neighbors (WMAN). Their bold stance on integration stabilized that community and was a national model for social justice.

12:2

West Mt. Airy Neighbors (WMAN)

Growing out of neighborhood concern about "white flight" and "block busting," this civic organization was founded in 1959 by George Schermer, the first Director of Philadelphia's Human Relations Commission and by an interracial group of 50 families. West Mt. Airy neighbors proved its mettle by successfully lobbying Philadelphia City Council to pass several key ordinances and by pressuring real-estate agents to stop contributing to white flight through prejudicial practices. This organization has also educated itself about zoning and used this tool to slow the destructive neighborhood trend of subdividing large houses into apartments or turning them into institutions. Several decades later WMAN published a handbook, *The Mt. Airy Quality of Life*, for block captains, activists and residents. It is particularly useful as a guide to community problem solving and as a primer on Philadelphia zoning.[1]

Like Chestnut Hill, Mt. Airy has been home to a number of professionals, academics, city officials and wealthy businessmen. Like Chestnut Hill, it is also divided between a wealthier west side, adjacent to the park, and the less affluent community on the east side of Germantown Avenue. Unlike Chestnut Hill, which was WASP and elitist in the years directly after World War II, Mt. Airy's early commitment to forceful action in the area of race relations, along with the diversity of WMAN membership, made this community a welcoming home for a multiplicity of people.[2]

Sometimes overshadowed in its achievements by the Chestnut Hill Community Association (CHCA), WMAN has preserved the Quaker legacy of social justice. West Mt. Airy remains a model of a stable, racially integrated community in the United States. After long years of economic decline, this community is having a renaissance, due in no small part to the recent efforts of WMAN to promote businesses along Germantown Avenue.

Before the establishment of WMAN, West Mt. Airy residents banded together in the Henry Home and School organization (a parent-teacher association) to enrich the public school curricula with after-school art classes and to ease racial tensions at the school. In 1953, they founded the Allen's Lane Art Center, which not only provided fully integrated after-school classes, but also a summer day camp. The center's large property, and stone house, called Medlock Wold, is on Allen's Lane between McCallum and Greene Streets. It was given to Fairmount Park by the Woodward family. This facility is near, but not actually adjacent to Wissahickon Park.

West Mt. Airy is the home of a number of religious, cultural and even commercial organizations that by their mission, diverse membership and programs reinforce the social justice mission of WMAN, and the tolerant, activist image of the community.

These organizations include the Lutheran Church on Germantown Avenue, the Unitarian Church and the Jewish Center on Lincoln Drive, and Weavers Way Food Cooperative across from the Henry School. In 1969, over 35 religious organizations banded together to create the Northwest Interfaith Movement (NIM), with a mission "to build a more just and sensitive community through advocacy and service." Weavers Way, a member-owned retail cooperative, founded in 1973, serves as an informal town hall, information exchange and social hub.[3] These local organizations also provide an extensive network of adult education classes, drawing people from all over the city and the northwestern suburbs.[4]

1. Cynthia Jackson-Elmoore, "The Role of Institutions in Community Building: The Case of West Mt Airy Philadelphia," in (ed.) Richard C. Hula, Barbara Ferman and Patrick Kaylor, *Nonprofits*, 93-120.

2. WMAN Website: wman.net/mtairybiblio.pdf.

3. Phyllis Knapp Thomas with photographs and maps by Dennis Johnson (both WMAN members), *Mount Airy in Philadelphia, A Pioneering Community*. This reference can be found in the Lovett Memorial Library, in the Mt. Airy branch of the Free Library of Philadelphia.

4. As one of the few integrated communities in the United States, West Mt. Airy has been the subject of academic research and numerous newspaper and magazine articles. Long-time West Mt. Airy Neighbors Board member Patricia Henning has compiled an extensive bibliography on Mt. Airy, which can be found at the WMAN Website: wman.net/mtairybiblio.pdf.

A number of organizations at the time attempted to restore Germantown to economic health. The most important of these organizations were the Germantown Historical Society, the Germantown Businessmen's Association, the Germantown Community Council, the short-lived Concern for Germantown, the Twenty-Second Ward Planning Committee and Colonial Germantown, Inc. Because all these volunteer civic associations were in competition with each other for very limited resources, they unwittingly contributed to Germantown's decline.

Perhaps the most far-reaching effort was the 1960 plan by Concern for Germantown called "A Proposal for the Revitalization of the Heart of Germantown," which recognized the need for an integrated social and economic plan. Perhaps the most misguided effort was the campaign by Colonial Germantown, Inc., led by local insurance executive Arthur O. Rosenlund, to make Germantown into a major tourist attraction. Beginning in 1946 and extending for nearly three decades, Rosenlund and a group of historic preservationists tried to rehabilitate the old Market Square at Germantown Avenue and School House Lane into what this development group called a "Miniature Williamsburg."[12] Most of the genuine colonial era buildings in the square had been demolished decades earlier. To create a colonial enclave, the group tore down distinguished Victorian structures, including the ornate, terracotta, polychromatic Germantown Mutual Life Insurance building by architect George T. Pearson (1847-1920), replacing them with bland Colonial Revival buildings. The miniature Williamsburg effort was a failure.[13]

Other important decisions made at the time ought to have spurred the rehabilitation of Germantown: the commitment by a major institution—Germantown Friends School—to remain in the community; the building of several new public schools; a new public library and improvements to Vernon Park. Despite these endeavors, the time was not right for Germantown. Its social capital had unraveled, and the forces of decline were too great for any single individual or group to reverse. Loss of its economic base and of its wealthy, powerful residents, lack of collaboration among civic groups and lack of leadership from local and municipal government (which was concentrating almost entirely on the problems of center city) meant that Germantown's decline would continue. Partly from a fear that Chestnut Hill would follow the downward trajectory of Germantown, and partly because of the lessons learned by civic groups there, the effort to revitalize Chestnut Hill was born.[14]

Chestnut Hill was fundamentally a residential community whose wealthier residents had either inherited money or made good livings downtown as lawyers, bankers, brokers and corporate executives. However, as in Germantown, the commercial spine had deteriorated by the early postwar period. Nearly 30 percent of the available floor space along Germantown Avenue was vacant, leaving only about 40 stores in operation. Low commercial rents—only 5 cents per square foot in some cases—left little incentive for landlords to improve their properties. Shop facades were disfigured by crumbling neon signs. There were 17 of them altogether north of South Hampton Avenue, one of which was over 10 feet high. Most of the original colonial and Victorian facades had been "modernized" to create shoddy storefronts, ruthlessly attached to the old buildings. The revival of Chestnut Hill began with cooperative efforts to rescue the commercial spine, spearheaded by the organizational genius and imaginative solutions of one crusading maverick—Lloyd P. Wells.

12:3

Lloyd P. Wells (1921–)

Lloyd Wells had a gift for building connections. He was tireless in his drive to find solutions and would not give up. When he ran into obstacles or seemingly insurmountable opposition, he created new organizations and invented novel strategies to achieve his ends. Through his leadership and vision he changed both the governance and the physical appearance of Chestnut Hill, saving the community from the decay that afflicted many sections of Philadelphia after World War II.

An outsider, Wells settled in Chestnut Hill in 1947 after his marriage into an "old" Chestnut Hill family. Being dyslexic and with no high school diploma, he believed that his employment potential was limited. Wells and two friends started a hardware store (Hill Hardware) just south of the intersection of Germantown Avenue and Bethlehem Pike.[1]

Wells was visionary and very persuasive and charismatic. He was also a man of strong opinions and a determination to do things his way. Ultimately, he angered a number of residents who saw him as arrogant and high-handed. In part because of lessening community support, he left Chestnut Hill for varying periods, moving away permanently in 1976. Now living in Florida and in Maine, he continues to work with others to keep the community's long running but continually threatened quasi-government from becoming prey to individual ambitions and national party politics. Difficult as ever, he continues to aggravate his enemies and alienate his friends.

In Maine, Wells has established the non-profit Center for Consensual Democracy, which works with grass-roots civic associations to provide ideas and information on the organization and effective management of local communities. He has recently co-authored a "how-to" manual called *Recreating Democracy, Breathing New Life Into American Communities*.[2] The focus of this manual is the revitalization of communities through more participatory local government.

1. Lloyd Wells, interview by David Contosta and Carol Franklin, March 2005.

2. Lloyd P. Wells and Larry Lemmel, *Recreating Democracy, Breathing New Life into American Communities*, Center for Consensual Democracy, 1998.

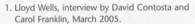

Lloyd Wells, in 1969, on left, discussing a new sign for an automobile repair garage on West Willow Grove Avenue, with Mary Lea Lowry (now Mary Lea Cope), then chair of the CHCA's aesthetics committee.
Source: *Chestnut Hill Local*

"Quasi-Government" The Chestnut Hill Community Association

Wells, a newcomer to Chestnut Hill, informed by painful but illuminating experiences working with civic organizations in Germantown and Center City Philadelphia, understood that the blight of Chestnut Hill's commercial district would spark the exodus of wealthier residents and erode the quality of life in the whole community. He also understood, like the leaders of the Philadelphia Renaissance, that political organization was a key to realizing physical and social renewal. In the late-1940s, he began to put together, piece by piece, what he called a "quasi-government" for Chestnut Hill. This extraordinary experiment in private community government, designed to supplement the administration of the larger municipality, may have been the first of its kind in the nation.[15]

The community would not only be governed by the City of Philadelphia, but also by a reorganized and more powerful Chestnut Hill Community Association. The association's board would now represent all segments of the community. To validate its authority, it would include 20 of the highest elected officers of local, non-profit institutions. In a reciprocal arrangement between the association and local non-profits, a member of the community association's board would sit on the board of each organization. The association's by-laws recognized and promoted this concept of "interlocking directorates."

The community association hired a manager and set up offices in a self-proclaimed "town hall" on Germantown Avenue, in the heart of the revitalized commercial district. The city administration, weighed down with its own burdens, was relieved to let residents of Chestnut Hill take the lead in solving their own physical and social problems. The community association was legally structured as a non-profit corporation (501 C3), but unlike most non-profits, this group delivered many of the services that ideally would be provided by Philadelphia city government—including zoning, land use, street improvements, traffic,

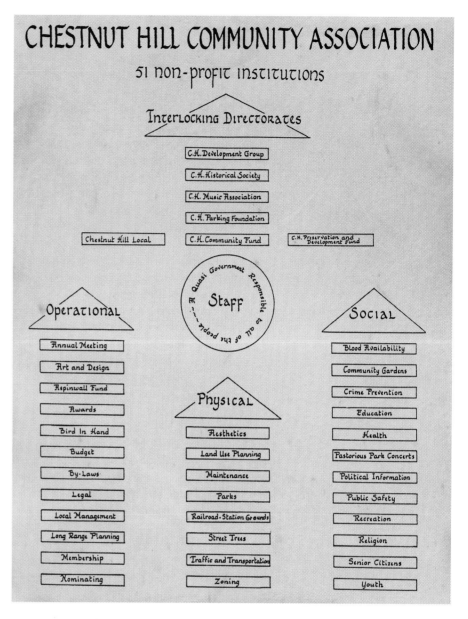

Chestnut Hill Community Association Organizational Structure. Source: CHHS

transportation, care of the aged, teen recreation, concerts and street fairs. These services would be paid for by specific fund drives as well as by a "quasi tax" (also called a "consensual tax") in the form of dues to the association.[16]

The community association, and the network of organizations cooperating with it, was designed to support and reinforce the renewal effort. The authority for this experiment, which functioned as a private government, depended on the consent of those who considered themselves "Chestnut Hill residents" (which often included those living in Mt. Airy or Springfield Township). The Chestnut Hill Community Association followed a Philadelphia tradition that had emerged with the city-county consolidation—the creation of Fairmount Park and later the Benjamin Franklin Parkway—in which civic and business leaders joined together to promote city, planning ideas.

Significantly, one of the first committees established by the reorganized community association was the Land Use Planning Committee in the mid-1950s. Rising land values and increasing property taxes in the post-World War II period encouraged the break-up of the large, old estates and the infill of every available piece of open space. These forces led to conflict and required a community forum to debate and find solutions to these property pressures.

The quasi-government succeeded in coming up with imaginative and attractive solutions to physical problems by persuading local residents to contribute their talent, professional experience, self-confidence and political connections These contributions were pro-bono and protected both individual interests and the overall quality of life in the community. Among these residents were a number of able architects and urban planners, including G. Holmes Perkins, then Dean of the University of Pennsylvania's School of Fine Arts and chair of the Philadelphia Planning Commission, and landscape architects such as Ian McHarg, Gerald Cope and Anthony Walmsley. Linked together through the interlocking directorates of the Chestnut Hill Community Association, local public service institutions and committed individuals formed "multistranded networks" of social capital that accomplished remarkable results.[17]

A Community Newspaper

To augment a strong and dedicated community association, committed to the public interest, Wells, with the aid of Fred Berger, founded a newspaper called the *Chestnut Hill Local*, first published in May 1958. Its objective was to allow Chestnut Hillers to develop an enlightened public policy on topics of concern, which could then be taken up by the community association board for resolution and implementation. This weekly newspaper was not to be a "house organ" or a local gossip sheet. Nor was it to support any political party or candidate.

The *Local* was owned and published by the community association with financial losses covered by the Chestnut Hill Development Group, a new business association founded by Wells. The newspaper was not intended to make a profit, but only to break even. The editors and staff began as volunteers, but were later paid. When the paper was well established, it generated annual profits of up to $80,000. This money was used to support the association's many physical and social improvement programs.[18]

For nearly 40 years, two crusading editors—Ellen Newbold and Marie Jones—fearlessly rooted out, exposed and discussed in depth, difficult community issues. It explored multiple potential solutions in lengthy editorials, encouraged lively exchanges of letters and rallied residents to take action. Under these editors, the newspaper never attacked community figures, but stuck rigorously to clarifying both sides of a community debate.

As a genuine community forum, the newspaper involved residents in a wide variety of issues that included adverse land use, the degradation of Wissahickon Park and repeated attempts by narrow but outspoken interest groups to takeover the community association and its public voice. In its heyday, the *Chestnut Hill Local* played a vital role in giving the community a sense of itself and confidence in its ability to recognize problems and to come together to solve them. This community organ was critical to creating and reinforcing community cohesion, and in maintaining an unspoken compact between the many different elements, encouraging them to work together for the benefit of all. That these compacts are fragile and easily destroyed has been demonstrated in recent years (2000-2009) by the unraveling of both newspaper and community government. In January 2009, this experiment in "quasi-government" was further undermined when the board of directors of the Chestnut Hill Business Association (CHBA) resigned from the CHCA.

12:4-5

Rehabilitating the Physical Fabric

From the beginning, Wells realized that the physical presentation of a community was a mirror of its health, and that conflicts between providing practical necessities and maintaining community character (such as between providing parking and creating an attractive pedestrian shopping area) would have to be resolved. Being a Chestnut Hill shop owner himself, Wells understood that the lack of nearby off-street parking was blighting the retail stores and preventing them from competing with the new shopping-centers in Flourtown, Lafayette Hill and other surrounding communities. He also understood the value of the "picturesque village on the hill." Recognizing the strength of the old main street model, Wells saw the importance of preserving the village structure—the continuity of a long, linear "Main Street," the walking scale and the intimate relationship between shop-owners and customers.

APPROXIMATE MID-BLOCK SEPARATION BETWEEN RESIDENTIAL & COMMERCIAL

COMMERCIAL ZONE

PARKING IN MID-BLOCK TYPICAL

GERMANTOWN AVENUE

Diagram showing the main street as a strip village and illustrating the ideal relationships between the commercial and residential districts. The community parking lots were created by individual landowners leasing their backyards to the Chestnut Hill Parking Foundation (CHPF) for $1.00 a year. The lots combined the backyards of several adjoining shops into one substantial parking lot for each block. These lots were landscaped and supervised by senior citizens hired by the CHPF.

Source: *CHCA, Land Use Guidelines*, revised 1982, drawing by Colin Franklin

Redevelopment of the Top of the Hill

In 1965, to further stimulate the renewal of Chestnut Hill, Lloyd Wells with the assistance of Nancy Hubby and others designed and implemented the Chestnut Hill Reality Trust. This for-profit organization was intended to be the redevelopment arm of the CHCA.

The trust was proactive. Its objective was to create a development arm of the community that would buy up decayed properties as they became available and hold these properties until they found enlightened developers and negotiated with them for an appropriate plan. This private

corporation was made up of local residents who raised money by selling shares. As key properties became available, the trust acquired and modified them, inserting new covenants into the deeds and re-selling the properties at cost.

The Realty Trust's first projects were the purchases of two blighted eyesores. The first site was an auto repair garage. The trust used this property to enlarge the commercial strip along West Highland Avenue, a side street just off Germantown Avenue, by building an early "mini-mall." The second project was the Top

of the Hill, located at the highest point of Chestnut Hill (and one of the highest points within the city) at the confluence of two arterial streets—Germantown Avenue and Bethlehem Pike. This area had been a commercial hub since the early 19th century.

The Top of Hill project involved buying the Acme supermarket and tearing it down, along with the purchase and demolition of the Grove Diner and the trolley station. Once the land had been cleared, a developer approved by the trust created an L-shaped set of shops that wrapped around the trolley loop.

Looking north on Bethlehem Pike towards Stenton Avenue, near the top of Chestnut Hill, c.1950. The area was then a clutter of billboards, a cacophony of overhead wires and large, undefined asphalt parking lots. The picture also shows a run-down Acme supermarket and an art deco gas station. Sadly, the art deco station was demolished and replaced in the 1960s with a Colonial Revival gas station. Several decades after the successful completion of the Top of the Hill project, this second gas station building was demolished and replaced with a Border's bookstore.
Source: CHHS

View looking north on Bethlehem Pike a half century later. The gas station has been replaced by a bookstore. The trolley loop remains, although buses have replaced the trolleys. A mini-mall was built on the site of the Acme supermarket. The church steeple is still part of the streetscape.

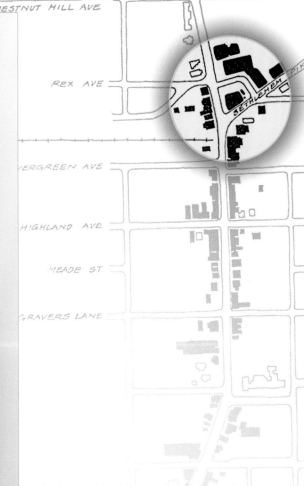

Trolley turn-around wrapped by new mini mall which embraced the trolley loop and created an L-shaped plaza. A second and smaller plaza was made two decades later to give a more defined entrance from the street.

At the top of the hill, Germantown Avenue forms a big "Y" at the intersection with Bethlehem Pike. The commercial district ends here at the highest point and at the nexus of two arterial routes, forming a "gateway" to Chestnut Hill. This area was the focus of a major redevelopment in the 1970s. Source: *CHCA, Land Use Guidelines*, revised 1982, drawing by Colin Franklin

Results of the Top of the Hill development showing the mini-mall and the bookstore. The bookstore that replaced the gas station has contributed to a sense of "commons," with its curving front facing the crotch of the "Y" and its extra wide sidewalk forming a little gathering place in the front of the building. The area has become the closest thing to a "town square" in Chestnut Hill.
Source: Photographs by CLF

Germantown Avenue in Chestnut Hill

The commercial spine in Chestnut Hill is successful, in part, because it is not simply a uniform line of buildings facing each other across a long, straight street. The avenue curves as it rises to the top of the hill, giving very different views as one moves along it. The building facades are broken by openings that draw the shopper into complex spaces off the main street.

This angled building creates a sheltered space at the side entrance of a main street shop. The plaza extends an outdoor café from an adjacent garden.
Source: Photographs by CLF

View along Germantown Avenue at the "Middle of the Hill."

A porous and variable streetscape keeps the main commercial spine lively and interesting from the "Bottom of the Hill" to the "Top of the Hill."

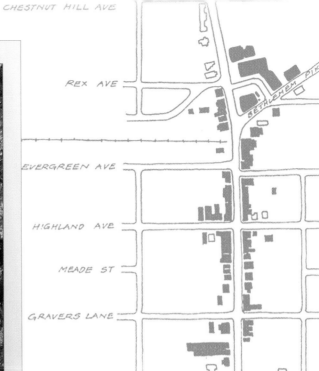

CHESTNUT HILL AVE

REX AVE

BETHLEHEM PIKE

EVERGREEN AVE

HIGHLAND AVE

MEADE ST

GRAVERS LANE

GERMANTOWN AVENUE

Map of Germantown Avenue in Chestnut Hill showing the spatial variety along the main street.
Source: *CHCA, Land Use Guidelines*, revised 1982, drawing by Colin Franklin

Small alcoves connected to the main street by alleyways contribute to the spatial and visual variety of what might otherwise be a uniform and unrelieved corridor.
Source: Photographs by CLF

To preserve the continuity of a small town main street, where cars are parked in front of the stores, Chestnut Hill could not follow the suburban strip mall model. To resolve the parking problem within a village context, Wells came up with the idea of joining the backyards (remnants of the lots that had once run back as narrow strips from both sides of the main commercial road) and combining these strips into long, linear parking lots paralleling the main street behind the stores. Wells proposed the idea of a non-profit parking company to the Chestnut Hill and Mt. Airy Businessmen's Association. When this group rejected the proposal, Wells and other merchants resigned from the association and formed the Chestnut Hill Development Group in 1953. With a new and supportive business organization behind him, Wells went door-to-door to sell the merchants on leasing their backyards for a dollar a year to create eight community parking lots. To pay for the initial construction of these lots, the merchants were asked to purchase common stock in what came to be known as the Chestnut Hill Parking Foundation. To pay for the upkeep and parking lot attendants, participating local businesses bought "tickets" and issued them to their customers for "free parking." The land on which the lots were built continued to belong to the owners of individual stores, who paid city property taxes on this land.

The public value, added by cooperating merchants, first stabilized and then significantly enhanced property values along Germantown Avenue. In exchange for advertising by development group merchants, Wells persuaded the local newspaper (then The *Herald*, a predecessor to the *Chestnut Hill Local*) to write articles explaining the importance of

View of a community parking lot on West Highland Avenue, late 1950s. These lots, made by combining the backyards of the shops, reached into the residential neighborhood where well-planted properties and alleys with hedgerows gave these parking areas a rural feel.
Source: *Chestnut Hill Local*

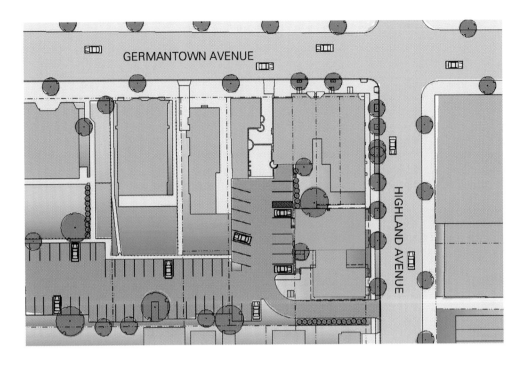

GERMANTOWN AVENUE

HIGHLAND AVENUE

Plan of community parking lot at East Highland Avenue. This plan shows how the backyards of the shops along Germantown Avenue were joined to form a large parking space.

Despite the addition of two new buildings on East Highland Avenue (shown in orange), in 2007, this plan shows that it is possible to insert new buildings and maintain the character of the existing fabric.
Source: Kreiger + Associates Architects Inc.

12:6–7

proposed improvements. Wells also pressured recalcitrant shop owners to cooperate with these proposals by telling them, sometimes disingenuously, that everyone else had agreed to participate.[19]

Throughout the commercial district, there was a conscious effort to restore and repair the green fabric. The treeless and dingy commercial spine was planted with street trees. In the parking lots, the remaining small groves and pieces of hedgerows were carefully preserved, and contributed to a "country" feel that was friendly and intimate. The development group retained the alleyways and created little walkways between some buildings as access to and from the new parking lots in mid-block.

There was a continuing effort to persuade landlords and business owners to remodel their facades and remove the unsightly neon signs. These renovations recognized and took advantage of the growing nostalgia for the small town main street, later celebrated at Disneyland and Disney World. Despite the fact that most of the buildings dated from the 19th and early 20th centuries, storeowners were encouraged to redo their fronts in a colonial style. These colonial facades were "fake," and again, as in Germantown, some beautiful Victorian buildings, such as the Chestnut Hill Hotel, were badly defaced in the process. Still, the "colonialization" of the avenue gave a uniform look to what Wells liked to call a "horizontal department store," and in the early 21st century these improvements have created a main street that is a pleasure walk, even if the character of some of the most interesting buildings has been lost.

Greening Barren Streets

One of Lloyd Wells' first steps in revitalizing the Business District was to "green" Germantown Avenue by planting trees. A tree committee was established and funded as part of the Chestnut Hill Development Group. Later this committee became a part of the Physical Division of the Chestnut Hill Committee Association. Carol Van Sciver was the chairperson of the Tree Committee and served until 1980. She was succeeded by Carol Franklin who served until 2000.

On Germantown Avenue the Tree Committee gradually replaced the ginkgos and callery pears planted earlier with canopy trees from the Wissahickon Valley—oaks, ashes, hickories (when available) and other native species. A second focus was the enlargement of the undersized tree pits by substituting a continuous tree trench or at least creating a larger hole for the tree.

Original planting on Germantown Avenue c. early 1950s. Source: CHHS

Left
Three decades later the tree committee enlarged the existing tree pits on Germantown Avenue to a minimum of 5 x 7 feet.

Right
Where possible, a continuous tree trench was installed. The trench was filled with renovated soil. Unit pavers allowed pedestrians to cross to the street and water to penetrate into the soil. Large openings for the trunk gave the tree room to grow.
Source: Photographs by CLF

Greening Open Spaces

As the Chestnut Hill Community Association Tree Committee evolved, the focus moved beyond the main commercial street to the barren, public spaces within the community, in particular to the large, asphalt parking lots around the railroad stations. During the decade between 1980 and 1990, the tree committee was able to "green" two station lots in partnership with the South East Pennsylvania Transportation Authority (SEPTA) that had taken over the regional commuter rail lines.

SEPTA initially resisted requests to give up land for planting. Eventually, through the efforts of an imaginative and supportive area manager and through the influence of Chestnut Hill residents who appealed to the CEO of SEPTA, the rail authority worked closely with the tree committee to ensure minimal loss of parking spaces. The community association contributed the money for these projects from the general fund and from additional funds from private donors.

The critical impetus behind the revival of the Chestnut Hill Tree Committee was Dorothy "Dottie" Sheffield. A powerful community activist, Sheffield started a very successful consignment shop called

Wyndmoor train station before—a sea of asphalt.

"Bird in Hand" in 1975 to raise additional monies for the CHCA fund. Sixty percent of the money earned went to the physical divsion and supported the tree committee in their major projects.

Wyndmoor train station after asphalt paving was removed to create large planting beds. Source: Photographs by CLF

Belgian Blocks

Germantown Avenue (Chestnut Hill's main commercial street) was originally dirt and gravel. In the 1920s, cut granite blocks were used to pave this street. These pavers were modelled after the original "Belgian Blocks" that were brought to this country as ballast in ships sailing from Europe to America in the 17th and 18th centuries. The granite block road reinforced Chestnut Hill's village atmosphere, emphasizing its age, character and connections to Europe.

When the City of Philadelphia threatened to replace these blocks with asphalt in the 1980s, the Chestnut Hill Community Association and other civic groups protested and forced the city to retain and replace the existing Belgian blocks on Germantown Avenue—from Cresheim Valley Drive at the bottom of the Hill to Bethlehem Pike at the top. The reconstructed street used concrete between the trolley tracks that ran down the center of the roadway and modern granite blocks for the remainder of the road.

City crews did not lay these blocks correctly. Instead of bedding them on a thick layer of wet cement, butted together with no mortar between each block, the cut stones were laid on a bed of dry mortar, with dry mortar sifted into the gaps between the stones. As a result, large areas of Belgian blocks have been dislodged by heavy traffic as well as by the freeze and thaw of water trapped between the blocks and the concrete base on which they were laid. Repairs were then made with asphalt, making the street look patchy. In 2008, the Pennsylvania Department of Transportation (Penn DOT) once again restored this portion of Germantown Avenue, again using cut granite blocks, and unfortunately, the same construction techniques.

Cobblestones on Germantown Avenue disappearing underneath asphalt "repairs." Photograph, c. 2000.
Source: CLF

The reconstructed roadbed of Germantown Avenue laid with modern cut granite blocks. Photograph, c. 1980s.
Source: *Chestnut Hill Local*

The Land Use Planning Committee

Making consistent land use decisions required a vision of the physical fabric of the community and a set of standards to support this vision. In 1976, the Land Use Planning Committee adopted and published a set of guidelines, revised and reissued in 1982. The goal of these guidelines was to preserve and enhance "the harmonious joining of its residential, commercial and institutional land uses, its generous endowment of green open spaces in balance with the intimacy of smaller, more contained urban spaces; its fine architectural tradition; and its excellent service by public transportation."[20]

The Land Use Guidelines formalized and reinforced many of the ideas that had been used to structure the community's physical development. It identified three residential zones in Chestnut Hill and made specific planning recommendations for each. There were also separate recommendations for historic preservation, open space, institutional areas, transportation systems and the commercial spine along Germantown Avenue. These directives did not have the force of law, but relied on community consensus and pressure on property owners to comply. When followed, these guidelines provided a very successful framework for evaluating, recommending or opposing new development.

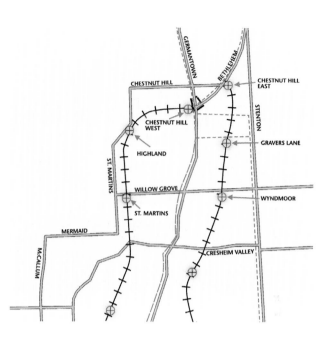

Chestnut Hill— a"New Urbanist's" dream town, is well served with transportation that takes residents into the city and out to the suburbs and the small towns beyond.
Source: CHCA, Land Use Planning Guidelines, revised 1982

Since the late 1950s, the refurbished commercial area of Chestnut Hill has flourished, with more than 120 active stores. Key elements of Chestnut Hill's original historical patterns and postwar "main-street" plans are still in place 50 years later. The commercial strip is lined with small stores whose facades abut the sidewalks and whose second and third floors are apartments. These apartments provide surveillance of the street when the stores are closed. Exceptions to this pattern—the schools, churches, public library and the Women's Exchange building—are set back with planted front gardens, and give a visual variety within the largely uniform streetscape.

The gray Wissahickon schist, putty-colored stucco, cobbled streets and tree-lined sidewalks tie the different architectural styles of the buildings together.[21] Despite many pressures to make changes that sabotage a healthy mix of commercial uses, Chestnut Hill remains a real community where people live, work, shop and play. Although there have been attempts to sabotage key recommendations of the Land Use Guidelines, Chestnut Hill remains a walkable community with continuous sidewalks rarely broken by driveways. It is blessed with a public transportation network of rail, buses and trolleys within a quarter mile of a majority of community residents. Most important of all, the commercial core still sits in a garden with forest fingers that connect to Wissahickon Park. Every public park, landscaped front, backyard garden and side court play a role in supporting this idea.[22] To this end, street trees cannot be tight, formal shapes, but need to overarch the streets and create the leafy green tunnels that mimic the structure of the forest.

12:8

View of the VFW building in 1966. The threat to remove the third floor of this 1859 building at 8717-19 Germantown Avenue led to the establishment of the Chestnut Hill Historical Society, one of the non-profit organizations that participated in the system of interlocking directorates under the Chestnut Hill Community Association.
Source: CHHS

For Wells, the Achilles heel of the community had been the run-down commercial district. If the commercial spine could not be revitalized, it would drag down the residential areas. The focus of his efforts was not the preservation of historic buildings or the reestablishment of historic integrity. Instead, he understood the power of the more modern concept of "branding" the community with a distinct and easily recognizable character. The initial revitalization spearheaded by Wells resulted in a new form of government for the community and the preservation, within a dense metropolitan area, of some of the most functional, flexible and attractive aspects of a village pattern. Following Well's retirement in 1976, other individuals and civic organizations took the lead on the increasingly complex issues of the last decades of the 20th century.

The Chestnut Hill Historical Society

Mounting interest in rescuing historic structures—and in restoring them correctly—led to the establishment of the Chestnut Hill Historical Society (CHHS) in 1967. The catalyst for founding this organization was the threatened removal of the third floor of the 1859 Veterans of Foreign Wars (VFW) building at 8717-19 Germantown Avenue. This building was one of the few good examples of Greek Revival architecture remaining in Chestnut Hill.

At this time, Wells and Nancy Hubby were developing the Chestnut Hill Realty Trust (CHRT), which was to become the redevelopment arm of the community association. Ann Spaeth, a newcomer to Chestnut Hill, seeing the wrecking ball demolishing the VFW's roof, protested to the editor of the *Chestnut Hill Local*, Ellen Newbold, who sent her to Wells and Hubby. Wells phoned Charles Woodward who agreed to contribute $1000 for

View of the VFW building after restoration. In 2007, the long-term tenant, Dobbins Rug Shop (formerly Dobbins Rug Cleaning Company), remained, but new flanking restaurants reflected stronger economic activity along the avenue.
Source: Photograph by CLF

MOREHOUSE '82

Source: CHCA, Land Use Guidelines, Revised 1982, drawing by Barbara Morehouse

an architectural plan for the restoration of the building. Hubby and Speath, armed with this plan, persuaded the VFW to sign a covenant allowing repairs to the roof and facade. Wells suggested creating the Chestnut Hill Historical Society as another interlocking directorate of the Chestnut Hill Community Association. With this organization as the legal framework, Hubby and Speath, joined by Shirley Hanson, then spearheaded a drive to raise the necessary funds.[23]

This group was committed to accurate historic restorations. Their interests moved beyond recreating a "main street village" character, to the identification and preservation of quality examples of the range of architectural styles represented in both the commercial core and in the residential neighborhoods. As part of its preservation program, the society agreed to accept easements on the facades of historic buildings along Germantown Avenue.

Filling Remnant Farm Fields and Developing Old Estates

During and after World War II, agriculture, supported by vast public hydro-electric projects, defense, service, tourism and technology industries combined with cheaper labor, drew population and resources to cities in the South and West. The large, undeveloped spaces within municipal boundaries and the new infrastructure built to accompany this boom also made this growth possible in the so-called Sun Belt.

Attitudes of the time—racial fears, dislike of the grimy, worn-out cities and the American dream of a single-family home with land—stymied growth in the older industrial cities of the Northeast and the Midwest. This growth was funneled either to these southern or western cities or to the undeveloped edges of the cities and to the suburbs of the Northeast.

In the far northeastern and far northwestern sections of postwar Philadelphia, large parcels of farmland still existed within city boundaries. The Philadelphia Planning Commission, searching for ways to bring economic vitality to a stagnant city, focused on downtown renewal and on encouraging development in these outer areas. The city opened up the far northeast by extending Roosevelt Boulevard (one of five parkways proposed in the early 20th century), and the far northwest by completing Henry Avenue into Roxborough.

In the communities bordering the Wissahickon, much of this undeveloped land was held in large estates. Postwar demand for new residential and commercial development, coupled with the aging and death of estate owners, and with high property and estate taxes, motivated descendents to sell or subdivide these parcels.

Germantown and Mt. Airy had been built out earlier. In Upper Roxborough, West Chestnut Hill and West Mt. Airy, the Houstons and the Woodwards had developed their large landholdings themselves. These families had contributed generously to the enlargement of Wissahickon Park and to the establishment of new community facilities. They fostered high quality design that continued to preserve the character of the community. In this tradition, Houston and Woodward heirs planned carefully and imaginatively for the reuse of their remaining properties. Unfortunately, other large landowning families often sold their properties without considering the impact of new development on the fabric of the community and particularly on Wissahickon Creek and its tributaries, building all the way up to the creek.

Two examples—Market Square/Chestnut Hill Village in East Chestnut Hill and a remaining farm field along Wissahickon Avenue below Allen's Lane in West Mt. Airy—illustrate the abuses of development in the immediate postwar period. Four examples—Cherokee Apartments, Krisheim, Druim Moir and Anglecot—show a more imaginative approach which adapts significant buildings and the unique terrain to new uses.

Map showing the three Houston Estates—Stonehurst in the middle is flanked by Krisheim to the south and Druim Moir to the north. By 1954, when this map was drawn, the mansion at Stonehurst had been torn down and the Cherokee Apartments built on the site of this estate.

Source: Franklin Survey Company, *Atlas of Philadelphia*, 1954

12:9—15

Market Square | Chestnut Hill Village

In the southeast corner of east side of Chestnut Hill, the Morgan estate, called "Wyndmoor," was an idyllic piece of countryside, with huge old trees including a 400-year-old "William Penn" oak. It was 85 acres of manor house, formal gardens, woodland and farmland, with about one third of the property outside the city in Springfield Township. The entire parcel lay within the Wissahickon watershed, with the southeastern side paralleling Cresheim Creek. The parcel bordered three neighborhoods—East Mt. Airy, East Chestnut Hill, in the city, and Wyndmoor, in adjoining Montgomery County.

In 1950, the heirs of Randall Morgan sold an option to Temple University to develop this large property. Alarmed at the possibility of massive institutional development, residents formed the East Chestnut Hill Neighbors, led by Joseph Pennington Straus, a prominent Philadelphia lawyer, to negotiate with Temple for plans that would be the least disruptive to the neighborhood. By 1954, after recent federal and state legislation gave universities new powers to obtain public funds and condemn land around their existing campus, Temple decided to stay in North Philadelphia. The university transferred its option on the Morgan tract to Meyer I. Blum, a member of the Temple Board, who proposed developing the site with a 50,000-square-foot shopping center and six high-rise apartment buildings. Beaten down by community pressure, Blum let his option expire, and Temple sold the property to a New York City developer, with no personal connections to Chestnut Hill.

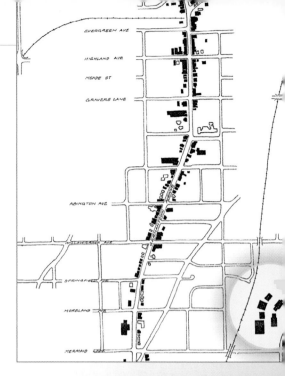

Plan showing the main street of Chestnut Hill and the new development of Market Square in the lower right-hand corner. The new development was not woven into the grid of the community but stood isolated in a "superblock." It was further isolated by the railroad tracks that ran through the site on a high embankment.
Source: *CHCA, Land Use Guidelines*, Revised 1982, drawing by Colin Franklin

Aerial View of the Morgan Tract, c. 1960. The mansion has been demolished and single family houses have been built on the Springfield Township portion of the old estate. The relic woodland and large canopy trees on the site that can be seen here were later cut down, including a centuries-old "William Penn oak," a tree that had been living when Pennsylvania's proprietor had first arrived. The strip between Mermaid Lane and Cresheim Valley Drive is being prepared for townhouses.
Source: *Chestnut Hill Local*

In 1955, the new owners, Summit Construction, proposed an even more ambitious plan, with 12 high-rise apartment buildings, a 100,000 square foot regional shopping center and a 400,000 square foot parking lot, increasing the density and impervious cover.

Needing support for rezoning, Summit was forced to negotiate with the community association and the East Chestnut Hill Neighbors. Talks dragged on for four years and finally, in 1958, Summit agreed to reduce the number of apartments, move the shopping center to the west end of the property against the railroad tracks, reduce its size and provide wide planting strips between the commercial and residential areas. Negotiations between the community association and the developer led to a scaled-down plan, but this revised plan still included a high-rise apartment, dozens of three-story garden apartments, townhouses and a 75,000-square foot shopping center. Nearly all the forest, which had once covered more than a third of the property, was cut down.

The site organization—building locations, roads, open space and parking lots—were drawn from the standard developer's lexicon of the 1950s and were unsympathetic to the patterns of the community. Building materials also failed to reflect or complement the local vocabulary. Instead of covering the exterior walls in affordable stucco, with occasional stone accents (used historically in the community), the new townhouses, shops and garden apartments were covered in vinyl siding and red brick veneer, keeping the residential

development from being visually integrated into the older Chestnut Hill community. This visual isolation reinforced the separation created by the site organization and made the development an alien and undesirable island.

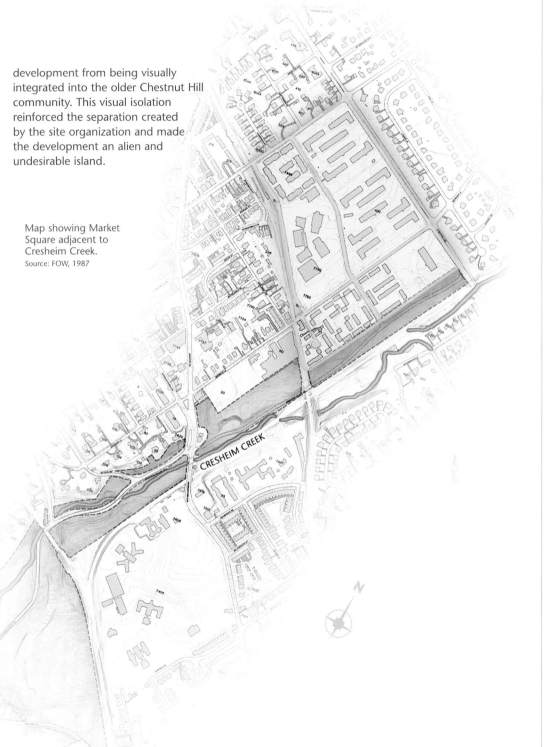

Map showing Market Square adjacent to Cresheim Creek.
Source: FOW, 1987

CRESHEIM CREEK

Market Square | Chestnut Hill Village *(Continued)*

The shopping center, originally designed as a "super block," was divorced from the street grid and backed up against the railroad embankment. A green open lawn around the shops, created to appease the community association, cut the shop fronts off from vehicular traffic. Philadelphia zoning ordinances at the time of the original development would not allow a mix of commercial and residential uses and there was none of the commingling of shops, houses and upstairs apartments that characterized Germantown Avenue.

The segregation of uses also isolated Market Square and separated it from the rest of the community, dividing the shopping center from the surrounding residences and from easy public or police surveillance. It quickly became the most crime-ridden area of Chestnut Hill. Without community foot traffic or automobile access, these stores suffered for 40 years.[1]

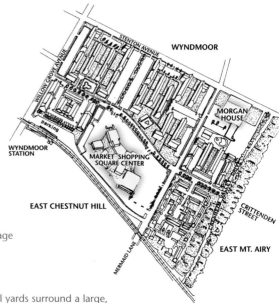

Plan of Market Square/Chestnut Hill Village
Source: Environmental Resources Group

At Chestnut Hill Village, townhouses with minimal yards surround a large, interior parking lot. Morgan House, the single apartment tower that was finally built, can be seen in the background.
Source: Photograph by CLF

View of the central open space at the Market Square Shopping Center, c. 1970s. The grassy mall between the two sides of the shopping center created a dead space that discouraged through traffic and activities. Source: *Chestnut Hill Local*

The most destructive aspect of this new development was its relationship to the park and to the adjacent Cresheim Creek. Although Randall Morgan had earlier given a small linear piece of his land in the city to Fairmount Park, his heirs sold the entire remaining property. Within city boundaries, the farm fields and forest remnants were converted to nearly 100-percent paving, creating a major source of stormwater runoff pouring into Cresheim Creek and ending ultimately in the Wissahickon. In this dense development within city boundaries, land not covered by buildings became parking lots for the townhouses, apartments and the shopping center. With almost total coverage, these "improvements" came nearly to the site boundaries, confining the park to a narrow and unusable corridor. On the east side, townhouses formed a wall against any penetration of the park into the site. On the west side, the railroad embankment made a "Chinese wall " against the rest of the community. On the north side, the townhouses blocked the potential of a shared open space or public route to Cresheim Creek.

Only a thin strip of trees protected Cresheim Valley Drive, the small parkway that follows Cresheim Creek, from the high-rise, the backs of townhouses and their huge parking lots. The opportunity to make the upper Cresheim Creek into a viable park, and to integrate it into the residential fabric, was never considered and the sense of Cresheim Valley Drive as a country road through parkland was badly compromised.

On the land once owned by Morgan outside city boundaries, in Wyndmoor, the impacts on Cresheim Creek were particularly destructive.

There, farm fields belonging to the original estate were converted into lots for single-family houses. Had the developers followed the example of the Houstons or the Woodwards in the lower Cresheim Valley, they would have donated the land adjacent to Cresheim Creek, either to create the beginnings of a municipal open space corridor or to be held as permanent, private open space. This open space would also have been integrated into the design of the development. Instead, on this portion of the Morgan Tract, the lots butt right up to the streambank, setting the precedent for the appalling abuse of the headwaters of Cresheim Creek in Wyndmoor.

Although Market Square and Chestnut Hill Village continue to trouble the Cresheim Valley and the larger community, time, which sometimes heals problems, has begun to heal this development. In the late 1990s, new owners redesigned the traffic flow to undo the "super block" and bring cars back through the space to reconnect with community streets.

The anchoring supermarket upgraded its building and attracts a wider range of customers, and better small stores provide higher-quality services to a broader community. The apartments and the houses have mellowed and the place is replanted and well-maintained.

Nonetheless, Market Square and Chestnut Hill Village demonstrate the unnecessarily high price that the community paid in an era when even well-heeled and powerful residents did not have the political and regulatory clout to compel large developers to respond to community concerns and radically revise their plans. Both the commercial corridor on Germantown Avenue and the Chestnut Hill Village/Market Square development are examples of high density, mixed use. However, this classic postwar shopping center, town house and apartment complex has brought severe environmental degradation, social isolation and a less than ideal quality of life.

1. Contosta, *Suburb in the City*, 201-209. Thomas A. Bell, "Negotiations Concerning the Development of the Morgan Tract," unpublished manuscript, Chestnut Hill Historical Society; Joseph Pennington Strauss, interview by Contosta, March 29, 1985.

Mt. Airy's Last Fields

"Suburban" development also crept into the remaining large properties in West Mt. Airy, filling the last, open fields adjacent to Wissahickon Park. In the late 1950s, at the intersection of Allen's Lane and Wissahickon Avenue poorly built, split level houses sited around cul-de-sacs replaced a long band of farm fields on the hillside just above the park. For the new residential development, the hillside was massively regraded, drainage channels obliterated and almost all the remaining hedgerows and old relic trees cut down. The developer scraped off and sold the topsoil, leaving only compacted subsoil for new planting. A large commercial chain allied to the developer supplied a standard landscaping package of three plants per lot—red, yellow and blue—generally a Japanese cherry, a forsythia and a Colorado blue spruce. This approach was in direct contrast to earlier residential development in the area, where local nurserymen, sympathetic to the Wissahickon forest,

created wonderfully usable outdoor rooms, planted with native species.

This project, although similar in some respects to the Morgan Tract in Chestnut Hill, was even more problematic. Like the Morgan Tract, the soil and most of the native vegetation were destroyed. Shoddy materials were used for both the buildings and the landscape. Because of the steep hillside in Mt. Airy, the buildings were cut awkwardly into the terrain. Volumes of stormwater ran off the impervious surfaces (roofs, pavements and lawns) into the park below, carrying sediment from poorly established lawns and bare areas, as well as herbicides and other chemicals into Wissahickon Creek.

Like Chestnut Hill Village/Market Square (on the old Morgan tract), this West Mt. Airy project created an island within the larger community that was uninviting and difficult to access. It missed an important opportunity to thread the park into the community.

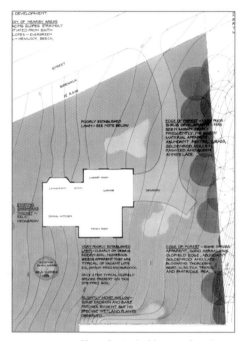

Plan of a typical house when it was first built, showing the site problems left by the developer.
Source: Andropogon, drawing by Rolf Sauer

This sloping hillside leading down from Wissahickon Avenue into the park was the site of a 1950s residential development in West Mt. Airy.
Source: GHS

Although this house was located directly adjacent to Wissahickon Park, the grading, placement of the house in the center of the site and the landscaping—all work to divorce the house from its context.
Source: Photographs by CLF

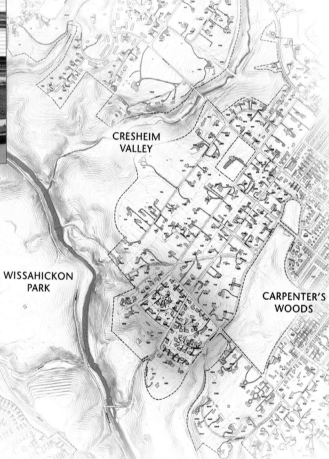

CRESHEIM VALLEY

WISSAHICKON PARK

CARPENTER'S WOODS

Map showing the Mt. Airy development above Wissahickon Park.
Source: FOW, 1987

Cherokee Apartments

In contrast to the conventional suburban development of the Morgan tract in Chestnut Hill, the Cherokee Apartments, begun in 1953, offered a different and more appropriate model for garden apartments and high-density development. At the Morgan Estate, ownership and operation rested in an out-of-state developer with no personal interest in the local community. At Cherokee, the Henry heirs maintained ownership of the property, both during and after its development, with their own corporation leasing and managing the buildings, creating a development that was responsive to both the social and natural context.

Taking their name from Cherokee Street, which runs along the east side of this 50-acre property in West Chestnut Hill, these apartments were built on the former Stonehurst Estate, owned by Sallie Henry. When she died in 1938, none of her children wanted to live at Stonehurst, and two years later her heirs demolished the house, with the idea of subdividing the land and selling it for building lots. Interrupted by the shortage of labor and building materials during World War II, plans for the Cherokee tract were finally revived with the building boom of the 1950s.

Oskar Stonorov (1905-1970) was commissioned by Donald Davidson Dodge (the spouse of a Henry heir) to design garden apartments for the property. Stonorov had studied with Le

Plan of the Cherokee Apartments, showing the use of the main estate roads to define the placement of the new apartment buildings. The map also shows the relationship of the site to the park.
Source: Franklin Survey Company, *Atlas of Philadelphia, 1954*

View of Stonehust Estate from Druim Moir, c.1880s. By the 1950s, the Wissahickon forest had filtered up from the valley and wrapped around the lawns and gardens of the estate. Source: CHHS

Corbusier and had come to Philadelphia as an important modern architect. He brought Louis I. Kahn into his office in the early 1940s, and his commissions included several Philadelphia Public Housing Projects. Stonorov was lionized as the bearer of Le Corbusier's legacy.

The buildings at Cherokee were long, plain three-story apartments. Neither the proportions nor the materials of the buildings were particularly elegant or well-detailed, and the interior rooms were pleasant but unremarkable. However, unlike the Morgan Estate, where the forest remnants were cut down, Gertrude Dodge insisted on preserving the estate trees and the road. Cornelia Hahn (Oberlander), the landscape architect, created the site plan that spared 90 of the largest and best trees and reused the estate roads. The site plan retained the original grades and terraced the buildings gracefully into the hillside.[1]

At the rear of the apartment buildings, the park-like setting of the old estate merged into Wissahickon Park. Over the decades, the surrounding forest has crept up into the site, and has given this development much of its quality—the sense that this dense complex was actually an intimate little village, embraced and infiltrated by fingers of the Wissahickon woods. Source: "Good Land Use + Good Architecture = Long Earning Life," *House and Home*, February 1956

Cherokee Apartments, showing the mature canopy trees anchoring the non-descript apartment buildings. Photograph, c. 1954.
Source: "Good Land Use + Good Architecture = Long Earning Life," *House and Home*, February 1956

Cherokee Apartments (Continued)

Stonorov himself had strong ideas about the contribution of the Cherokee Apartments to the community: "[It] is a project for park living with the conveniences of a big apartment laid flat among the trees— a new form of estate living. [It is] something really domestic, where people can feel at home—not consider themselves transients between apartments."[1] Stonorov also told the *Philadelphia Evening Bulletin* in June 1953, just as ground was being broken, that each of the units would have direct access to the outdoors, either by a terrace on the first floor or by a balcony on the second.[2]

In developing the Cherokee Apartments, a portion of the estate garden was donated to the Nature Conservancy as a forested, public open space directly adjacent to Wissahickon Park. This piece of property preserves the headwaters of a small tributary that runs along ValleyGreen Road.

Views of the back of the Cherokee Apartments in 2007, showing the Wissahickon forest as the principal feature of the landscape.
Source: Photographs by CLF

A second piece of the old Henry Estate, which included the formal gardens of the former Stonehurst mansion, was sold to private owners who built a new house on this property. The owners, Ronald and Roberta Berg, renovated the historic garden, with its pools, terraces and trellises.

1. "Good Land Use + Good Architecture = Long Earning Life," *House and Home*, February 1956, 162-66.

2. *Philadelphia Evening Bulletin*, June 20, 1953.

Views of the old Stonehurst Mansion gardens after renovation.
Source: Photographs by CLF

Krisheim

Following the death of Gertrude Houston Woodward in 1961, Krisheim—the Woodward Estate—became a conference center for the Presbyterian Church. High costs made it difficult for the church to maintain the facility, and in 1985 Charles Woodward, the youngest son of George and Gertrude, bought back the property, specifically to keep the house from being demolished. This purchase also kept the remaining 11 acres of park and gardens surrounding it from being subdivided.

The Presbyterians had done considerable damage to the house by installing big open bathrooms on the upper floors and by gutting the first floor kitchen and butler's pantry. Woodward made a decision to restore the ground floor to the plan of the original family home and to divide the upper stories into rental apartments.

At the rear of the Krisheim mansion, large double doors open onto a series of terraces that step down into the garden and from there into the park. Looking from the entrance hall out through these doors, there is a spectacular view into the Wissahickon Valley.

The rescue of Krisheim saved both the house and the early 20th-century gardens, which had been designed by the Olmsted Brothers. The most recent owner, Charles Woodward II, has continued this restoration work. Lynch Martinez, Architects, designed the elegant restoration of the ground floor of the house. Claire Yellin, a granddaughter of Samuel Yellin, located the original drawings for Krisheim and used them to replicate lost or damaged ironwork. Artisans from the Mercer Tile Works, in Doylestown, repaired or recreated damaged tiles.[1]

Krisheim after restoration, seen from the back looking up from the Wissahickon Valley.
Source: Photographs by CLF

1. David R. Contosta, *A Philadelphia Family: The Houstons and Woodwards of Chestnut Hill,* (Philadelphia 1992), 138; *Chestnut Hill Local,* March 1, 8, 15, 1984; *Philadelphia Inquirer,* April 4, 1986.

2. James P. Dodrill, Jr., Interview by David Contosta, February 22, 2003.

Garden Restoration

The seemingly impractical, but very imaginative decision to keep the ground floor at Krisheim open as Woodward family space, and later as a common space for the tenants of the apartments, preserved the important connection between the house and the gardens, and between the house, the gardens and the Cresheim Valley.[2]

The simple, elegant gardens, designed by the Olmsted Brothers, c. 1910, step down into the valley below in a series of formal terraces that become broad, shadow lawns and finally turn into meadow and woodland that blend into the park. Robert Flemming, a Chestnut Hill landscape architect, designed the beautiful and sensitive restoration of the gardens.

View of the terraced gardens looking back to the house.

Garden bench at Krisheim on a terrace above a shadow lawn that grades into Wissahickon Park.
Source: Photographs by CLF

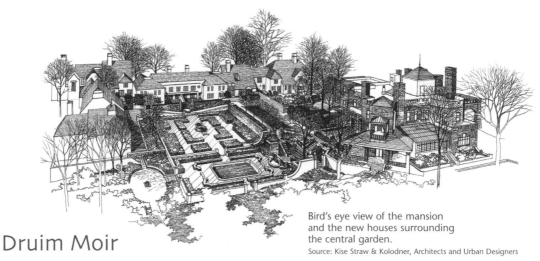

Bird's eye view of the mansion and the new houses surrounding the central garden.
Source: Kise Straw & Kolodner, Architects and Urban Designers

Druim Moir

After the death of Samuel F. Houston in 1952, Druim Moir was donated to the Episcopal Church as a home for retired clergy. The front part of the property was given to Springside School (formerly located at Norwood and Chestnut Hill Avenues) as a new campus.

When the church opened Cathedral Village, a much larger facility in Upper Roxborough, retired Episcopal clergy and their spouses could move there. Druim Moir was no longer needed. Sarah L.O. Smith, a granddaughter of Sam Houston, and her architect husband James Kise,

Plan of Druim Moir development
Source: Kise Straw & Kolodner, Architects and Urban Designers

purchased Druim Moir and carefully sub divided the house vertically into three smaller units, selling them as attached houses on their own lots.

On the grounds, Kise designed a number of connected houses that appeared to extend out from the old mansion, some of them grouped around the restored formal gardens that had been designed by Robert McGoodwin after World War I. As his model for these connected houses, Kise used the Gate Lane development in the French Village, also designed by McGoodwin. Each of the units at Druim Moir had its own land and

Front of Druim Moir flanked by a small wooded tributary valley in the left rear of the photograph. Source: Photograph by CLF

Rear of Druim Moir showing
the central garden on a
terrace below the mansion.
Source: Kise Straw & Kolodner,
Architects and Urban Designers

shared an interest in 10 common
acres. The new houses and their site
plans were modern demonstrations of
the Wissahickon style.[1]

The project has been enormously
successful. The houses on the Druim
Moir grounds form an intimate
community, similar to the Houston
and Woodward developments of the
1920s, where groups of houses form
courts, and the walls extend to
enclose sheltered garden rooms in the
front. The new houses, built of stucco
and Wissahickon schist, extend out
from the old mansion and gradually
attenuate into the landscape.

1. Daivd R. Contosta, A Philadelphia Family: The
   Houstons and Woodwards of Chestnut Hill,
   (Philadelphia, 1992), 172; Philadelphia
   Inquirer, March 2, 1980; Philadelphia Evening
   Bulletin, March 29, 1981; Chestnut Hill Local,
   January 24, February 2, 1981.

New houses at Druim Moir, which reach out, like a wing of the old mansion, to
embrace the formal garden. The Wissahickon forest frames this garden on the left.
Source: Photograph by CLF

New houses at Druim Moir.
Source: Kise Straw & Kolodner, Architects and Urban Designers

Anglecot

An interest in private preservation developed in conjunction with the founding of the Chestnut Hill Historical Society and the conservation of public buildings. Victorian architecture, despised during the first half of the 20th century, when the revival of colonial styles held people's imagination, gradually came back into favor in the 1960s. This interest may have been a new iteration of Romanticism, at a time when irregular and organic forms were again appreciated.

Anglecot was the Chestnut Hill residence of Charles A. Potter, a linoleum manufacturer. Built in 1883, the mansion was one of Philadelphia architect Wilson Eyre's earliest residential designs. Eyre (1858-1944) was an important country house architect, known at the time for his playful, shingle-style designs. He was a clever promoter and helped found the Philadelphia T-Square Club. He was also a founding editor (in 1901) of *House & Garden*, a magazine that featured many houses in the Wissahickon style.[1] His designs have been described as an "assembly of calculated asymmetries."[2] They were welcoming, informal and picturesque.

Anglecot is unusually sited at the angle of two Victorian residential

Anglecot, shortly after construction, at the "angle" of two streets. Photograph, c. 1883. Source: CHHS

streets—Prospect and Evergreen Avenues. The front entrance, at the point of junction, gives the house its name, "Anglecot." After World War II, this elegant structure was turned into a nursing home. Richard Snowden, a Chestnut Hill developer, with a strong interest in historic preservation, purchased this neglected and rundown estate just 100 years after it had been built.

Snowden converted the mansion, carriage house and stables into condominiums, subdividing these structures very imaginatively. The design preserved the character and integrity of this historic house. Along with Druim Moir and Krisheim, the Anglecot project set a model for the community to recycle its large houses.

These former "white elephants" were too large for a single owner and too difficult to be economically retrofitted for modern use. Many of the largest houses in Chestnut Hill were neglected and often abandoned. Some, like Compton, the mansion at the old Morris Estate (now the Morris Arboretum of the University of Pennsylvania), were torn down. In 1982, Snowden had Anglecot listed on the National Register of Historic Places.

1. Website: design.upenn.edu/Eyre/Eyrebio.html
   A professor at the University of Pennsylvania's Department of Architecture in the 1880s, Eyre told his students, "Do not have theories. No artist has any business with them. If you don't work from inspiration, you can get no aid from theories."

2. Sandra L. Tatman and Roger W. Moss (Eds.), *Biographical Dictionary of Philadelphia Architects: 1700-1930* (Boston, 1985), 253-54.

Anglecot readapted, showing the high quality restoration that has brought out the quirky character of this wonderful house. The architectural integrity has been carefully preserved, despite making it into a number of condominium units. Photograph, 2008.
Source: Photograph by CLF

Anglecot *(Continued)*

View of Anglecot stables,
which were also made into
condominiums. The estate
landscape is captured and
preserved between the two
buildings—the mansion
and the stables.
Photograph, 2008.

Source: Photographs by CLF

Rear view of Anglecot showing the "assembly
of calculated asymmetries."
Photograph, 2008.

Richard Wood Snowden (1957–)

Richard Snowden has been one of the major figures responsible for a wide variety of preservation efforts in the larger Wissahickon community. Born in Philadelphia, Snowden belonged to an "old" Chestnut Hill family. He moved to Lake Oswego, Oregon (outside Portland) when he was five years old and grew up there. In 1985, several years after graduating from Kenyon College, he founded Bowman Properties, with financial backing from his family, in particular from his grandmother, Virginia C. Wilmsen (1908–2004). Together, they believed that land conservation and historic preservation were compatible components of a successful real estate business, if each given transaction was handled within a viable financial structure. As partners, Snowden and his grandmother were involved in all aspects of a project, from initial plans to appropriate plantings. Within a dozen years, their land development and building management firm became one of the largest property owners in Chestnut Hill.

Snowden has been committed to high quality restorations. He has been extraordinarily sensitive to the architectural and landscape fabric of the Wissahickon style. His projects have gone far beyond the expectations of most commercial development. Like Lloyd Wells, Snowden realized that to keep the unique character of Chestnut Hill, there needed to be an imaginative reintegration of old and new. He also understood that for investors to be willing to put money into Chestnut Hill, they needed to turn a profit.[1]

Snowden has angered many people in the community by allowing some of his commercial properties to stand empty for years. However, he has also imaginatively restored a number of deteriorated properties along Germantown Avenue, creating new stores and office complexes with extensive gardens and courtyards. The associated green spaces have been gifts to the street and extended a sense of the forest into the commercial corridor. He coupled these real estate ventures with a broad support for public policies such as the Chestnut Hill Land Use Guidelines and the Chestnut Hill National Historic District Application, which he wrote in collaboration with Shirley Hansen, Nancy Hubby and Jefferson Moak.

One of Snowden's early projects was the adaptive reuse of Anglecot, designed in 1883 by the celebrated Philadelphia architect Wilson Eyre. Later, in the mid-1990s, he began to buy up and renovate large properties adjacent to the Wissahickon Valley, reselling these properties with open space and facade easements. Initially, he conveyed these easements to the Chestnut Hill Historical Society, and later to the Philadelphia Historic Preservation Corporation and the Preservation Alliance for Greater Philadelphia. The *Philadelphia Inquirer*, in a series of muckraking articles about easements, was critical of Snowden and others for the tax savings that they gained from these transactions. This criticism failed to recognize the benefit to the entire community of preserving open space, or of the need to provide financial incentives to induce owners to part with development rights.[2]

Like George Woodward and Lloyd Wells, Snowden can be seen as an outsider/insider. All three men grew up outside Chestnut Hill, but were connected to the community through family ties. As partial outsiders, they brought a new perspective, representing three distinct generations in the life of the community. Each in his own way has been a key force in shaping the physical fabric, and each has been passionately committed to making Chestnut Hill an exceptionally livable community.

These men were often stubborn and outspoken and pushed for change, and their leadership provoked considerable opposition. Like Woodward and Wells, Snowden has a tendency to get angry at the organizations that oppose him and to establish alternatives more in line with his own views. These shakeups can be beneficial to the community bureaucracy (which tends to become stagnant and corrupt), or they can undermine fragile community institutions.

Having accomplished so much and with many private business concerns to attend to, Snowden withdrew from leadership of public policy, at a time when the community badly needed his vision and multiple talents. However, by 2009, to offset the economic downturn, he returned to active intervention on Germantown Avenue, renovating and re-adapting several important historic buildings. He has also bought the abandoned Ford dealership. Snowden is active in planning both this site and Border's Bookstore, two big, empty sites which could remain unused, or offer huge opportunities to the community.

1. Richard Snowden, telephone interview by Contosta, January 29, 2004; interviews by authors, April 19 and May 10, 2008.

2. *Philadelphia Inquirer*, February 25, 26 and 27, March 3, 2002.

Prosperity and Pressures

Alexis de Tocqueville said in *Democracy in America* that an aristocratic society has no need for people to combine or to act together, because the word of a single, powerful individual is enough to make things happen. In a democracy, individuals are weak and need to create voluntary associations to achieve their public goals.[24]

In Chestnut Hill, inventive explorations of residential and commercial development suggested alternative directions for future planning and design in Northwest Philadelphia and beyond. Most significantly, Chestnut Hill's innovative physical solutions to neighborhood deterioration were coupled with a highly effective example of the power of social capital—with its experiments in "quasi-government" and "consensual democracy." Equally important, was the determination of several Chestnut Hill families to preserve the best qualities of their estates in concert with new uses, and to contribute substantially to increasing parkland within the community.

Unfortunately, gains are fragile and easily destroyed. Chestnut Hill's success in rehabilitating a deteriorating social and natural fabric demonstrates the need to encourage a participatory community conversation. Finding solutions that look—Janus-faced— both forward and backward is critical to dynamic community growth. Threats to the physical fabric and threats to a productive, structured community dialogue occur and reoccur. When a community loses interest and momentum, individual and institutional self-interest takes over and past successes can be quickly obliterated.

An Environmental Sensibility

1950-1976

13

13 An Environmental Sensibility
1950-1976

"Council finds that development within the Wissahickon Watershed has led to increased flooding of the Wissahickon Creek and its tributaries, and has increased the hazards of erosion, siltation and channel enlargement within the Wissahickon Watershed. To prevent such adverse conditions and the degradation of the environment, it is necessary to impose environmental controls to protect the health, safety and general welfare, to improve water quality and to achieve environmentally sound land development within the Wissahickon Watershed. These controls shall apply during and after construction and shall encompass all construction, site clearing and earth moving within the Wissahickon Watershed and shall promote a regional approach to the protection of the Wissahickon Watershed."

Philadelphia City Council, Bill #14-1603.2, Environmental Controls for the Wissahickon Watershed, 1975

An understanding of the Wissahickon as a forest ecosystem—influenced by forces both within and well beyond the valley—gradually emerged as an environmental consciousness grew nationally and new dangers to the valley were recognized. In the past, users and stewards (with the exception of the Lenni-Lenape) had seen the valley as separate and unconnected elements (rocks, water, trees and animals), or as dramatic scenery that inspired romance and devotion. With new scientific knowledge, there was a growing awareness that the forest was a complex and dynamic system, and a nascent understanding that this system was fragile and under siege.

After the hiatus of the war years, the civic organization formed to protect Wissahickon Park—the Friends of the Wissahickon (FOW)—resumed its stewardship slowly. New major projects—infill of the last open fields in Mt. Airy, adaptation of some of the largest estates in Chestnut Hill, combined with the development of the Henry Avenue corridor in Roxborough, reengaged the FOW and initiated a decade and a half of innovative measures to protect the park. The implications of these projects forced the FOW to reach out to the community and build bridges with other organizations and constituencies, broadening its social networks and political clout.

By the mid-1970s, there was a nation-wide revival of interest in comprehensive planning—this time with a new environmental component. Specific threats to Wissahickon Park would consolidate this interest and lead to the first legislative attempts in Philadelphia to ensure that already protected natural lands remained healthy, functioning ecosystems.

The Environmental Movement

Concerns about the human impact on nature have deep roots in the past. Environmental historian Kirkpatrick Sale pointed to the romantics of the first half of the 19th century and to the naturalists and activists of the early years of the 20th century "as different as John Muir. . . and Gifford Pinchot," who shared "an active concern for the natural world and alarm at its various perils. . . ."[1] Later important figures—Aldo Leopold, Rachel Carson, Paul Erlich and Ian McHarg, among others—would join these historic voices to create the modern environmental movement.

13:1

Ian Lennox McHarg (1920–2001)

A Chestnut Hill resident and long-time advocate of the Wissahickon and its ecological issues, Ian McHarg was a seminal landscape architect, regional planner, and educator. In many ways, this man created the discipline of environmental planning and changed the way in which a landscape would be understood.

Born in Clydebank, Scotland, some ten miles from Glasgow, a city he called "a sandstone excretion cemented with smoke and grime," McHarg joined the British army, served as a paratrooper in World War II, and by the end of the war, at age 25, had risen to the rank of major. Although he had not attended college, McHarg enrolled in the Harvard University School of Design after the war and earned graduate degrees in landscape architecture and city planning. He then returned briefly to Scotland.

G. Holmes Perkins, another Chestnut Hill resident and Dean of the School of Fine Arts of the University of Pennsylvania, built the departments of architecture, landscape architecture and fine arts into some of the best programs in the United States. Perkins invited McHarg to found and chair the department of landscape architecture and regional planning, a position that he held from 1955 to 1986.

As chair, McHarg transformed a sleepy horticulture curriculum into a regional planning and design department with its foundations in ecology. This department became a magnet for the whole university community and it would revolutionize the profession of landscape architecture.

In 1959, McHarg created a lecture series called "Man and the Environment," which brought lecturers, from poets to physicists (as many 14 Nobel Prize winners participating in one year), to talk about all facets of the human relationship with nature. The course was adapted as a 12-part television series on CBS called "The House We Live In," which McHarg wrote, produced, and hosted. In 1967, he published *Design With Nature*. This seminal book demonstrated, with case studies, his thesis that an in-depth ecological understanding was the most practical and moral basis for planning and design.

One of the first to recognize and call attention to the lack of environmental knowledge in these disciplines, McHarg saw that the physical, biological and social sciences were fragmented and rarely brought together to give an integrated view of a site and the processes that shaped it. Although he worked painfully, first by hand, and later with the large, awkward "Intergraph" computer, the McHargian "layer cake" was the precursor to computerized "geographic information systems" (GIS), such as Arc–View, a critical tool in analyzing regional sites.

McHarg was also a practicing landscape architect, who co-founded the Philadelphia firm of Wallace, McHarg, Roberts and Todd with planner David Wallace. After twenty bumpy but extremely creative years, McHarg was involuntarily retired from the firm by his partners and the office continues to exist under

Ian McHarg, with author Carol Franklin, 1996.
Source: Photograph by Colin Franklin

the name of WRT.

McHarg made Penn's department of landscape and regional planning world famous and changed the lives and focus of generations of students. He was a charismatic and powerful public figure, who walked and talked with politicians, artists, Native American elders and famous scientists.

Living adjacent to the Wissahickon, he understood its great value to the city. Brilliant, poetic, hilariously funny and often forceful and abrasive, McHarg went straight to the heart of environmental issues. His vision of an ecological foundation for architecture, engineering and landscape architecture was well ahead of his time, pre-dating and pre-visioning the sustainable design movement. His holistic vision of design has yet to be realized.[1]

---

1. For obituaries for McHarg, see the *Philadelphia Inquirer*, March 7, 2001, the *New York Times*, March 12, 2001 and the *Pennsylvania Gazette*, May/June 2001. For more on Ian McHarg's life, see his autobiography, *A Quest for Life* (New York, 1996).

Postwar affluence had brought the "synthetic revolution" of "plastics, fibers, chemicals, pesticides, detergents, [and] nuclear power," along with suburban sprawl, increased air and water pollution and the alarming disappearance of wilderness and open space.[2] In his 1958 book, *The Affluent Society*, economist John Kenneth Galbraith focused on the recurrence in this postwar period of the traditional American tension between progress and despoliation.

The growing disaffection with the consequences of progress created an audience for a remarkable series of books. In 1962, Rachael Carson's *Silent Spring* documented the devastating effects of the insecticide DDT on bird populations and implied, by extension, the "toxicity" of human progress. *The Population Bomb* (1968) by Paul Ehrlich, a neo-Malthusian, warned that exploding human populations would overwhelm earth's resources and seriously damage the balance of nature. *Design With Nature* (1967) by Ian L. McHarg, a Chestnut Hill resident and an internationally known landscape architect and regional planner, maintained that civil engineering, building and landscape design should respond to (rather than obliterate) the integrity and patterns of each place.

Earth Day, first celebrated on April 22, 1970, and conceived as a "National Teach-in on the Crisis of the Environment," focused public concern on the deteriorating natural world. Its prescient organizers understood that the environmental crisis was the most serious threat confronting humanity. This first Earth Day was a nation-wide program of lectures, discussions, singing, dancing, and appropriate foods to highlight this crisis and heighten awareness of the issues. Based on a format first used by opponents of the Vietnam War, and growing out of some of the same dissatisfactions, Earth Day ultimately became a "mainstream event" now observed by tamer groups across a broad political spectrum.[3] A growing body of literature and public debate about environmental issues eventually led to legislation. In 1964, Congress passed the Wilderness Act, which over the next four decades would set aside 106 million acres of forests, grasslands, rivers and seacoasts. Congress created the federal Environmental Protection Agency (EPA) in 1969, and a year later state legislators established Pennsylvania's Department of Environmental Protection (PDEP), later the Pennsylvania Department of Conservation and Natural Resources (PA DCNR). Although funding and enforcement fell short of expectations, these new laws and new agencies were the result of a growing environmental awareness that would have an enormous positive impact on local, regional and national environments.[4]

The FOW: A Slow Awakening

Directly after World War II, Wissahickon Park appeared to be in remarkably good heath. The period of WPA projects had ended only a few years before, in 1943. During this period shelters, bridges, dams, roads, retaining walls and trails were repaired or built.[5] Planting done by various New Deal agencies and by the FOW, along with natural regrowth, had begun to close gaps in the tree canopy created by the chestnut blight and the loss of many hemlocks. New diseases and pests had not yet arrived, or were not yet present in suffi-cient numbers for their impacts to be recognized. At this time, very few people were actually using the park, and the majority of these park users were still from the immediate neighbor-hoods. Most of the activities were still the relatively genteel recreations of the Victorian era. There was some vandalism, theft of plants and dumping, but not in alarming proportions. Personal recollections and photographic records of the period show a fairly healthy, mature forest with recognizable and diverse plant communities, as well as a full range of successional landscapes—woodlands, old fields and meadows—rich in species.

From the first, the FOW had concentrated its efforts in the park on the east (Chestnut Hill/Mt. Airy) side of the creek, largely ignoring the Roxborough side (except for Valley Green). This neglect stemmed partially from the fact that Upper Roxborough remained mostly in farms, but it also grew out of the deeply embedded prejudices of the White Anglo Saxon Protestant (WASP) upper middle class of West Chestnut Hill/West Mt. Airy, which had founded and directed the organization. Little effort was made to seek out or encourage typical Roxborough residents—working class, mainly Catholic, with Irish, Polish or Italian backgrounds—and persuade them to join this organization dedicated to park stewardship. This concentration on just one side of the creek weakened the effectiveness of the organization. In addition, after World War II, when Wissahickon Park was in relatively good condition, the FOW believed it was enough to concentrate their efforts on overseeing the Valley Green Inn. As a result, the FOW was slow to appreciate threats to the park resulting from the extension of Henry Avenue into Upper Roxborough. By the late 1950s, after ten years of development in the surrounding communities, FOW members finally began to recognize the new pressures on the valley and initiated a decade and a half of innovative, protective measures. This renewed civic activism reflected the larger environmental paradigm that engaged the nation in the 1960s and early 1970s.

13:2

Gaspar Lopez (1897–1984)

After hiring and firing a number of unsuccessful managers for the Valley Green Inn, the FOW finally selected Gaspar Lopez in 1958. Although the focus on Valley Green has been widely criticized as a weakness of the FOW, finding a genial proprietor enhanced the inn's role as the heart of the park.[1]

For nearly a quarter century, from 1958 to 1982, Lopez personified the inn for many visitors. In those days, the restaurant managers were required to live on the second floor of the building to provide surveillance. An Argentinian from Mendosa, Lopez began his career

in the restaurant and hotel business in Philadelphia, working at the Bellevue-Stratford Hotel during the 1920s. Later he managed two now defunct Philadelphia hotels, the St. James and the Stephen Girard.[2]

Lopez saw the inn as his home and himself as the innkeeper. He welcomed guests dressed in an immaculate black tuxedo and created an atmosphere of old-world hospitality. This outfit made a bizarre juxtaposition between Lopez's dressing as the maitre d' at a fancy downtown hotel and his role as the host of a little country inn.

In contrast to Lopez's very proper and rather formal image, the waitresses at Valley Green, like so many emblematic waitresses in Philadelphia's restaurants of those days, had worked at the same establishment for innumerable years. They were either grandmotherly sorts shuffling about in carpet slippers, or middle-aged women with teased, bleached-blond hair. They chewed gum and called you "hun."

The food—bland, overcooked, and plunked down in front of the customer—was also typical of

In 1950, the FOW revised and reissued the map of the park and its trails, which the organization had first published a decade earlier.[5] This map showed the park embedded in its surrounding neighborhoods, the park boundaries, its constituent parts, the trail network and noteworthy features—both natural and cultural. Giving the park a widely available image allowed communities around the park to see themselves as an integral part of the valley and helped both residents and outside visitors to appreciate the FOW as an important player in park stewardship.

In the early 1960s, in line with the growing awareness of the importance of cultural landscapes, the FOW applied to the U.S. Department of the Interior to designate it as a "*National Historic Landscape*" under the Historic Landscape Initiative created by Congress. This legislation was intended to draw attention to landscapes of national significance and focused attention on sites that should be preserved and protected from inappropriate uses, vandalism and insensitive development. Congress believed that by highlighting the scenic, economic, ecological, social, recreational and educational opportunities of these landscapes, Americans would come to acknowledge the character and beauty of their country. Rooted more deeply in a unique place, they would better understand themselves as a nation.[6]

In 1964, Wissahickon Park became one of the first of seven sites in the United States to receive recognition as a National Historic Landscape. The official dedication took place in May 1966. A plaque, set into a large rock near the door of the Valley Green Inn reads, "This site possesses exceptional value in illustrating the natural history of the United States of America."

Philadelphia cuisine before the restaurant renaissance of the 1970s. Despite the food and the service, inn patrons were attracted by the look and feel of a hostelry nestled in the valley, with its hallways and walls lined with furniture and tools donated to the inn in the 1930s by Samuel Fleisher, and by the roaring fire on cold winter days in the large country fireplace.

It was during Gaspar Lopez's management that exaggerated claims about the historicity of the inn reached their zenith. A pamphlet distributed during the 1960s claimed, miraculously, that, "The original hostelrie was in existence in 1683, frequented by Pastorius and by millers and farmers. . . . In 1778 Washington and Lafayette were reputed to have dined here on their way from [the] Barren Hill Camp to Germantown."[3] These assertions probably flowed from Lopez's lively imagination and aggressive marketing strategies, even though several researchers had already proven that there had been no inn, or any other building on the site, before 1850.[4]

1. The FOW Board Minutes for January 27, 1958, reported that "the proprietor [of the Valley Green Inn] has been rude and unpleasant on several occasions to members. After Lopez had been hired, the FOW Annual Report for 1959 stated, "Valley Green Inn is under excellent new management."

2. For an obituary of Gaspar Lopez, see *Chestnut Hill Local*, February 16, 1984.

3. Pamphlet, *Valley Green Inn*, from 1960s, CHHS.

4. See Chapter 7 of this book for a discussion of when Valley Green Inn was actually built.

Harold D. Saylor (1892–1981)

Harold D. Saylor was the inspiration and organizing force behind the designation of Wissahickon Park as a National Historic Landmark. A member of the FOW from 1928 until his death more than 50 years later, he was president of the organization from 1966 to 1972, and a member of the Fairmount Park Commission for three decades, beginning in 1950. Intensely interested in local and regional history, Saylor also served as president of the Historical Society of Pennsylvania and the Germantown Historical Society. As an amateur naturalist, he frequently walked the Wissahickon and gave many talks in support of the park system. A lawyer by profession, he was a judge of the Philadelphia's Orphans Count, and was known affectionately as "Judge Saylor," both on and off the bench.[1]

Judge Harold Saylor. Photograph c. 1970.
Source: Urban Archives, Temple University Libraries, Philadelphia, Pa.

1. *Chestnut Hill Local*, May 26, 1966; FOW Board Minutes, November 2, 1966, October 3, 1972. A good feature article on Judge Saylor appeared in the *Chestnut Hill Local*, November 25, 1976 and in the *Legal Intelligencer*, January 10, 1966. For an obituary see the *Germantown Crier*, (Winter 1981), 18.

A decade later in concert with the growing environmental movement, the FOW gave a platform to nationally prominent speakers living in the region, who presented cutting edge ideas about water pollution and forest ecology. At the annual meeting in June 1970, Ruth Patrick, who founded the Division of Environmental Research at the Philadelphia Academy of Natural Sciences, gave the first annual lecture on pollution in the creek and its tributaries.[7] The FOW published these lectures as pamphlets and distributed them to members and other interested parties.

The Henry Avenue Corridor

Long years of isolation, dictated by topography, and several failed attempts to make transportation connections across the valley, had kept much of Roxborough rural. Henry Howard Houston owned more than 2,000 acres of Upper Roxborough, and with his death, his estate now managed the property. Over time, both Houston and the estate had put forward a number of projects for these extensive landholdings. All these projects would include—and, in fact, depend on—major changes in the regional transportation network.

Panoramic view of Upper Roxborough at the end of World War II, looking towards Chestnut Hill. The photograph shows the mosaic of farm fields, hedgerows and small woodlots characteristic of the rural landscape in this area.
Source: University of Pennsylvania Archives, Houston Estate Papers

Ruth Patrick Hodge (1908–)

Born in Topeka, Kansas, Ruth Patrick received her Ph.D. from the University of Virginia. She attributed her great love of science and the natural world to the intense interest her father had taken in showing her the marshes and rivers of her native city. She began her career as a limnologist with Philadelphia's Academy of Natural Sciences in 1933, founded its division of environmental research in 1947 and became chair of the academy's board of trustees in 1973. She was an advisor on water pollution to President Lyndon Johnson and a science advisor to three Pennsylvania governors. For many years, she was the only woman at the Academy of Natural Sciences, then a male bastion. She suffered prejudice and campaigned throughout her professional career for the equality of women in science.

Patrick's major contribution to the environmental sciences was to demonstrate how to use the amounts and varieties of freshwater organisms as indicators of water quality, rather than relying on chemical and physical analysis alone. Specifically, she devised a system that correlated the numbers and types of algae with siliceous cell walls—called diatoms—present in a stream or other waterways, to measure the amount and type of pollution present. Later, identification and measurement of these organisms would become an important tool for detecting and studying acid rain and radioactive contamination. Patrick's methods are still used throughout the world.

Called the "Queen Bee of Limnology" by Ian McHarg, Patrick is a long-time resident of the Wissahickon Valley, living just beyond Chestnut Hill and above the park. At the time of this writing she is 102 years old and still occasionally goes in to work at the Academy of Natural Sciences.[1]

1. *Philadelphia Inquirer*, February 19, 1989; *Chestnut Hill Local.* May 6, 1993.

Ruth Patrick at the Stroude Water Resources Research Station. Photograph, 1974.
Source: Urban Archives, Temple University Libraries, Philadelphia, Pa.

Drawing of a diatom.
Source: Hilda Carter-Lund and John W.G. Lund, *Freshwater Algae* (Bristol, U.K., 1998), 3rd printing

The city golf course at Walnut Lane and Henry Avenue. On the golf course, the greens and the fairways are separated by a hedgerow of black locust (*Robinia pseudoacacia*) and white ash (*Fraxinus americana*) that marks the boundaries of old, terraced farm fields.
Source: Photograph by CLF

13:5-6

In the 1890s, Houston had proposed a railroad from Chestnut Hill, paralleling Bells Mill Road and connecting across the valley. With the Depression of 1893 and Houston's death two years later, this cross-valley railroad scheme was abandoned.

Growing automobile traffic in the 1920s spurred a second project to connect the two sides of the valley. Access to a proposed new high bridge would begin just off Germantown Avenue at Hartwell Lane in Chestnut Hill, cut through Pastorius Park and the golf course of the Philadelphia Cricket Club and cross the creek to Cathedral Road in Upper Roxborough. Later plans showed this route continuing west across the Schuylkill River into Lower Merion Township and the Main Line suburbs. This bridge connection was a critical part of architect Paul Cret's 1926 plan for Andorra—another unrealized development proposed for the Houston Estate in Upper Roxborough.

The Great Depression of the 1930s and World War II froze significant change, but with the postwar building boom, the Houston Estate lobbied heavily to get the city to open this undeveloped area by extending Henry Avenue, which then ended just beyond the Walnut Lane Bridge in Lower Roxborough. This road was named after Alexander Henry, Mayor of Philadelphia from 1858 to 1862. His brother had married the daughter of Henry Howard Houston.

When completed, Henry Avenue was a four-lane arterial with high traffic volumes. Previously, the street pattern in Upper Roxborough had been an irregular grid of small farm lanes following field boundaries, with one central connector, Ridge Avenue. Henry Avenue now enabled the intensive development of Upper Roxborough. The new development would change the nature of the existing road network and the connection of the community to the park.

Along Henry Avenue, the community had two very different relationships to parkland. From Walnut Lane to Wise's Mill Road, the park was relatively broad and flat. Here the new arterial ran directly along the park edge. During and after World War II, the park commission allowed city departments to use this flat land for public puposes—a high school, golf course and ball fields. North of Wise's Mill Road, park boundaries did not abut Henry Avenue. The extensive land on the plateau in this area remained in private hands and was available for concentrated development.

At a width of 120 feet, Henry Avenue was a divider and not a uniter. The width of this road, and the large volume of traffic it carried, created a barrier between community and park. The new houses built along the roadway reinforced this separation. Long rows of duplexes, with garages facing the street, and three-story garden apartments, formed a solid phalanx of buildings that made visual and physical community access to the park very difficult. The forested fingers along the tributaries of Wissahickon Creek were either cut off by the road or surrounded by a "wall" of houses. Similar to Chestnut Hill and Mt. Airy, tributaries outside the park in Roxborough were originally in private hands. However, unlike the communities on the east side of the valley, Roxborough tributaries remained in farmland until the dense residential development of the postwar era. In the rush to build, most of the Wissahickon Creek tributaries were buried and covered over. As a consequence, these little streams and their corridors could not pull the park into the neighborhoods like the Cresheim, Carpenter and Monoshone Creeks on the other side of the valley.

Walls Against the Park

Along the Henry Avenue corridor, there are many barriers between the community and the park—the width of Henry Avenue itself, the solid row of houses, garages facing the street (with their driveways cutting off the sidewalk), and the almost treeless yards.

Three views of Henry Avenue.
The black and white photograph is c. 1976.

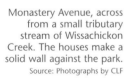

Monastery Avenue, across from a small tributary stream of Wissachickon Creek. The houses make a solid wall against the park.
Source: Photographs by CLF

"Gradient of Wildness"

Map of the Wissahickon Valley showing the adjacent communities—Lower and Upper Roxborough on the west side and Mt. Airy and Chestnut Hill on the east. Although Roxborough has more actual parkland, the tributary streams are cut off by Henry Avenue and do not generally bring the park into the community. The tract housing, garden apartments and apartment blocks also form a wall against the park. In contrast, in West Mt. Airy and West Chestnut Hill, the largest houses and properties are located nearest the park, creating a "Gradient of Wildness." This gradient makes a gradual transition from the natural lands of the park to the dense commercial strip along the ridge road (Germantown Avenue). Source: FOW, 1987

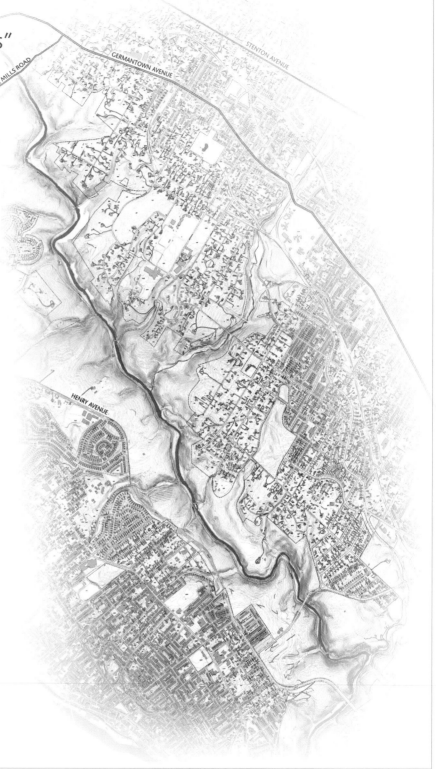

Aerial view of Chestnut Hill at Bells Mills Road, showing how the forest fingers extend up into the community, through the large properties at the edge of the park.

Aerial view of Upper Roxborough at Bells Mills Road, showing how the suburban layout abruptly cuts off the park. Source: Photographs by Colin Franklin

Andorra Homes and Shopping Center

After World War II, the Houston Estate proposed a number of plans for its vast holdings in Upper Roxborough. This area at the northern end of what would become the Henry Avenue Corridor was known as Andorra. In 1857, Richard Wister gave the name "Andorra" (taken from the Spanish province of that name) to his country estate and deer park in Upper Roxborough. The name stuck and was later adopted by the Andorra Nurseries.

In 1946, the United Nations was looking for a site for its permanent headquarters in the United States. A number of American cities competed to be the chosen site. Philadelphia offered a 400-acre tract in Fairmount Park on the Belmont Plateau overlooking the Schuylkill River along with the 2,000 acres of the Houston Estate in Roxborough. The Belmont Plateau would be used for the U.N. headquarters, while the Roxborough portion would be used for staff housing. This project was scuttled when John D. Rockefeller, Jr., purchased and gave the U.N. a 17-acre tract along the East River in New York City.

After the collapse of the U.N. bid, the estate offered to sell some of the Roxborough property to Temple University for a new campus. Instead, Temple took an option on the Morgan property in Chestnut Hill, with the idea of moving its operations there. It later made the commitment to remain in North Philadelphia.

A typical house in the Andorra Homes development.
Source: Photograph by CLF

Eero Saarinen's 1948 Plan for Andorra

The estate then hired Eero Saarinen, the noted Finnish architect, to make a plan for their extensive holdings—over four square miles. This plan proposed new roads, some 5,000 residential units (including single family and twin houses and garden apartments) and two shopping centers on Ridge Avenue. Each shopping center would be connected to Chestnut Hill by a major road and bridge. To access the proposed bridges over the Wissahickon Valley, Lincoln Drive would be extended through Chestnut Hill to connect with the access road for the Cathedral Road Bridge at Pastorius Park. The upper portion of Lincoln Drive would become a major connector to Bethlehem Pike and to the northeastern suburbs of Springfield and Whitemarsh Townships. When this proposal collapsed, Sam Houston, principal trustee of the estate, concluded that modest housing—for this historically working and middle class area of the city—was the most realistic possibility.[8]

At Andorra, small and affordable houses were woven into the street grid. These houses had a charming cottage-like quality that created a sense of an American small town, while the stucco finish reflected the vocabulary of the east side of the valley (Germantown, Mt. Airy and Chestnut Hill). Sam Houston drew up a set of guidelines to preserve the character of this development, which governed the distance between the houses, their size, height and sight lines. After his death, these guidelines were taken over and enforced by the Andorra Homes Civic Association.

Located too far away to walk comfortably to the historical, commercial strip in Roxborough along Ridge Avenue, Andorra Homes lacked a main street shopping district. In place of the stores that lined Ridge Avenue, and to compete with the gigantic projects in the suburbs, the Houston Estate built the Andorra Shopping Center.

13:7–10

Following postwar suburban models, this early shopping center was a modest, slightly distorted L-shaped arrangement. It was later enlarged to form an elongated U around a huge, rectangular parking lot. Saarinen's plan showed greenways to connect the park, the new community and the shopping center, but these corridors were never realized.[9] Preserving the headwaters of the two main Wissahickon Tributaries (Bells Mill Run and Cathedral Run) would have allowed these little streams to "finger" up through the neighborhoods, bringing together living, shopping, work and play—all cradled within the amenity of the forested Wissahickon Valley. Instead, there is little connection between the park in the valley and the community on the plateau.

Aerial photograph of Upper Roxborough. The Andorra Homes can be seen above. The Andorra Shopping Center (under construction) can be seen in the lower left. The oversized Cathedral Road borders the shopping center site.
Source: University of Pennsylvania Archives, Houston Estate Papers

The Andorra Shopping Center showing the elongated U-shaped footprint of the buildings and the extensive parking lot. Photograph, 2007.
Source: Photograph by CLF

In contrast to West Chestnut Hill and West Mt. Airy, the site, now converted from field and woodlot into paved surface, carried stormwater runoff and pollutants from the large flat rooftops and the massive shopping center parking lot directly into Cathedral and Bell's Mill Runs. Over the last half-century since this development, the volume and velocity of stormwater entering these tiny creeks during heavy storms has gouged out the creek bottoms and undercut their banks.

Land that did not become the Andorra Homes and Shopping center—much of the remainder of the Houston property in Upper Roxborough—was sold to other developers. Initially, these developers built a series of typical, mid-20th-century subdivisions—uniform boxy, ranch houses, evenly spaced, set in a matrix of lawn, on wide streets ending in cul-de-sacs. Where the houses backed onto Wissahickon Park, this arrangement blocked the forest from becoming a part of the lots and from moving into the fabric of the community.

Eero Saarinen's 1948 Plan for Andorra

Image from the Saarinen brochure for the Houston Estate. It shows the Houston lands and portions of Chestnut Hill, Upper Roxborough and adjacent Montgomery County. The land inside the blue square was slated to become housing and two shopping centers.

Image from the brochure prepared by Saarinen for the Houston Estate. The map shows that the proposed Andorra development was a logical trajectory for urban growth and would be located in an area well served by transportation corridors linking Center City to Northwest Philadelphia and to the suburbs beyond.

Source: University of Pennsylvania Archives, Houston Estate Papers

Image from the Saarinen brochure for the Houston Estate. It shows the context of the 1948 plan for 5,000 houses and two shopping centers in Upper Roxborough. Three major loops are formed by new arterial roads. The top loop encircles Layfayette Hill in adjoining Montgomery County. The middle loop crosses Wissahickon Creek at two places and joins Roxborough with Chestnut Hill. The lower loop circles the proposed community of "Cathedral Hills" (that took its name from the unfinished Episcopal Cathedral). All three loops connect to bridges that cross the Schuylkill River to the Main Line. The plan was conceived as a "model community," with highways, shopping centers, schools, churches and houses.

Source: University of Pennsylvania Archives, Houston Estate Papers

Eero Saarinen's 1948 Plan for Andorra

Shortly after World War II, the
Houston Estate hired Eero Saarinen,
the noted Finnish architect, to make a
plan for four square miles in Upper
Roxborough.

The detailed site plan shows:

1. Shopping and office facilities with a community center to serve
   a projected population of 15,000.

2. High density housing—200-300 acres around the center.

3. Schools and churches.

4. Fingers of dedicated green open space separating the lobes of the plateau.
   Single-family houses were proposed adjacent to these fingers. The most
   southern of these green strips connects to Wissahickon Park at Wise's
   Mill Road.

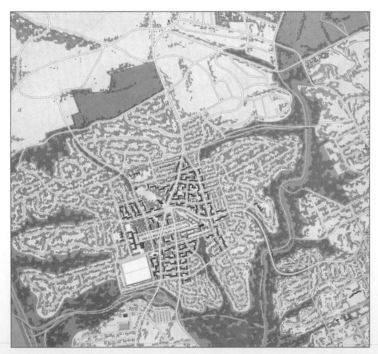

Plan for Andorra by Eero Saarinen, 1948.
Source: University of Pennsylvania Archives, Houston Estate Papers

Detail of plan.

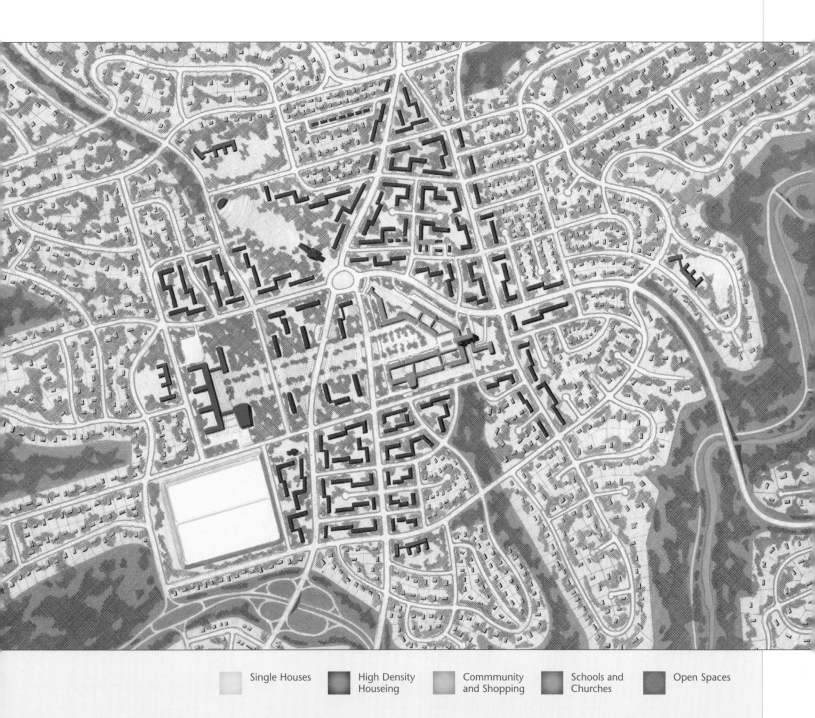

Single Houses   High Density Houseing   Commmunity and Shopping   Schools and Churches   Open Spaces

Eero Saarinen's 1948 Plan for Andorra | Cathedral Road

Saarinen's plan included new roads, over 5,000 residential units (single-family, twin houses and garden apartments) and two shopping centers on Ridge Avenue. Each shopping center would be connected to Chestnut Hill by a major road and bridge.

One part of the Saarinen plan was realized—the construction of Cathedral Road in Upper Roxborough. This road was once a small rural lane running a short distance between farm fields. In the 1930s, the Episcopal Diocese of Pennsylvania began building

a cathedral on the adjacent land. Construction of the cathedral was interrupted by the war and never resumed. The surrounding land ultimately became the site of "Cathedral Village," a retirement community, and the portion of the cathedral that was built is now

The proposed Cathedral Road Bridge. This bridge would have crossed the Wissahickon Valley into Chestnut Hill, connecting to an extension of Lincoln Drive above Pastorius Park. Source: University of Pennsylvania Archives, Houston Estate Papers

Aerial photograph showing the proposed route of Cathedral Road on the Chestnut Hill side. This road would have followed West Gravers Lane and skirted the Cricket Club Golf Course to cross Wissahickon Park and join Cathedral Road on the Roxborough side.
Source: University of Pennsylvania Archives, Houston Estate Papers

used as a parish church. In the early 1950s, in anticipation of the proposed new bridge across Wissahickon Creek, Cathedral Road was constructed with four lanes and a median, to create an arterial similar to Henry Avenue. In 1959, the Philadelphia City Council approved the construction of a single bridge, but residents in both Chestnut Hill and Roxborough opposed it. They feared the proposed cross-valley connection would take too much land and bring huge volumes of traffic. Their opposition forced the city to abandon the bridge proposal.

A small tributary of the Wissahickon, Cathedral Run, parallels the bottom piece of the road, below Courtesy Stables. Although it extended only a few blocks through a small residential neighborhood, Cathedral Road was now as big as an interstate highway. Stormwater funnels down the pavement, creating severe, negative impacts in the park and on Cathedral Run. Where the road ends abruptly in the park, the banks of this stream are blown out and the steep slopes of the valley badly eroded.

Aerial photograph of the proposed site of the Andorra Homes and Shopping Center. This photograph shows how open and rural Upper Roxborough remained at the time. The yellow lines show the projected extension of Henry Avenue and the proposed route of Cathedral Road. This road runs along the tiny tributary valley of Cathedral Run. The upper portion of this stream, partially in farm fields, could have been incorporated into the design as a green connection to houses and park. Photograph, c. 1948.
Source: University of Pennsylvania Archives, Houston Estate Papers

Samuel Frederic Houston (1866–1952)

The only surviving son of Henry Howard Houston, Sam Houston became the principal trustee of his father's estate in 1895. Approximately 2,000 acres of land in Upper Roxborough were among the assets of this estate. Unlike land his father had bought and developed across the valley in Chestnut Hill, these properties suffered from the isolation of Upper Roxborough. Without a railroad line or good roads into the area, they were too remote from Center City for an easy commute.

By the 1940s, increasing real estate taxes led Houston to market this undeveloped land to large institutions. He entered into serious discussions with the Philadelphia Veterans Hospital, Temple University and the United Nations, but for a variety of reasons, each potential buyer ultimately decided against a Roxborough location.

In 1950, shortly before his death, Houston launched Andorra Homes and the adjacent Andorra Shopping Center. The stuccoed "cottages" on small lots sold for reasonable prices, and were successful socially and environmentally. This modest development on relatively flat land created a dense but pleasantly wooded neighborhood near Wissahickon Park, unlike the lawns and driveways of later, larger houses which ate into the steep valley walls.

Houston was an important but largely unrecognized community benefactor. He was a generous supporter of St. Martin-in-the Fields Church, where he was the rector's warden for 63 years. By paying the mortgage and taxes of the Philadelphia Cricket Club during the Great Depression and World War II, he may have saved this facility and its large open space from being sold and subdivided.

Surviving Sam Houston were his three daughters: Edith Brown, Margaret Meigs and Eleanor Smith. The sisters created the Houston Foundation, endowed by Edith Brown to support Druim Moir. In 1967, Margaret Meigs and Eleanor Smith donated 500 acres in Upper Roxborough for a new conservation institution called the Schuylkill Valley Nature Center (later renamed the Schuylkill Environmental Education Center), located just below Ridge Avenue, in the Schuylkill watershed.

Samuel Houston.
Photograph, c. 1920.
Source: Author's collection

The Andorra Natural Area

The remaining Houston property in Upper Roxborough, including the site of the old Andorra Nurseries, was inherited by the children of Sam Houston. Operation of the nurseries continued until 1961. When the business dissolved, a majority of the 1,400 acres located outside the city in Montgomery County was sold for housing developments. The property inside the city reverted to the Houston Estate.

The Tree House, the Environmental Center at the Andorra Natural Area.
Source: CHHS

In 1977, Eleanor Houston Smith, one of Sam's daughters, and her children (Lewis, Sam, Meredith, Sallie, Mary Minor and Eleanor) sold the 100 acres of the original nursey tract to Fairmount Park for approximately $375,000. This addition, bounded by Bell's Mill Road, Forbidden Drive and Northwestern Avenue, extended the park to the city's edge on the Roxborough side. The Smiths, with an imaginative strategy of purchase and donation, then returned the purchase price to the park commission as a perpetual endowment for the Andorra Natural Area. In 1981, the park commission bought adjacent land to make a total of 210 acres added to the park.[10]

The gift of the old Andorra Nurseries tract was the last major donation of land to Wissahickon Park in the 20th century. It continued a remarkable tradition, from a remarkable family. The acquisition of the old Andorra Nurseries tract filled out the last portion of the Wissahickon Valley within the city and a critical portion of Wissahickon Park. Private development of this piece of land would have obliterated the entrance to the gorge from Montgomery County and seriously compromised the park experience.

The Andorra Natural Area also preserved Andorra Run where it joins the Wissahickon Creek at Harper's Meadow. This tributary originates in the adjacent Springfield Township panhandle, on a large, private tract, which has tantalizingly held out the potential of extending parkland into Springfield Township.

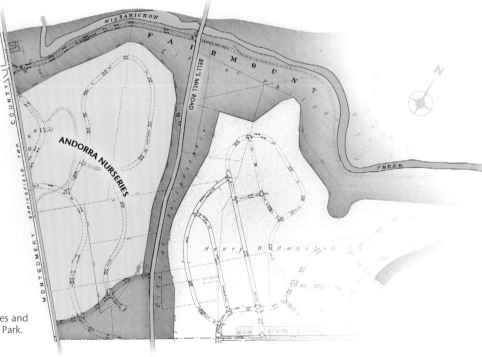

Map showing the location of the Andorra Nurseries and the site of the Andorra Natural Area in Fairmount Park.
Source: Franklin Survey Company, *Atlas of Philadelphia*, 1954

Cathedral Road

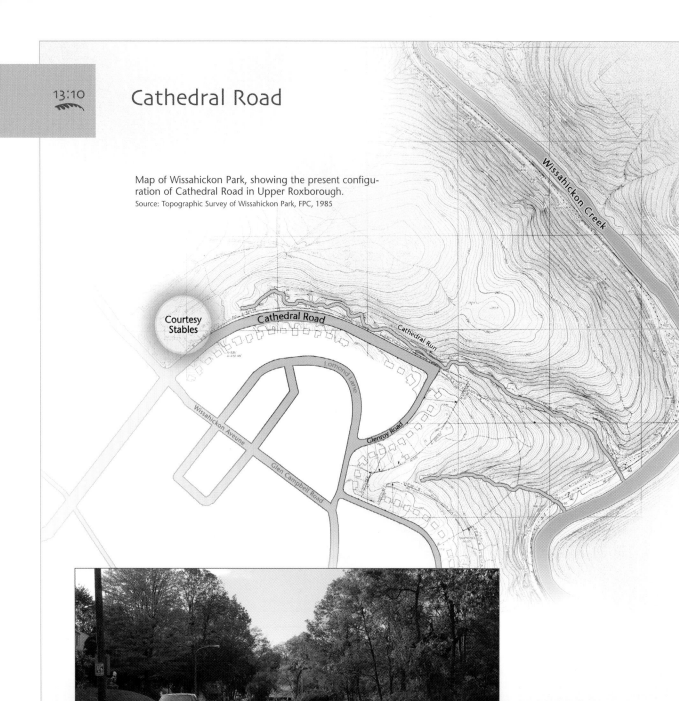

Map of Wissahickon Park, showing the present configuration of Cathedral Road in Upper Roxborough.
Source: Topographic Survey of Wissahickon Park, FPC, 1985

Courtesy
Stables

Cathedral Road

Cathedral Run

Lomond Lane

Wissahickon Avenue

Glen Campbell Road

Glenroy Road

Wissahickon Creek

Cathedral Road in Andorra, Upper Roxborough.
Bordered by park on one side and houses on the
other, the 4-lane cartway is inappropriately wide
for its present use as access to a small residential
enclave and entrance to the park.
Source: Photographs by CLF

1.

2.

3.

4.

5.

1. Healthy Cathedral Run above the stormwater outlet at the foot of Cathedral Road.
2. The foot of Cathedral Road where stormwater is funneled into the Wissahickon Park.
3. The deep gully formed by stormwater ripping out the sides of the tributary valley of Cathedral Run.
4. View up Cathedral Run from the park, showing a scoured and ripped out stream channel.
5. Close-up of the scoured stream channel, showing exposed roots and the undercut bank. The large trees on the edge of the stream bank are about to topple into the run.

A Threat to the Park Entrance at Wise's Mill Road

13:11–12

Just before the important gift of the Andorra Nursery property, and at the height of the new environmental consciousness, another critical piece of Roxborough, along Henry Avenue, was threatened and ultimately acquired as parkland. The top of Wise's Mill Road, where it joins Henry Avenue, is the only entrance to the center of Wissahickon Park from Roxborough. It is a direct access to Valley Green. The tiny tributary—Wise's Mill Run—flowed down the steep hillside along Wise's Mill Road, emptying into Wissahickon Creek, just north of the Valley Green Inn.

Wise's Mill Run. Photograph, c. 1910.
Source: GHS, Jellet Scrapbooks

This beautiful little stream had already been compromised in the 1960s by the construction (north of the intersection of Henry Avenue and Wise's Mill Road) of a massive high-rise apartment complex called "Henry on the Park." These five-story apartments formed long monolithic blocks at the western edge of the park. Since new zoning ordinances required these towers to provide one parking space per resident, the buildings were surrounded by mammoth parking lots. The resulting impervious cover (parking lots plus the roofs of the buildings) funneled stormwater into Wise's Mill Run. The speed and force of this concentrated water created deep gullies in the hillside and tore up the little stream.

One of the large, rectangular apartment blocks at "Henry on the Park," directly above Wise's Mill Run.
Source: Photograph by CLF

HENRY AVENUE (UNDER CONSTRUCTION)

RIDGE AVENUE

WISE'S MILL ROAD

On the property adjacent to the "Henry on the Park" complex, the Kaplan brothers, Seymour and Bernard, proposed to develop two additional apartment blocks, one ten and the other 11 stories high, with a total of 400 dwelling units. Like its neighbor, the roof and parking lot surfaces would generate huge volumes of stormwater runoff. Following the engineering methods of the day, this runoff would have been collected in pipes, dumped into Wise's Mill Run,and from there carried into Wissahickon Creek.

The Save the Wissahickon Committee, headed by FOW board member Dorothy Persichetti, was organized to oppose this project. Persichetti was the wife of the world famous musician and composer of American classical music, Vincent Persichetti, and they lived on a small inholding in the park—an old farmhouse above Wise's Mill Run. She persuaded the FOW to support the Save the Wissahickon Committee and to contribute over $2,000 to fight the developers in court.[11]

In the 1930s, the area surrounding Wise's Mill Road was almost entirely farmland. The majority of the farmland northwest of the road was held by the Hilltop Land Company, and later became "Henry on the Park," a massive apartment complex. Thirty-five acres southeast of Wise's Mill Road had been purchased by the park in 1902. Grading for the extention of Henry Avenue can be seen in the center of the picture. Aerial Photograph, 1938.
Source: FPC

Roxborough's Entrance to the Park | Wise's Mill Tract

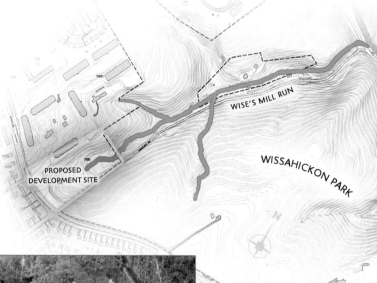

WISE'S MILL RUN

WISSAHICKON PARK

PROPOSED
DEVELOPMENT SITE

This old farm was once part of the proposed development tract on Wise's Mill Road. Farm remnants include a spring-house and farm building foundations. The area is the location of the damp, marshy headwaters of Wise's Mill Run.

Map of Wissahickon Park, showing Wise's Mill Road, Wise's Mill Run and the area of the proposed Kaplan developmemt.
Source: Topographic Survey of Wissahickon Park, FPC, 1985

Wise's Mill tract (now a part of Wissahickon Park). In the background, one of the seven, large rectangular "Henry on the Park" apartment blocks can be seen.
Source: Photographs by CLF

Wise's Mill | The Sad Story of a "Protected" Stream

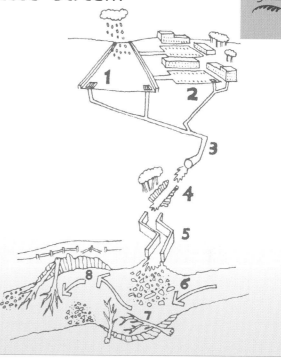

1. To accommodate new development Henry Avenue becomes a four-lane arterial.

2. New high density, high-rise apartments, with large parking lots, are built at the edge of the plateau adjacent to the steep slopes of Wissahickon Park.

3. Stormwater runoff is collected and piped from the roofs and parking lots and is discharged into Wise's Mill Run, a tributary of Wissahickon Creek.

4. Where the water is discharged, the increased volume and velocity erodes deep gullies in the hillside.

5. Park staff armor Wise's Mill Run with concrete to prevent increasing erosion.

6. Stormwater carries sediment into the run. This sediment builds deltas and destroys aquatic habitats in Wissahickon Creek.

7. The increased volume and velocity of the concentrated stormwater cuts into the streambank.

8. Trees on the eroded banks topple, further destabilizing the creek channel.

Source: *Chestnut Hill Local,* April 9, 1981, drawing and text by Rolf Sauer

One of the most vocal and active members of Persichetti's committee was architect Rolf Sauer, a founding partner of a local landscape architecture firm, Andropogon Associates, Ltd. (later Andropogon). He had already made a name for himself as a community activist, fighting air pollution by forcing the closure of the Manayunk incinerator. Sauer illustrated, step by step, the impacts of stormwater on the creek and on the park, from the proposed apartments. Published in *The Chestnut Hill Local*, his drawing helped to highlight, as the major environmental issue, the increased volume and velocity of the stormwater runoff.

Peter Hearn, an attorney representing the Save the Wissahickon Committee, summed up the community opposition by saying that the projected apartments would adversely affect "the public health, safety and general welfare . . . and substantially [impair] the scenic beauty and water quality of Wise's Mill Run and the Wissahickon Creek."[12] To reinforce their position, the committee brought in experts from the newly established Pennsylvania Department of Environmental Protection (PDEP) to review the site. The PDEP recommended a comprehensive study of the impacts of this project and the creation of regulations and guidelines for development in the valley. The City of Philadelphia agreed, refusing to grant the necessary building permits until this study was completed.[13] Lawsuits, zoning hearings and legal appeals kept the project in limbo for another decade, finally discouraging the Kaplan Brothers and eventually allowing the city to purchase this critical property in 1983 for $675,000.[14]

The Walter Biddle Saul School for Agricultural Sciences

Parkland in the lower section of the Henry Avenue corridor was characterized by lobes of plateau separated by tributary valleys. On the lobe directly south of Henry on the Park—and separated by the valley of Wise's Mill Run—the city chose the old farm fields above Wissahickon gorge as the site of the Wissahickon Farm School, founded in 1943. Today, the institution is a vocational school and the largest agricultural high school in the United States. Before the era of charter schools, this farm school was a unique part of the Philadelphia public education system.[15]

The Fairmount Park Commission rented the school site to the board of Education for a dollar a year. In 1966, the school district renamed the school the Walter Biddle Saul High School of Agricultural Sciences, to honor a prominent Philadelphia lawyer, Mt. Airy resident and former president of the Philadelphia Board of Education, who was a strong supporter of the school during its early years.

The multi-building complex is located on a 130-acre campus. On the community side of Henry Avenue, there are academic and agricultural buildings, an arboretum and athletic fields. On the park side, there is a working farm where students raise poultry, cows, pigs, sheep and horses. Barns on this farm are bordered by the school's golf course, nursery, field crops and pasture areas.

As it evolved, Saul School has recognized the possibilities of its unusual role in the city, teaching urban children agriculture, horticulture and ecology. Aquaculture is one of the school's specialities. It includes training in aquatic ecology, aquatic ecosystem issues, management and protection. The tradition of hands-on learning, which provides experiences outside the classroom, goes back to Saul's founding. In the 1940s, students participated in FOW-sponsored reforestation programs. The school has also had a composting program that makes soils from farm wastes and now incorporates mulched leaves from Fairmount Park, provided free to community gardeners. In recent years, the students have regularly monitored water quality in the Wissahickon Creek near the campus, assisted with trail maintenance, clean-up and fence repair in the park and have worked with the Pennsylvania Department of Fisheries to stock the creek with fish.

Saul's curriculum suggests the possibilities of a more effective use of the Wissahickon Valley with a new emphasis on the management of urban wildlands in its curriculum. The school could integrate academic courses in ecology, urban horticulture, and restoration with their "service learning" component. This focus would allow students to identify and tackle community problems and become "ecologically literate" citizens and professionals.

View of Saul School looking southwest towards Henry Avenue. Wissahickon Park is adjacent to the school on the far left. Despite unsympathetic 1950s and 1960s buildings, the school grounds preserve a little of the pastoral landscape of Upper Roxborough.

Source: Photograph by CLF

Environmental Planning

Along Henry Avenue, all of the significant tracts next to Wissahickon Park—Andorra, Henry on the Park, the Wise's Mill Tract and Saul School—were developed without an overall, coordinated plan for the corridor. With the successful battle to save the Wise's Mill tract, there was pressure on the city from the state and local citizens to include environmental regulations with other land use planning controls. The Wissahickon Watershed Ordinance (Bill #14-1603.2), enacted by the Philadelphia City Council in 1975, was the direct result.

This very forward-looking piece of legislation created controls within the zoning code for a special district (or zoning classification)—the Wissahickon Watershed. The new district would encompass the area generally bounded by Ridge Avenue, Schoolhouse Lane, Germantown Avenue, Mt. Airy Avenue and the Montgomery County Line. The environmental controls would be administered by the Philadelphia City Planning Commission, then under Marty Soffer. They included limitations on impervious coverage, regulations for building on steep slopes and standards for erosion control. Detailed development guidelines for building in the valley adjacent to the park were issued in a companion report—*The Wissahickon Watershed Development Guide*—published by the Philadelphia Planning Commission in 1976. Both the guide and the ordinance were written by Robert Coughlin (a Chestnut Hill resident) and Thomas Harmon of the Regional Science Research Institute, with advice from a task force of local citizens and officials from both state and city governments.[16]

The ordinance and guide grew out of the recognition that standard zoning ordinances were inadequate to address problems in the Wissahickon watershed. Philadelphia's first zoning code, adopted in 1933, had been modified in 1962 to expand the number of classifications or districts and to reflect new land uses, unknown when the code was initially developed. The 1962 zoning ordinances "were designed only to regulate development in accord with traditional planning concepts, such as density, land use relationships, light and air...and did not deal directly with protection of the natural environment. . . . To prevent the further degradation of Fairmount Park and the Wissahickon Creek a new kind of environmentally based development control has been devised."[17] The ordinance addressed the problems of "silted streams, eroding hillsides, and washed out trails" by: "1. requiring the preparation of earth moving plans, 2. limiting the extent of impervious ground cover, 3. controlling construction on steep slopes, and 4. requiring setbacks from water courses," and explained in detail how to accomplish these goals.[18]

The guide also emphasized the relationship between environmental quality and the exceptional beauty of the Wissahickon Valley neighborhoods. It urged preservation of the cultural landscape and incorporated aesthetic policies, advocating the continuing use of the best local development traditions. "Concern for the environment of the Wissahickon Watershed includes the man-made as well as the natural elements .... Standards for good site planning and architecture are not easily defined or quantified, however, since buildings are an important part of our surroundings, their proper design is a matter of public interest."[19]

13:13

Wissahickon Watershed Special District

**RECOMMEDED RESTRICTIONS
ON IMPERVIOUS COVERAGE
(% OF ALL LAND)**

COVERAGE LIMITED TO 20% MAXIUM

COVERAGE LIMITED TO 27% MAXIUM

COVERAGE LIMITED TO 35% MAXIUM

COVERAGE LIMITED TO 45% MAXIUM

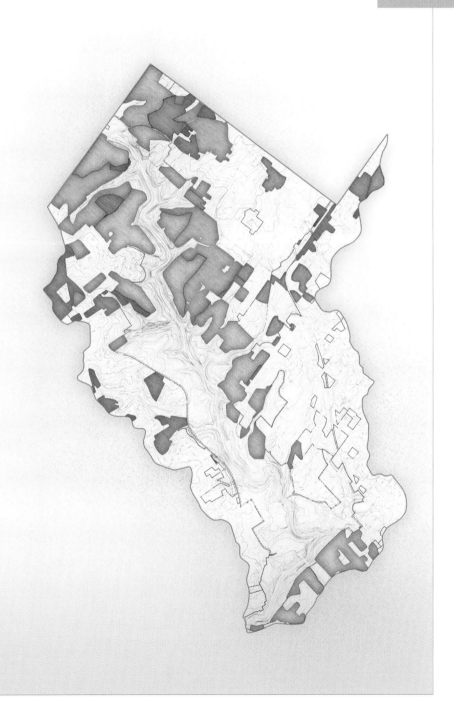

Wissahickon Watershed Special District, the first
environmental zoning in the City of Philadelphia. The
map shows the boundaries of the new zoning district
and the restrictions on impervious cover within this
area. The goal of these new regulations and policies
was to control development in the neighborhoods
surrounding Wissahickon Creek—Roxborough,
Chestnut Hill, Mt. Airy and East Falls—the only areas
of Philadelphia given such protection.

Source: Map by the Regional Science Research Institute, for the
Philadelphia City Planning Commission, 1976

An Environmental Sensibility

An environmental consciousness emerged in the context of a growing scientific understanding of the natural world and the reaction to the excesses of "prosperity and progress." From the early 1950s through the mid-1970s, individuals and organizations concerned about the Wissahickon Valley began to see the park and its immediate surroundings as part of an integrated system.

Each of the communities bordering the Wissahickon in the post-World War II period succumbed, in varying degrees, to suburban models that did not respect the terrain, the native vegetation or the building traditions of the area. Upper Roxborough, still rural at the end of World War II, was particularly impacted. The result was a legacy of awkward, often shoddy and environmentally destructive development, poorly integrated into the earlier fabric.

New and revitalized community organizations emerged to fight threats to the valley. The Wissahickon Watershed Ordinance and the accompanying *Development Guide* initiated bold new ways of looking at and preserving the valley. A few skilled and persistent individuals identified problems, focused the discontent, organized protests and envisioned viable solutions. Civic activists and donors of both land and money multiplied their effectiveness through public-private partnerships. Without the intervention of the Pennsylvania Department of Environmental Protection and the cooperation of city agencies (such as the Philadelphia Department of Licenses and Inspections, the Philadelphia Zoning Board of Adjustment and the Philadelphia Planning Commission), the protest against the development af Wise's Mill Road could not have succeeded. Without cooperation from the Fairmount Park Commission, the coordinated private donations and public land purchases would not have been possible.

The Wissahickon in Crisis

1975-1990

14

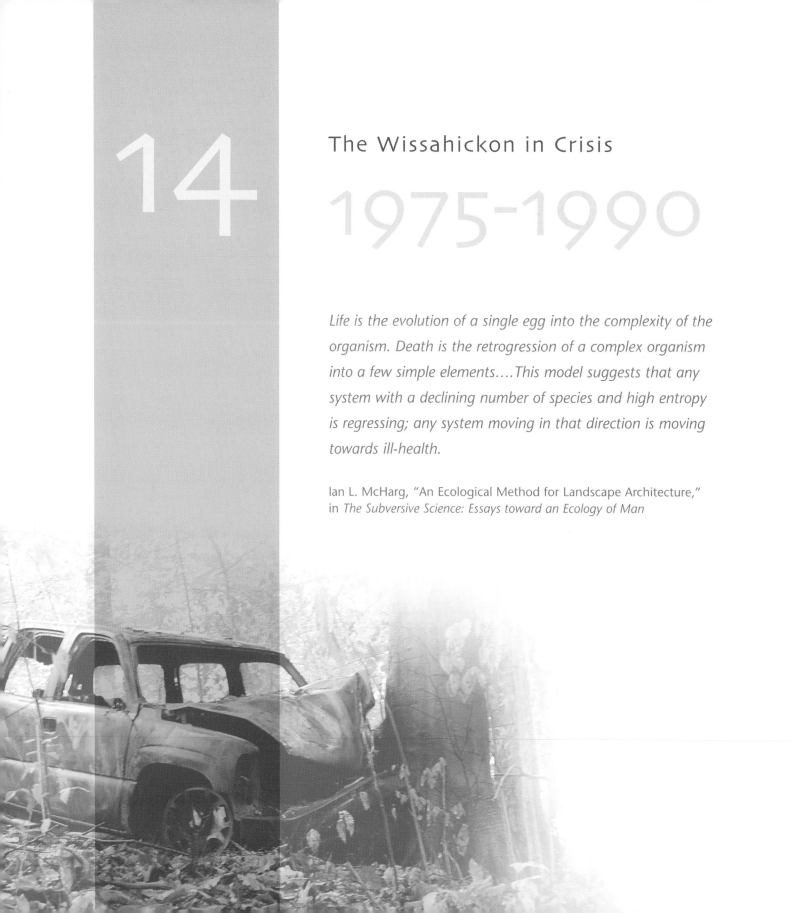

14

The Wissahickon in Crisis

1975-1990

Life is the evolution of a single egg into the complexity of the organism. Death is the retrogression of a complex organism into a few simple elements....This model suggests that any system with a declining number of species and high entropy is regressing; any system moving in that direction is moving towards ill-health.

Ian L. McHarg, "An Ecological Method for Landscape Architecture," in *The Subversive Science: Essays toward an Ecology of Man*

While the growing environmental awareness of the last decades of the 20th century led park advocates to a slow recognition of the Wissahickon forest as an ecosystem, it became increasingly evident that this system was deteriorating. Ironically, as the era of environmental awareness waned (in a reaction that was both local and national) the valley itself suffered from a combination of destructive impacts and a lack of focused, informed stewardship.

By the 1970s, Philadelphia was a city with both a shrinking population and a shrinking economic base. In this context, the Fairmount Park Commission experienced continuously declining budgets and was unable to enhance or even to maintain its vast park system. Equally as crippling, a citywide political blindness to the vital importance of Fairmount Park turned the attention of city officials to other arenas. A succession of Philadelphia mayors, both competent and incompetent, had little interest in the park system. Park budgets shrank, relatively and in real dollars, over the next decades. Inadequate funding meant an ever-smaller park staff, faced with an ever-growing backlog of maintenance. The postwar Fairmount Park staff, drawn from horticultural schools of the time, had no state-of-the-art expertise in natural resource management. Once hired, they received little training in this field, and, as a result, were unable either to identify or to solve contemporary park problems.

By the late 1970s, a decline of environmental activism locally reflected the nationwide backlash against the environmental reforms of the 1960s. The election of conservative presidents like Ronald Reagan, whose secretary of the interior, James Watt, undid much of the environmental progress of the previous years, helped to institutionalize this backlash.

During this period, new forms of recreation became widely popular around the United States and in the valley. Mountain biking, jogging, rock climbing and cross-country skiing reflected a general dedication to the pursuit of vigorous physical exercise apparently linked to a growing obsession with health and beauty. These activities gradually superseded (but did not completely replace) the older and gentler pastimes of walking, horseback riding, sleighing, ice-skating, picnicking, fishing, dabbling in the creek, leisurely bike riding, painting, photography and poetry writing. At the same time, a far greater number of people from a wider set of cultural backgrounds, discovered the opportunities of the park. More strenuous activities, greater numbers of people, and conflicting ideas of appropriate park use, would all help to unravel the fabric of the park.

By the mid-1970s, park infrastructure—bridges, roads, paths, and trails—were badly in need of repair, as were other parts of the built landscape—shelters, guard rails, gardens and water features. Dumping and vandalism, always something of a problem, grew worse, as users discarded the increasingly elaborate packaging of the postwar period. This problem expanded as park staff shrank and were unable to clean up all of the litter.

Cumulative environmental impacts, which were to grow increasingly worse over the next decades, also helped to unravel the ecosystem of both the middle and lower valley. Severe erosion, the chemical, physical and biological collapse of the soil, changes to the hydrologic cycle, the disappearance of native wildflowers, songbirds and small mammals, the assault of invasive plants and new pests and diseases, were all manifestations of widespread ecological decay.

Decline of the City and the Park Commission

As many businesses and residents left for the suburbs, or for other parts of the country, Philadelphia's population declined from 1.95 million in 1970 to 1.6 million in 1990, and then to just over 1.5 million in 2000.[1] In this last census, Philadelphia was one of only two major cities in the United States, the other being Detroit, which failed to gain population. With the exception of certain gentrified neighborhoods near center city, and middle-and upper-middle-class neighborhoods in the far northwestern and northeastern parts of the city, those who remained behind were generally the poorest and the least skilled.

Responding to a decline in revenues, Philadelphia's city government continued its policy of cutting back on park funding. Between 1955 and 2000, the number of park employees in Philadelphia declined from 1,302 to 229, a rate far faster than the city's decline in population. While the city's population fell by approximately 28 percent during this period, the Fairmount Park staff declined by a shocking 82 percent. In 2003, the park appropriation from the city was just $14 million, an amount that represented less than half of one percent of the total municipal budget, despite the fact that the park system made up about 12 percent of the city's land. These disastrous cuts made it difficult for park staff to do more than mow grass and pick up trash. The staff, educated in "horticultural park maintenance" of a previous generation, was unprepared to recognize or tackle these new threats.

By the end of the 20th century, Philadelphia was spending only $13.00 per resident on parks, making it 19th in spending out of the 25 largest municipal park systems in the United States. When compared to the 11 largest systems in the country, Fairmount Park fared even worse. In 2001, Philadelphia spent the fewest dollars per park acre—just $1,890 compared to the $14,421 spent by Cleveland, and the $37,578 spent by top-ranked Chicago. In the ratio of park acres to maintenance staff, Philadelphia, at 40.6 acres per employee, was also in last place among the 11 major park systems. Furthermore, Philadelphia's poor record compared very unfavorably to cities with far fewer acres per park employee—Cincinnati's 10 acres and Chicago's 2.3 acres.[2]

14:1–2

14:3

City Government Grows | City Population Declines

As of 2007, Philadelphia's population was 1,448,394 people. Since 2000, the city's population has declined 4.56 percent.[1]

According to the *Philadelphia Inquirer*, "Three factors dominate why city government costs more. First, city employees' wages and benefits have increased at a greater rate than inflation. Second, the city spends more on social services programs for the poor. Third, crime has grown dramatically, requiring more public-safety employees."[2]

Although the population has declined, the city budget has doubled, and the number of city employees per 1,000 residents has grown, but Fairmount Park budgets and park staff have declined.

1. Website: bestplaces.net/city/Philadelphia
   _PA-54260000000.aspx.

2. *Philadelphia Inquirer*, February 2, 2003.

POPULATION

Since 1960, the city's population has declined by nearly 500,000 people ...

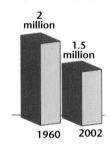

Population declined 25 percent during the 40-year period.

... yet the number of city employees per 1,000 population has grown ...

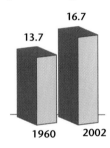

This information is for employees paid out of the general fund, which is the city's main budget.

... causing the city budget to double ...

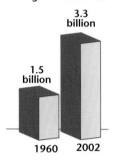

The budget Richardson Dilworth proposed in 1960 totaled 1.5 billion in today's dollars. The budget the city is operating under in 2002 totals $3.3 billion.

FAMILY INCOME

In 1960, four out of five people in Philadelphia earned a middle-class income, and less than one in five was poor ...

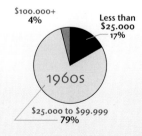

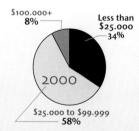

... but by 2000, only three of every five people were in the middle class, and the percentage of families that were poor doubled.

Source: *Philadelphia Inquirer*, February 2, 2003

City Government Grows | City Population Declines (Continued)

CRIME AND LAW ENFORCEMENT

With a rise in poverty has come a rise in crime, and an increase in efforts to fight crime.
(Data are per 1,000 population in Philadelphia for 1960 and 2002.)

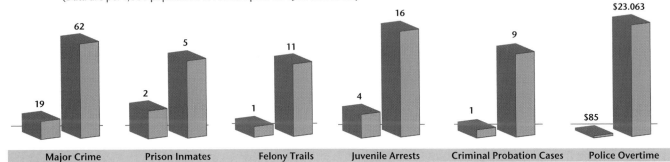

19 / 62	2 / 5	1 / 11	4 / 16	1 / 9	$85 / $23.063
Major Crime	**Prison Inmates**	**Felony Trails**	**Juvenile Arrests**	**Criminal Probation Cases**	**Police Overtime**

CITY WORKFORCE

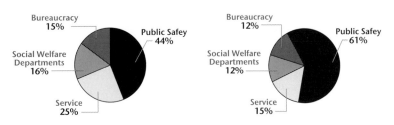

1960 pie chart:
- Bureaucracy 15%
- Public Safey 44%
- Social Welfare Departments 16%
- Service 25%

2002 pie chart:
- Bureaucracy 12%
- Public Safey 61%
- Social Welfare Departments 12%
- Service 15%

**Deployment of City jobs has changed.
Now, six out of 10 employees work in public safety ...**

Job deployment in 1960 ...   ... and in 2002.

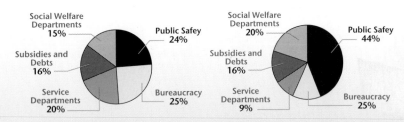

1960 budget pie chart:
- Social Welfare Departments 15%
- Public Safey 24%
- Subsidies and Debts 16%
- Service Departments 20%
- Bureaucracy 25%

2002 budget pie chart:
- Social Welfare Departments 20%
- Public Safey 44%
- Subsidies and Debts 16%
- Service Departments 9%
- Bureaucracy 25%

**... and 44 cents of every dollar in the general fund is spent
on those public safety jobs.**

Budget breakdown in 1960 ...   ... and in 2002.

Mayor Richardson Dilworth spent
millions on infrastructure improvement; he also
hired more city employees, and raised their
wages, paying for it all by increasing taxes.

Source: *Philadelphia Inquirer*, February 2, 2003

Park Facts

PHILADELPHIA PARKS ALLIANCE I Philadelphia Parks by the Numbers
IN PROFILE: Fairmount Park Commission and Philadelphia Department of Recreation

How does Philadelphia measure up when compared with other cities?

City	Population	Total Park Expenditure	Expenditure Per-Resident
Seattle	57,911	$152,448,993	$266
San Francisco**	739,426	$186,484,899	$252
Minneapolis	372,811	$56,328,061	$151
Cincinnati	331,310	$46,176,411	$139
Chicago	2,842,518	$390,961,599	$138
New York	8,213,839	$812,057,360	$99
Cleveland	452,208	$43,227,398	$96
Denver	557,917	$52,296,630	$94
Atlanta	483,108	$43,756,158	$91
Phoenix	1,461,575	$124,634,565	$85
Boston**	596,638	$45,190,179	$76
Dallas	1,213,825	$71,271,546	$59
Detroit	886,671	$50,800,000	$57
Philadelphia	1,463,281	$82,258,038	$56
Dept. of Recreation (PDR)		$62,959,755	$43
Fairmount Park (FPC)		$19,240,283	$13
Baltimore	640,064	$33,469,825	$52
Pittsburgh**	316,718	$15,682,033	$50
Houston	2,076,189	$85,421,145	$41
Los Angeles**	3,844,829	$128,725,919	$33

AVERAGE $101.94

Total Park-Related Expenditure Per Resident, by City, **Selected Cities - (FY '05)** Source: Center for City Park Excellence, Trust for Public Land

* Total expenditure includes both operating and capital expenditure, but excludes stadiums, zoos, museums and aquariums. If acity has more than one agency, expenditures are combined.
** Indicates estimate based on prior year's information.

City	Population	Total Park Acres	Employees Per-1000 Acres
Cleveland	1,272	3,117	408
San Francisco**	1,544	5,773	267
Chicago	3,002	11,860	253
Oakland	608	3,082	197
Seattle	989	6,050	163
New York	5,748	38,147	151
Pittsburgh**	412	2,838	145
Boston**	616	5,496	112
Minneapolis	580	5,359	108
Detroit	620	5,890	105
Atlanta	401	3,829	105
Los Angeles**	2,218	23,749	93
Baltimore	383	4,905	78
Philadelphia***	669	10,600	
Dept. of Recreation (PDR)		1,400	357
Fairmount Park (FPC)		9,200	18
Phoenix	1,476	38,040	39
Houston**	1,024	56,405	18

AVERAGE 163.5

Number of Non-Seasonal Park Employees per 1,000 Acres, by City, **Selected Cities - (FY '06)** Source: Center for City Park Excellence, Trust for Public Land

* Total park acres include city, county, metro, state and federal acres within the city limits.
** Indicates estimate based on prior year's information.
*** Includes park acres for FPC and PDR only.

Source: Philadelphia Parks Alliance, December 2007

Park Facts   *(Continued)*

PHILADELPHIA PARKS ALLIANCE I Philadelphia Parks by the Numbers
IN PROFILE: Fairmount Park Commission and Philadelphia Department of Recreation

How does Philadelphia measure up when compared with other cities?

FAIRMOUNT PARK COMMISSION (FPC) PROFILE FY '07	FAIRMOUNT PARK COMMISSION STAFFING TRENDS	FAIRMOUNT PARK RANGER STAFFING TRENDS

FAIRMOUNT PARK COMMISSION (FPC) PROFILE FY '07

- Fiscal 2007 Operating Budget: $12.9 million
  (0.34% of the City's total budget)
- Fiscal 2006 Capital Budget: 0
- Land Area: 9,200 acres, or 10% of the City
- 63   Neighborhood and Regional Parks
- 40   Playgrounds
- 1   Day Camp
- 113   Tennis Courts
- 155   Athletic Fields
- 40   Basketball Courts
- 1   Recreation Center
- 469   Structures
- 215   Miles of Recreational Trails
- 30,000   Individual Volunteers
- 80   Friends Groups

FAIRMOUNT PARK COMMISSION STAFFING TRENDS

1970   637 Employees
1975   489 Employees
1980   433 Employees
1985   411 Employees
1990   304 Employees
1995   233 Employees
1999   215 Employees
2000   219 Employees
2001   219 Employees
2002   217 Employees
2003   206 Employees
2004   201 Employees
2005   179 Employees
2006   169 Employees
2007   169 Employees

FAIRMOUNT PARK RANGER STAFFING TRENDS

1971   525 Fairmount Park Guard Police
2004   18 Fairmount Park Rangers
2005   16 Fairmount Park Rangers
2006   18 Fairmount Park Rangers
2007   18 Fairmount Park Rangers

Data from the Fairmount Park Commission

PHILADELPHIA DEPARTMENT OF RECREATION (PDR) PROFILE FY '07

SOURCE OF FUNDS
General Funds
$37,389,655
Fees Retained by the Agency
$413,366
State & Federal Support
$6,592,673
Capital Income Total
$10,766,289
(General Capital Project Fund)
$30,000
(PICA Capital Projects Fund)

EXPENDITURE
Ground & Facilities,
Maintenance & Repair, $12,793,901
Recreational Programming
& Activities $25,278,480
Capital Construction / Acquisition
(General Capital Project Fund)
$10,766,289
(PICA Capital Projects Fund)
$24,750

TOTAL

Agency Acreage in City	1349
Acreage as percent of City	1.57%
Acres per 1,000 residents	0.899
Number of Recreation Centers	162
Outdoor Pools	78
Indoor Pools	8
Baseball Fields	316
Football/Soccer Fields	156
Tennis Courts	215
Basketball Courts	292
Hockey Courts	52
Neighborhood Parks	76*
War Memorial Parks	8
Ice Skating Rinks	5
Miles of Bikeways/Greenways	0
Number of Full Time Employees	457
Seasonal Employees	1,837
Part Time Employees	130
Rec Center Advisory Councils	169
Parks Friends Groups	50
Spray Grounds	4

*Number from Philadelphia Green, Pa. Horticultural Society

DEPARTMENT OF RECREATION STAFFING TRENDS

FY 2000   613 Full-time Employees
FY 2002   575 Full-time Employees
FY 2003   593 Full-time Employees
FY 2004   586 Full-time Employees
FY 2005   511 Full-time Employees
FY 2006   469 Full time Employees
FY 2007   457 Full time Employees

Data from the Department of Recreation

Source: Philadelphia Parks Alliance, December 2007

The Park System—Underfunded and Understaffed

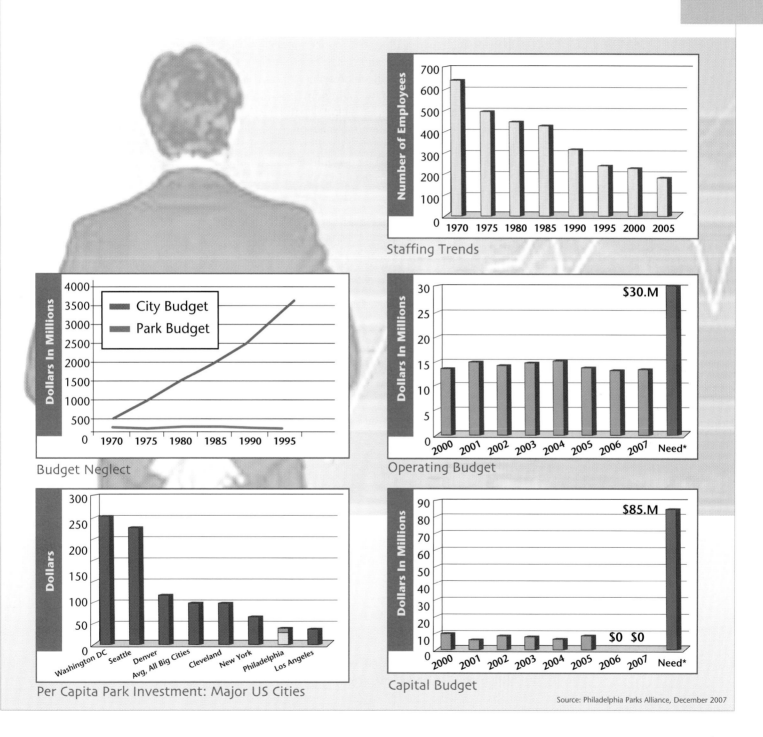

Staffing Trends

Budget Neglect

- City Budget
- Park Budget

Operating Budget

$30.M

Per Capita Park Investment: Major US Cities

Capital Budget

$85.M

$0 $0

Source: Philadelphia Parks Alliance, December 2007

Besides financial problems, the park commission continued to suffer from bureaucratic and political difficulties. Peter Harnik, in his book *Inside City Parks*, which compares the strengths and weaknesses of the nation's largest park systems, writes that much of the money for parks in Philadelphia went to the Department of Recreation for playgrounds, ball fields and other facilities. The park commission itself was starved for funds to conduct even routine maintenance and certainly had no funds for capital improvements. The total adjusted budget for the Philadelphia Recreation Department in 1998 was approximately $48 million, as opposed to the Fairmount Park Commission that received just $21 million.

By the mid-1980s, the recreation department had more staff members and more facilities per capita than any other in the nation. According to Harnik, "Too many [recreation] centers [in Philadelphia] were created as political favors to city council members, and more than a few employees landed jobs as a result of cronyism rather than merit." When a budget crisis hit the city in the mid-1980s, the bloated recreation staff had to be cut from 1,200 to 489.[3]

Disbanding the Fairmount Park Guard

The Fairmount Park Guard was another casualty of budgetary constraints and political disregard for the value of urban wildlands. The guard, formed in 1868, patrolled the entire park system and enforced regulations. For over a century, these guardians were integral to park operations and park stewardship—curbing bad behavior, reporting problems and caring for both visitors and creatures.

Captain Everett Stringfellow and Fairmount Park Mounted Color Guard. Photograph, c. 1940s.
Source: CHHS

Citing budgetary constraints, Mayor Frank Rizzo disbanded the park guard, ending this distinguished legacy. The change was a three-stage process. In September 1968, the guard's official title became the Fairmount Park Police. Then, in February 1972, the park commission agreed, under pressure from the mayor, that these new park police should answer to the city police commissioner. By May 1972, the park police were merged into the city's police department and disappeared as a separate entity.

Twice daily trips along Forbidden Drive by police in patrol cars were no replacement for the guards on foot or on horseback, who spent their whole day as a presence in the park. Before the merger, approximately 525 guards had patrolled 7,731 acres of parkland. They were assigned on a long-term basis to one of seven park districts and were well-known and liked in their jurisdictions. After the merger, only a handful of city police patrolled both East and West Park, as well as the Wissahickon.[4]

Disengagement of the FOW

In the 1960s and early 1970s, FOW efforts had increased community understanding of environmental problems in the park. The organization had participated in citywide environmental legislation and had partnered with the Wissahickon Valley Watershed Association (WVWA), the stewardship organization in the middle valley, on regional planning initiatives.

Unfortunately, the next generation of the FOW gradually closed these doors. This later group loved the park as much as their predecessors. They made important contributions—keeping park history alive, removing graffiti and trash and operating and maintaining the Valley Green Inn. For this group, however, it seemed that the original FOW mission had been fulfilled with the preservation efforts of the past, and they did not understand the crucial difference between "conservation" and "restoration," or realize that what the founders of the FOW had conserved was now falling apart. They rejected the regional focus of the previous decade and turned inward to small-scale, local projects. Failure to recognize a wider spectrum of problems meant that there was no civic discussion or leadership to solve these issues. Elitism and a narrowness of focus would stultify the FOW and exacerbate the crisis in the valley.

Vandalism, Dumping, Littering and Arson

Paper, plastic, construction debris, discarded tires, abandoned cars and motorcycles have been problems in American parks for many years. In the Wissahickon, littering and "short dumping" became increasing problems after World War II, a symptom of an affluent, throwaway society.

Vandalism took a number of forms. Short dumping of everything from trash to old refrigerators at the edges of the park became a terrible problem from the early 1960s onward. Increased amounts of trash led to higher fees to dispose of materials in landfills, encouraging people to use the park as a free dumping area. Abandoned cars were pushed over the sides of the valley or driven into the creek. When stocking of trout resumed in the early 1970s, littering became a major problem. In fishing season, fishermen with six packs of beer and considerable gear left the creek banks strewn with cans and plastic bags.

14:4–5

As the park sank into neglect, rocks were spray painted and the heads of statues were lopped off. The old WPA structures were covered with graffiti or stripped of their shingles. Plants, especially evergreens—hemlocks, laurels, and Christmas ferns—were dug up and taken for private gardens. Arson, a minor problem in the 1970s, became increasingly destructive. In the spring of 2008, a new composting toilet was smashed and a new tool shed (a repaired WPA structure) had its roof burned. Graffiti, littering, dumping, vandalism and arson compromised the "primeval" experience, making the park feel like a dangerous and derelict urban setting—no longer a "place apart."

During the late 1970s, the park commission itself was guilty of a form of dumping when it allowed debris from city projects, including the midtown tunnel, to be used to "improve" trails at Kitchen's Lane and those opposite Valley Green. Park staff bulldozed

14:6

Vandalism

Decreasing park budgets and cuts in staff made maintenance and enforcement of park rules more difficult. In 2007, Patricia Crossan, manager of Fairmount Park District #3, which covers the northwestern region, had only nine maintenance staff and one supervisor to manage about 2,300 acres of the Fairmount Park system. The responsibilities of her staff include Wissahickon Park, as well as several small, separate parks (such as Pastorious Park), all the buildings within District #3, 24 picnic sites,10 sports fields and seven playgrounds.

Of all the areas in Wissahickon Park that suffer from littering and vandalism, Devil's Pool has been a recurring problem. This area, at the confluence of the Cresheim and Wissahickon Creeks, has been a special and beloved area since the gatherings of the Lenni-Lenape. Renowned for its picturesque rock cliffs, overhanging hemlocks and a deep, dark pool called Devil's Pool, this area is no longer designated an "official" picnic site by the park commission. Since the old, elevated, wooden walkways have rotted and have not been replaced, the main trail along Wissahickon Creek no longer crosses Cresheim Creek. This break, in a once continuous trail along the east side of the valley, represents a major interruption in park circulation. Park visitors are now forced to scramble down a steep rocky slope, wade across Cresheim Creek and clamber up the other side of another steep rocky slope. The desire to continue along Wissahickon Creek has created unauthorized trails and damaged the vegetation. The lack of access has also made maintenance very difficult.

As the culture of park users has changed, the Devil's Pool area has attracted a rowdier crowd. Crossan said in an interview with the *Chestnut Hill Local*: "It's my worst area. ... and it's an absolutely uncontrollable situation for the Commission....Park rangers are scared to approach the large drunken parties, and the only deterrent is to arrest them."[1]

1. Kristen Palzulski, "Vandalism and Litter Sully

Graffiti on rocks at Devil's Pool.
Source: Photograph by David Soffa

Devil's Pool?," *Chestnut Hill Local*, July 20, 2006

Graffiti on the piers of the Walnut Lane Bridge. Many undersides of the large bridges in the park have been defaced.
Source: Photograph by CLF

Arson

Arson has been a recurrent problem in the park. One of the newly repaired WPA structures (off Kitchen's Lane) was set on fire. Arsonists also recently burned the roof off the newly reconstructed tool shed located where the park trail extension of Rex Avenue meets the creek.

WPA Guard House, at Allens Lane, burned to the ground. By 2007, this pavilion was rebuilt.
Source: Photograph by Edward Stainton

The burned tool shed at the bottom of Rex Avenue. By 2009, this little building was repaired.
Source: Photograph by CLF

Dumping

Like many parks and open spaces, Wissahickon Park has become an illegal dump site. Cars are pushed over the hillsides or are driven down the old mill roads and abandoned in the park.

Dumping of "organic materials" —dirt, leaves, grass clippings, Christmas trees and dead plants—is often thought to be harmless. People believe that they are simply returning natural materials to the forest. In fact, dumping at the edge of the woods is extremely destructive. Tree roots and the ground layer itself, which require air, are smothered. Weeds are carried in and take root in the soil piles. Disturbance encourages the spread of invasive exotic plants. Mulch piled up against tree trunks causes the bark to rot and the trees to die. The heat of composting leaves and grass kills the microorganisms in the living soil.

This rubble from the crosstown tunnel in center city Philadelphia was used to "repair" park trails. As the path erodes, these materials are exposed.

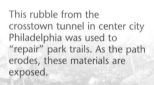

Piles of leaves and organic matter dumped at the edge of Wissahickon Park.
Source: Photographs by CLF

and widened the narrow forest trails on the upper slopes of the valley, using bricks, asphalt and chunks of cement as fill. This dumping has caused uneven surfaces, as fill materials continue to push up, and voids form where the ground has settled. Protests in May 1981 by William Klein, then director of the Morris Arboretum, environmental activist Sioux Baldwin and several community groups finally halted these "improvements," but this activity revealed the depths of indifference by city authorities to the park system.[5]

More People, New Activities

The countercultural revolution of the 1960s rejected the artificial and stressed the healing powers of nature. A new generation embraced the body as natural and good, and it was no longer considered vain and selfish to cultivate health and fitness. These attitudes merged with America's long love affair with youth. John Naisbitt in his book, *Mind Set!*, suggests that one consequence of the shift, from an industrial age to an information age, is the increasingly sedentary nature of work: "This shift has meant that we have become …more and more concerned about what we do with our bodies and what we put into our bodies, [and has created] an extraordinary era of body awareness."[6]

Greater and greater numbers of people were now enjoying the park—in sharp contrast to the 1940s and 1950s, when Wissahickon Park was almost empty. A nation-wide desire to look good, eat a healthy diet and exercise in a natural setting helped to alter park usage from the more traditional and genteel activities to more aggressive new sports. More active users created noticeable new impacts, particularly on the sensitive valley slopes of the gorge.

By 1983, there were approximately 200,000 mountain bikes in the United States and by 1990, some 15 million. Heavier shock absorbers gave bikers better access to rugged terrain. Improved gears permitted them to go up and down steeper slopes.[7] The narrow, upper trails of Wissahickon Park gave bikers technical challenges set in a beautiful forested landscape, all within 30 minutes of the center of the fifth most populous city in the United States.

A desire to improve performance, demonstrate prowess, and "feel alive" often led bikers to "pioneer" difficult territory, make grueling climbs, leap logs, ride along rocks, and careen down hills. As a result, "rogue" trails (undesignated pathways) were opened up and previously inaccessible, fragile areas were sometimes damaged. Growing numbers of mountain bikers on the upper trails also brought conflicts with pedestrians and equestrians.

Left
Bikers gather for a ride in Wissahickon Park.
Source: Photograph by Jon Pierce, Philadelphia Mountain Biking Association

Right
Biker and climbers begin young.
Source: Photograph by CLF

Decline of the Forest and the Park

The living forest is the foundation of all park experience. By the 1970s, the park was increasingly beloved by an ever-greater numbers of users, but the forest was under attack from many sources. The ecosystem of the valley was unraveling—losing not only its individual components—but also the structure and the richness of its plant and animal communities.

The ancient forest giants, with their trunks almost touching, were long gone, and by the mid-1970s, a radical change in species composition had occurred. The American chestnut (*Castanea dentata*) had vanished and the Canadian hemlock (*Tsuga canadensis*) was in severe decline. New and more virulent diseases and pests were afflicting other important canopy and understory species. Invasive exotics and opportunistic natives (both plants and animals) were replacing the major species of the earlier forest. Large native predators were gone. Amphibians (frogs, toads and salamanders) and the songbirds of the forest interior were dwindling significantly. The ground was increasingly eroded and covered with sparse leaf litter or mats of coarse, aggressive plants. The soil was thin and compacted. The thick matrix of organic materials rotting on the forest floor had vanished, and with it, the damp, spongy ground with its spectacular carpets of wildflowers and the masses of ferns.

Too Much or Too Little Water

On the plateau above the park, infill gobbled up much of the open land, greatly increasing the amount of impervious surface (roads, sidewalks, driveways, parking lots and even turf areas). Although the gorge in the lower valley was preserved in parkland, some neighborhoods adjacent to the park had at least 30 to 40 percent impervious cover—especially on the Roxborough side.

14:7

Impervious cover has a strong impact on the health of streams. Studies have shown that when hard, impermeable surfaces cover more than 10 percent of a watershed, stormwater runoff degrades the streams.[8] In addition, the park is the downstream recipient of the problems created by this increased runoff in the middle and upper valley.

In the middle valley, extensive development replaced fields and woodlots. Only a few areas were preserved as public open space. With weak legal protection and no coordinated plans, floodplains were encroached on, low areas and wetlands filled, tributaries and drainage channels buried. This familiar litany, the result of greed,

14:8-9

thoughtlessness, corruption and ignorance, allowed almost any available site to be used for building. With greater amounts of impermeable surface, rainwater and snowmelt, which would normally soak into the ground, ran over the land with increasing volume and velocity.

In the engineering paradigm of the postwar era, precipitation was treated as a nuisance, to be carried away as quickly as possible from developed areas. Regulations mandated an extensive network of curbs, inlets and pipes to capture stormwater and funnel it to the nearest waterway. Gradually this "plumbing" network replaced the natural drainage. This new system of "collection and conveyance" has resulted in a number of negative consequences.

Stream Health and Impervious Surfaces

Sensitive:
Under 10% impervious surface. Potentially still capable of supporting stable channels and good to excellent biodiversity.

Impacted:
11 to 25% impervious cover. Urbanization leads to significant impacts on stream health.

Non-supporting:
More than 25% total impervious cover. Impacts on stream quality include eroding banks, poor biological diversity and high bacterial counts.

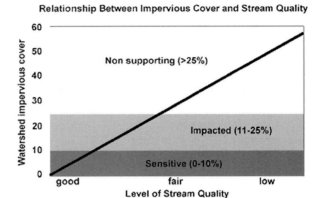

Relationship Between Impervious Cover and Stream Quality

Relationship between Stream Health and the Percentage of Impervious Surface
Source: .epa.gov/watertrain/protection/index2.html Stream Health

Source: Tom Schueler, "The Importance of Imperviousness" in *The Practice of Watershed Protection*, Center for Watershed Protection (Ellicott City, Md., 1994), 90-111

Hydrologic Cycle

The first diagram shows the destination of precipitation after falling on an undisturbed acre of land in the piedmont of Eastern United States (as in the forest of the Lenni-Lenape). The figures shown are for a one-year period, with an average of 45 inches of precipitation.

The second diagram shows the destination of precipitation after falling on a developed acre of land (as in a typical postwar suburban development). The figures shown are for a one-year period, with an average of 45 inches of precipitation.

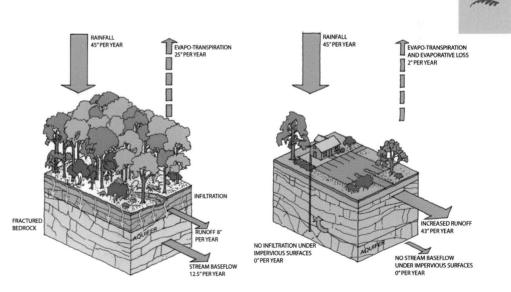

Source: Diagrams by Cahill Associates, Environmental Engineers, redrawn by Colin Franklin

A Sequence | The Consequences of Mismanaged Stormwater

A terrible reminder of the power of badly managed stormwater to compromise the small, precious preserved valleys, which are part of Wissahickon Park and the open space systems of the middle valley, came in the early morning of August 1, 2004. A large local storm dumped six inches of rain into the lower valley in just a few hours.[1] Arriving on the heels of one of the wettest Julys on record, the ground was too saturated for the new rainfall to sink in. In Wissahickon Park, torrents of water, gathering speed as it moved down the steep hillsides, carried tons of mud, rocks and vegetation into the creek.

The trail leading from the upper parking lot to Valley Green Inn collapsed into the little stream beside it, and the Valley Green Road buckled. At the extension of Rex Avenue, leading down to the Indian Statue, one side of the road was blown out and torn to pieces, the banks of the little tributary were washed away and a number of large trees were uprooted. All through the park, bridges were undermined and collapsed. Deep new gullies were carved out along the trails. Old wagon roads became stormwater conduits. Channeling water from impervious surfaces above the park, many of these roads were washed out and impassable.

On the Roxborough side (the most densely developed community in the lower valley and the one with

1. Stormwater runoff flows off impermeable surfaces (roofs and steep driveways) and moves with great volume and rapid speed down the hillside.
Source: Photographs by CLF

2. This picture shows the end result of stormwater flowing out of a single stormwater pipe. The water discharged at the top of the slope rapidly cuts a deep gully, exposing tree roots and destabilizing the trees.

the greatest amount of impervious paving), every small tributary became a muddy torrent. These small streams carried masses of rock and sediment down onto Forbidden Drive and left broad deltas of debris. Behind Valley Green Inn, an intermittent stream that began high above on Ridge Avenue flooded the new addition of the inn, covering the floors with several inches of mud. Wise's Mill Run and the Cathedral Road tributary sent avalanches of water, mud, and rocks down the hill into the park. When this heavily laden water arrived at the bottom of the valley, debris blocked the culverts under Forbidden Drive. These culverts then became elongated dams, causing the water to gouge new channels across Forbidden Drive and dump record amounts of sediment and pollutants into the creek.

In a second storm on September 28, 2004, communities upstream in Montgomery County were pounded with over ten inches of rain, innun-dating the creek in the lower valley with a torrent of floodwater that rushed through the channel at 17,000 cubic feet per second. In the lower valley, the flow in Wissahickon Creek on a normal day is 40 to 70 cubic feet of water per second.[1]

---

1. *Philadelphia Inquirer*, August 2, 2004; Mark A. Focht, telephone interview by Contosta, August 4, 2004. The six inches of rain on August 1, 2004 was measured by the gauge at the Tree House at the Andorra Natural Area.

3. Where gullies are formed in the hilside and erode below the water table, the gully carries water away from the plateau, preventing ground water recharge. It also acts as a "French drain," dewatering the adjacent slopes and lowering the water table still further below the entire hillside.

4. Many of the canopy and understory trees of the Wissahickon Valley, such as beech (*Fagus americana*), tulip poplar (*Liriodendron tulipifera*) and dogwood (*Cornus florida*), have shallow root systems and depend on a water table near the surface to survive drought. If the water table is lowered permanently (because it has not received recharge from rainfall), these trees will not survive.

5. Soil eroded from gullies, and from the hillside, is carried into the creek and its tributaries where the increased volume of water tears away at the banks, enlarges the channel, cuts the stream down to bedrock and brings increased silt, damaging aquatic life.

The Consequences of Mismanaged Stormwater *(Continued)*

This tiny tributary flowing into Wissahickon Creek along the road to Valley Green Inn
shows the ravages of the storm of September 2004.
Source: Photograph by Colin Franklin

Trail Erosion

Stormwater runoff problems have been exacerbated by the alignments of some park trails. Old mill roads had run perpendicular to the steep valley walls right down to the stream. With the creation of the park, they became part of a larger trail system.

These trails, which ran straight up and down the valley, became conduits for stormwater. Like the pipes that carry stormwater to the stream, these trails also concentrate the volume and increase the velocity of the water—magnifying the damage. During a storm, fast moving water tears down these conduits, stripping away the soil, sometimes down to bedrock. Many of these old mill roads have become gullies as deep as five or more feet.

Even the main park path, Forbidden Drive, is repeatedly damaged by stormwater runoff. This runoff causes the banks of the creek to collapse, taking with it trees, guardrails and path edges.

Source: Photograph by CLF

One of the most important of these negative consequences has been streams that have little or no water in dry periods or are badly flooded when it rains. Streams that suffer these major fluctuations of flow are called "flashy." In the Temperate Eastern United States, flashy streams have become the norm because concrete, asphalt and even well-maintained lawns are largely "impermeable" and do not allow water to soak into the ground. Because rain water does not have the opportunity to soak down into the water table, ground water levels are lowered and there is little water to seep gradually into the channel and refill the stream.

In an opposite effect, during storms, runoff from the surrounding impermeable land arrives quickly at a channel that is already swollen from upstream flow. These increasing amounts of water arriving at the stream, at a greater speed and with greater force, generate more frequent and more intense flooding.[9]

The channel of a healthy stream is gradually shaped over time to hold the average yearly flow in the stream. Water that fills the banks to the top of the channel is called "mean annual flow." When excessive amounts of water arrive at a stream in a storm, the stream begins to cut down and deepen the channel to accommodate this additional water. When the channel reaches bedrock, the stream then widens out to carry the larger volume of water. This reshaping of the channel signals a stream in trouble.

14:9-10

The Wissahickon Creek and the tiny streams that feed into it show all the characteristics of badly degraded urban waterways. Many banks of tributary streams in the Wissahickon Valley are steep and raw-sided, with exposed tree roots.[10] The small headwater streams that drain areas of only 20 or 30 acres have "downcut" their channels as much as four to six feet. These radical changes in the configuration of a healthy streambed have occurred because of greatly increased and accelerated runoff from areas developed as little as 10 years ago.

Dead and Dirty Water

Many pollutants continue to threaten the health of Wissahickon Creek and its tributaries. Soil brought down from construction sites and eroded areas above the creek mixes with soil eroded from the undercut channel to bring sediment into the stream. This sediment replaces the clear, deep pools with silty shallows.

Stormwater runoff also brings other pollutants—nitrates and phosphates (from fertilizer), ammonia and bacteria (from animal feces), salts, pesticides and herbicides (from yards, gardens and golf courses), oil and gasoline (from cars and trucks) and the occasional spill of toxic chemicals (from adjacent industries)—to degrade water quality.

Raw sewage is another major contaminant, especially during rainstorms. In Philadelphia, as late as the 1980s, only 40 percent of the streets were connected to "separate" sewer systems (with one pipe for stormwater and another pipe for human waste). The remaining network (generally in the older parts of the city) carried both sewage and stormwater in the same pipe. This system is called a "combined sewer" or "CSO." In big storms, these pipes could not handle the increased volume of water, and raw sewage spilled into the streams. High bacterial counts and the strong smell after heavy rains were unmistakable evidence of raw sewage in Wissahickon Creek.[11]

Although the Wissahickon Creek in the lower valley does not have a combined sewer system, it does have an interceptor wastewater sewer that runs parallel to the creek. Like all sewers, this interceptor can leak, allowing small amounts of raw sewage to enter the stream. In addition, water in Wissahickon Creek is augmented by partially treated sewage from five Montgomery County municipal treatment plants. According to the Philadelphia Water Department, "During dry weather—especially in summer when creek flow is diminished—on those hot, sultry days in July, the water flowing in the Creek may well be 90 percent treated effluent from these plants."[12]

Even "treated" discharge presents problems for Wissahickon Creek. Phosphorus and nitrogen—both components of human waste—are not completely removed. High levels of these nutrients fertilize aquatic plants and cause them to grow rapidly. As they grow, they suck up all the dissolved oxygen (DO) in the water. Deprived of oxygen, a wide variety of aquatic organisms die.

According to the Pennsylvania Department of Environmental Protection (PA DEP), in their October 2006 report, "Much of the Wissahickon Creek watershed is listed on the State's Integrated Water Quality Monitoring and Assessment Report list of impaired waters (303d) with impairments due to problems associated with elevated nutrient levels, low dissolved oxygen concentrations, siltation, water/flow variability, oil and grease, and pathogens…. Because of the significant volumes of treated wastewater assimilated by this stream, most of the sites exhibit low species abundance comprised of fish taxa characterized as pollution tolerant and generalist feeding guilds. The community lacks an abundance of top-predators, which is indicative of an unbalanced fishery. Wissahickon Creek is impacted by many sources including municipal and industrial wastewater discharges and non-point sources from both residential and agricultural land use." However, the PA DEP also notes that there are "indications that the basin's water quality conditions are not irretrievable." Some tributaries have a higher water quality. Water flowing from these tributaries into the main stem of the creek has improved conditions. Supporting scientific studies indicate that fish populations are improving downstream. In the lower reaches of the creek, bass (*Micropterus*

Head of American eel (*Anguilla rostrata*). Photograph from *DC Nature*.
Source: Website: lazy-lizard-tales.blogspot.com/2009/03/freshwater-eels-anguillidae.html.

salmoides) populations and stocked trout (*Salmo trutta*) occasionally live several seasons and reproduce. Perhaps the most hopeful sign is that the American eel (*Anguilla rostrata*), a migrating native fish, has been found in the lower and middle parts of the creek.[13]

Soil Is Not Just Dirt

The soil nurtures and supports all life in the forest ecosystem. Without a healthy soil, there is no forest. By the 1980s, many biological, structural, textural, and chemical changes appear to have taken place in the soils of the lower and middle valley.

Healthy soil is not just dirt, but a "biological soup" made up of inorganic material, decaying organic matter, water, air and billions of organisms of different sizes. Microorganisms—tiny animals and plants, as well as fungi (*eukaryote*) and bacteria (*prokaryote*)—too small to be seen by the naked eye, are essential to the structure and functions of the soil.

In the soil, the cycling of nutrients takes place mainly in the top two feet where air, water and food allow organisms to thrive. Healthy soil must be a loosely packed mixture of solids and voids to permit all this activity. Void spaces hold water and atmospheric gases (chiefly oxygen, nitrogen and carbon dioxide). When the soil is compressed by trampling, the network of pore spaces and soil aggregates are crushed and there is no longer any room for biological activity or for the soil to hold water and gases.[14]

Healthy soil is home to a very active community of microorganisms. These tiny plants and animals, as well as insects and burrowing creatures, break down dead or dying plant and animal life. This process of decomposition releases carbon dioxide into the air and nutrients into the soil.

Fungi are essential to the decomposition of woody plants. A forest, unlike a field, is composed primarily of woody plants. As Leslie Sauer explains in her book, *The Once and Future Forest*, "While herbaceous litter is primarily cellulose, the litter of the forest becomes increasingly higher in lignin, the woody component of plants."[15] Fungi of all sorts (as well as beetles and many other microorganisms) break down lignin into essential nutrients. Research has shown that fungi predominate in healthy forests, whereas in agricultural fields or grasslands, bacteria predominate.

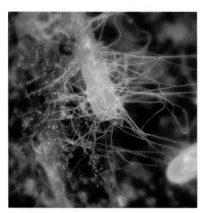

Mycorrhizae fungi on plant.
Source: Website: extension.iastate.edu

Mycorrhizal fungi in particular have an essential, cooperative association with woody plant roots. They act as extensions of the root hairs and greatly increase water and nutrient-absorbing surfaces. This partnership enables both plants and fungi to survive in nutrient-poor soils.

Millions of years of weathering have removed most of the phosphorous from older soils, such as those in Southeastern Pennsylvania. Phosphorus is a critical building block for genetic material. In the soils of the Wissahickon Valley, this mineral is often unavailable to plants, and the only access to phosphorous is in the leaf litter. Mycorrhizal fungi capture this phosphorous and make it available to woody plants.[16]

Most urban forests have lost fungal biomass. Fungi still predominate, but the ratio of fungi to bacteria has declined severely. Acid rain, nitrogen deposition, chemical changes and displacement caused by invasives and pollution are some of the reasons why this balance has shifted.[17] Almost certainly, the forest of the Wissahickon Valley is also suffering from this problem, although no soil studies have been undertaken.

New Pests and Diseases

New pests and diseases further unraveled the forest ecosystem. Most forest pests are insect infestations, which consume leaves, stems, and/or bark, weakening or killing their hosts. Diseases kill plants by affecting their ability to absorb and circulate nutrients. Woody plant diseases are spread by many pathogens—bacteria, viruses, fungi, nematodes and others. Pests, such as the elm beetle (*Scolytus multistriatus*), often serve as carriers of diseases. Environmental factors can stress and weaken plants, making them more susceptible to both pests and diseases. These factors include global climate change, urban heat blankets, acid rain and the disruption of natural, cyclical events.

During the first half of the 20th century, the chestnut blight destroyed a species that had once covered the upper slopes and ridges of the Wissahickon Valley. During the second half of the century, the wooly adelgid (*Adelges tsugae*) infestation, coupled with a scale (*Fiorinia externa ferris*), has eliminated many of the Canadian hemlocks (*Tsuga canadensis*). Both adelgid and scale originated in Asia and were brought in on ornamental plants. Pests and diseases, by diminishing or eliminating key tree and understory species, have radically changed the composition, structure and function of the historic forest.

Invasive Exotics

Continuous disturbance of the lower and middle valley—farming, logging, industry, commercial and residential development, pests, diseases, pollution, misuse, fragmentation, stormwater mismanagement, acid rain and finally climate change—have made the remaining natural lands very vulnerable to invasion by exotic plants and animals. While the impacts of rampant invasive exotics and the effects of native species out of balance are now widely recognized, in the early 1980s, these problems were neither seen nor understood.

Exotic plants were a part of the ecosystem even before European settlement in the Middle Atlantic region, carried east across the continent by Native Americans. European settlers also brought in a variety of plants from their homelands. Later exotics came from many sources and were often introduced with the best of intentions. The United States Department of Agriculture (USDA) Soil Conservation Service (now the Natural Resources Conservation Service, NRCS) imported a number of plant species for windbreaks, erosion control and cheap cattle feed. Nurseries and botanical institutions brought in others as the latest and most appealing ornamental plants.

Not all exotic plants and animals move out of gardens or agricultural areas and take over natural lands. Some remain tamely where they were planted and do not reproduce on their own. Other plants spread vigorously and thrive outside their original range.[18] However, with each new plant and animal introduction, it is difficult to tell how they will behave in the long run. In the Wissahickon Valley, the burning bush (*Euonymus alata*) was a seemingly harmless garden ornamental that over time has multiplied aggressively to become a major menace. In contrast, Norway spruce (*Picea abies*), a species of spruce native to northern Europe, has been widely planted, but has never reproduced locally. A plant or animal is most likely to become an invader if it comes from a parallel ecosystem. Species from other temperate, deciduous forests are the most likely to adapt to conditions in the Wissahickon Valley.

Both plant and animal invaders are "highly adaptable generalists," and flourish under almost any conditions. Carried into environments similar to their home ranges, but where many of the natural controls of their original habitats are not present, invasive exotics often become wildly successful and out-compete native species. In the process, genetic diversity is lost and the intricate and often interdependent connections of an ecosystem are unraveled. According to Chris Bright in his book, *Life Out of Bounds*, "Bioinvasion, the spread of exotics, is fast becoming one of the greatest threats to the earth's biodiversity. As a global threat of extinction, bioinvasion may rank just behind habitat loss, and increasingly, these two forms of ecological decay appear to be merging into a single syndrome. As more and more habitat is bulldozed away, the remnant natural areas grow ever more vulnerable to invasion."[19]

When invasive exotic vines cover the forest floor and choke out young seedlings or drape over saplings and understory trees, the natural trajectory of forest development is blocked. The landscape becomes static and the complex, layered structure of the forest is homogenized and its functions as food, shelter and breeding areas for native wildlife are lost.

Since the early 1950s, invasive exotics have increased exponentially in variety and numbers in the Wissahickon Valley, replacing native species that have shaped the character of the forest for centuries. Not surprisingly, the worst invasions of exotic plants occur along corridors of disturbance. From there, they move into the forest, along roads, paths, adjacent developed edges and areas of construction.

Although the focus by scientists and laypersons alike has been mainly on biological invasions above ground, these invasions can also occur beneath the soil. Non-native earthworms, as well as soil-dwelling pests and pathogens, have become a serious problem in the urban forests of the Middle Atlantic region. Studies have shown that non-native earth worms help to create a more hospitable climate for invasive plants. According to a research

Recognizing Disturbance | A Healthy Forest

In a healthy forest, the rich ground layer includes ferns, wildflowers and tree and shrub seedlings. The gap in the canopy is small, and the surrounding canopy trees are well on their way to closing this hole.
Source: Photographs by CLF

Signs of a healthy forest.

1. **Distinct forest layers:** Ground, shrubs and understory form visible layers under the canopy trees.

2. **A dynamic landscape:** Young plants can be seen everywhere, and there is reproduction in all layers.

3. **Birth, growth, maturity, death and rebirth:** In a healthy forest, recycling is a key process that adds to the sense of burgeoning life.

Fungi, under the leaf litter, are one important sign of a healthy forest.

team, "In the case of earthworms, much of their effect occurs because of their role as ecosystem engineers. They are capable of substantially changing the physical and chemical characteristics of the soil ..., with consequences for the entire soil foodweb, nutrient distribution, and even ... plant communities."[20]

Not surprisingly, Roxborough, with the densest and most conventional building patterns, has some of the worst problems with invasive exotics. Because the plateau is wider on the Roxborough side, more land was cleared for farming and was later available for development.

Recognizing Disturbance | An Unhealthy Forest

Signs of disturbance in a forest.

1. **An absence of distinct forest layers:** Heaping vines and broken branches blur the architecture of a healthy forest.

2. **A static landscape:** Little or no reproduction of native plants and vigorous reproduction of invasive aliens.

3. **Disruption of normal lifecycles, both in the whole landscape and in individual plants:** Wholesale death or damage should be a red flag of disturbance.

Eroded and compacted soil inhibits forest growth.

A severely disturbed forest in the lower Wissahickon Valley. Distinct forest layers are missing. Invasive exotic vines have smothered the forest floor, making regeneration difficult. The vines have distorted the growth of the trees and shrubs. Large holes in the canopy have developed where trees have died and have not been able to reproduce.

For the construction of Henry Avenue, hundreds of trees were cut and thousands of tons of fill were brought in. In the process, the removal of the original topsoil, and the mixing of the soil layers, destroyed the seed banks of local, forest plants. Seeds of invasive exotics came in with the new fill or were blown in from adjacent areas, finding opportunities to grow on the exposed subsoil. Invasive plants took hold along the forest edge and traveled from there deep into Wissahickon Park along the trails, which were themselves often lines of disturbance.

Invasive Exotic Worms

According to Peter Goffman who is studying exotic worms at the Cary Institute of Ecosystem Studies, "In most forest soils, the deep litter layer provides critical habitat for forest floor species. This layer exerts strong controls on nutrient cycling, nutrient retention, and seed germination. Exotic in the northeastern U.S., earthworms can transform the forest floor, impacting all of these processes."[1]

The Northeastern Temperate Deciduous Forest evolved without earthworms because they were driven south by the cold in the last ice age, 10,000 years ago. While the glaciers stopped in northern Pennsylvania, it appears that it was too cold in the Wissahickon Valley for native earthworms to survive.

Worms and their eggs probably first arrived in Southeastern Pennsylvania during the colonial period. They came in with the rocks and soil in ship ballast and on imported plants. New immigrants continued to bring in plants and soil. Later, nurserymen brought worms from both Europe and Asia on their plant stock. Fishermen contributed to this proliferation by using foreign worms as bait. Birds and the shoes of park visitors also helped spread these worms throughout the Wissahickon Valley.[2]

The European worm most often found is the nightcrawler (*Lumbricus terrestris*), a big worm. It is an "anecic" species that burrows deep into the soil pulling leaf litter down with it. Asian worms (generally *Amynthas hawayanus*) are smaller, and stay close to the surface, often living in the duff layer. According to Dennis Burton, Director of the Schuylkill

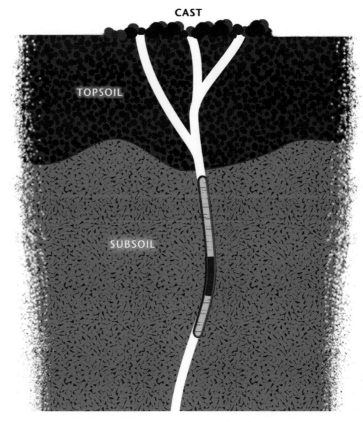

CAST

TOPSOIL

SUBSOIL

Center for Environmental Education, these worms are "like a rototiller running around the surface of the forest."[3]

Anne Bower, assistant professor of biology of the school of health and science at Philadelphia University, has been studying worms at the Schuylkill Center for Environmental Education for a number of years. She has found that, in rural areas, there are only two worms in every three square feet, but that urban forests have, on average, 89 worms in the same area.[4]

The results of USDA scientist Richard Pouyat's studies of New York City forests in the 1980s found that

exotic worms feed on the leaf litter that covers the soil, rapidly turning it into mulch in as little as one year, instead of the five years normally required for decomposition by native fungi.[5]

Leaf litter acts like a protective skin, retaining moisture, allowing small creatures to travel without drying out, protecting roots and microorganisms, preventing erosion, deterring pathogens and promoting seed germination. Ants and salamanders are reluctant to cross bare areas to transport the seeds of woodland wildflowers, reducing the opportunities for wildflower seeds to germinate in the nutrient rich refuse piles around an ant hill, or to be carried to new locations.[6]

Invasive exotic worms also change the chemistry of the soil. They secrete calcium carbonate, which makes the acid soil of the lower Wissahickon more alkaline. By rapidly converting leaf litter into mulch, worms create a microenvironment favorable to bacteria. These bacteria produce abnormally high levels of nitrates in the soil. Research has shown that high nitrates favor the proliferation of exotic vegetation, since native species are less able to process high levels of this naturally occurring chemical.[7]

1. Peter Goffman "Exotic Earthworms & Northern Temperate Forests" and "Invasion of North Temperate Forest Soils by Exotic Earthworms," Cary Institute of Ecosystem Studies. Website: ecostudies.org/people_sci _groffman_earthworms.html.

3. Anne Raver, "The Dark Side of a Good Friend to the Soil," *New York Times*, March 15, 2007.

3. Dennis Burton, quoted in Ibid.

4. Anne Bocherie, Lecture to the Friends of the Wissahickon, Conservation Committee, February 20, 2008.

5. Richard Pouyat, Lecture, "Earthworm Effects on Forest Soils: The Good, the Bad, and the Ugly." State of the Forest Symposium: Ecological Issues Regarding Highlands Forest Degradation & Restoration. Conservation Foundation, Morris County Cultural Center, N.J., October 3, 2002.

6. Albert J. Meier, Susan Power Bratton, David Cameron Duffy, "Biodiversity in the Herbaceous Layer in Appalachian Primary Forests," in Mary Bird Davis (ed.), *Eastern Old Growth Forests* (Washington, D.C., 1996), 50, 53.

7. Katalin Szlavecz, Sarah A. Placella, Richard V. Pouyat, Peter M. Groffman Csaba Csuzdi, Ian Yesilonis, "Invasive Earthworm Species and Nitrogen Cycling in Remnant Forest Patches," *Applied Soil Ecology* 32, 2006, 54-62.

The diagram on the opposite page shows earthworm "engineering" in forest soils. Scientists at the Cary Institute of Ecosystem Studies are exploring the decline in the depth of materials that traditionally constituted the forest floor and the redistribution of organic matter in the soil profile following earthworm invasion.
Source: Drawing based on diagram in Peter Goffman, "Exotic Earthworms & Northern Temperate Forests" and "Invasion of North Temperate Forest Soils by Exotic Earthworms," Cary Institute of Ecosystem Studies
Website: ecostudies.org/people_sci_groffman_earthworms.html

The European worm most often found in the Wissahickon Valley is the nightcrawler (*Lumbricus terrestris*), a big worm. The other most commonly found worm is a smaller, Asian species (*Amynthas hawayanus*).
Source: Photograph by Anne Bocherie

Farm fields in Roxborough, no longer used for agriculture after World War II, did not go through historical succession and return to healthy forest. The increasing environmental impacts of the period made healthy change to the landscape impossible. The Andorra Natural Area and the fields north of Saul School have become dense tangles of invasive exotics. Parallel to the Roxborough experience, construction in the middle valley has repeated this destructive dynamic, and the most disturbed areas of the middle valley are properties allowed to return to forest in the post-World War II period.

The Return of the Forest | Change over Time

1. Abandoned cropland—not a "blank slate."

2. Annual and biennial meadow—a continuous carpet.

3. Perennial Meadow—shifting mosaics.

4. Early Woody Old Field—mounds and thickets.

5. Late Woody Old Field—copses and groves.

6. Young Woodland—The closing of the canopy.

Diagrams showing historical "succession" (or change in the natural landscape over time) in the piedmont of the Eastern United States. This process has been seriously disrupted by an explosion of invasive exotics and opportunistic natives.
Source: Andropogon, drawings by Colin Franklin

Opportunistic Natives

Not all takeovers by either plants or animals are the result of the introduction of non-native species. Some native species—once part of an ecosystem in balance—have exploded in their populations and have had a destructive influence on large areas of Wissahickon Valley. Changes in habitat, loss of predators and government policy have all contributed to this problem.

By the early 1900s, the white tailed deer (*Odocoileus virginianus*) had been virtually eliminated in Pennsylvania, chiefly through hunting. The Pennsylvania Game Commission (established in 1895) actively worked to reintroduce and encourage this animal. Supported by hunters, the commission adopted a conservation model. In this model, game animals, like cutover forests, could be replenished and restored by legislative action and governmental agencies.

It took several decades for deer to return to Southeastern Pennsylvania (from the northern parts of the state), because these animals generally stay in the place where they are born, with only about 15 percent migrating each year. "Road kills" of deer in the Philadelphia area from 1971-93 indicate that the deer population grew from 40 in the period 1971-74 to 924 in 1990-93, an increase of 22 times in just two decades. The number of antlered deer shot by hunters in adjoining Montgomery County was another indication of the resurgence in the local deer population, with this figure climbing from just two in 1930-34, to 395 in 1960-64 and to 1,598 in 1990-94.[21]

Ideal conditions for deer exist throughout the Wissahickon corridor. Forest edges, thickets and glades and meadows and farm fields adjacent to woodlands offer an abundant supply of food. From late January through early March, deer congregate in stands of evergreens to seek shelter from wind, deep snow and cold temperatures. In the Wissahickon, these stands are generally hemlock (*Tsuga canadensis*), rhododendron (*Rhododendron*) and mountain laurel (*Kalmia latifolia*). With a "no hunting" policy within the city and the surrounding suburbs, and no natural predators, the deer population exploded by the late 1980s.

The most significant impact has been on the forest itself and the creatures that depend on it. Deer will eat any vegetation if they are hungry enough. They will stand on their hind legs to a height of five or six feet to strip whatever shrubs or small trees are within reach. Where overpopulation continues unchecked for a number of years, deer will eat everything—wildflowers, shrubs and tree seedlings, even stripping the bark from mature trees. Vegetation is unable to reproduce, and the absence of plants (at or near the ground) eliminates cover and food for forest insects, birds and small mammals. Songbird populations in particular (among the country's most endangered species) decline as deer eliminate their habitat and many of their feeding sources (the seeds and berries of the shrub and understory layers). Forests in Japan, overpopulated with deer for decades, are as barren as a moonscape. In the Wissahickon Valley, by the 1980s, deer had eaten most of the wildflowers, stripped the shrubs to a browse line of five to six feet and eliminated the seedlings of the canopy trees. Eventual loss of the forest means the loss of all the plants and animals that are dependent on it. If a forest cannot reproduce, it is doomed.

Loss of Plant and Animal Diversity | Deer Impact

The healthy, mature forest is multi-layered and provides food and shelter for forest birds, insects, reptiles and mammals. Excessive numbers of deer, browsing trees and shrubs up to a height of six feet, have jeopardized the resources required by other equally important members of the natural plant and animal community.

"Just as a deer herd lives in mortal fear of wolves, so does a ...[forest] live in mortal fear of its deer. And perhaps with better cause, for while a buck pulled down by wolves can be replaced in two or three years, a range pulled down by too many deer may fail of replacement in as many decades."[1]

Wiped out in successive periods, white tailed deer (*Odocoileus virginianus*) have returned to Eastern United States in large numbers since the 1970s. With the Pennsylvania Game Commission favoring this animal and with a general delight in being able to see this beautiful creature, few anticipated the devastation of the forest caused by the explosion of the deer population.

In this photograph, deer have eaten the ground layer bare and have stripped the shrub layer, leaving only a tiny head on the older mountain laurels (*Kalmia latifolia*). As the deer get hungrier, they will begin to eat the bark of the trees and kill them.

A forest heavily browsed by deer cannot survive. With all the seedlings eaten, it cannot reproduce itself.

1. Aldo Leopold, quoted in Richard Nelson, *Heart and Blood: Living with Deer in America* (New York, 1997), 122.

Source: Photograph by Colin Franklin

Deer also transmit Lyme disease, a debilitating infection from a spirochete (*Borrelia burgdorferi*), transmitted by the bite of the deer tick (*Ixodes dammini*). These ticks have a two-year cycle. The eggs hatch into larvae, which feed on mice and birds. They molt into nymphs and lie dormant during their first fall and winter. In the second year, the nymphs feed from May through July, transmitting the bacteria to humans or large animals. In the fall, the nymphs molt into adults. The females feed on deer and then mate, lay eggs and die. For humans, Lyme disease, if untreated, can spread to the joints, the heart and the nervous system. Similar to the infection caused by the syphilis spirochete, Lyme disease seems to proceed in stages. In the late stages, it can become well established in the brain and cause a very disabling diffuse encephalopathy and death.[22]

Loss of Keystone Species

Keystone species are those organisms crucial to maintaining the structure and function of their ecological communities.[1] These species should be given priority in conservation efforts.

"Such an organism plays a role in its ecosystem ... analogous to the role of a keystone in an arch. While the keystone feels the least pressure of any of the stones in an arch, the arch ...collapses without it. Similarly, an ecosystem may experience a dramatic shift if a keystone species is removed, even though that species was a small part of the ecosystem ...biomass or productivity."[2]

Some keystone species, like the american beaver (*Castor canadensis*) with their pivotal role in creating wetlands, are relatively easy to recognize.

The concept of keystone species may be less useful for the Eastern Deciduous Forest, where the major keystones in the historical ecosystem, such as the large predators—wolves, (*Canis lupus*), bears (*Ursus americanus*), and cougars (*Puma concolor*),

as well as other components, such as the passenger pigeon (*Ectopistes migratorius*) and the American chestnut (*Castanea dentata*)—have been missing for many years.[3] While the forest ecosystem has adjusted, it is greatly diminished. In addition, the meaning of these losses is still poorly understood.

In their article, Mills, Soule and Doak suggest several different categories of keystone species. These catagories include:

Predators: Removal of predators in the Wissahickon Valley has allowed the white tailed deer (*Odocoileus virginianus*) and small mammals, like the eastern grey squirrel (*Sciurus carolinensis*), to multiply beyond the carrying capacity of the system.

Prey: With few predators, herbivores multiply and eliminate food and shelter for other members of the ecosystem—from birds to butterflies.

Pollinators and Seed Dispersers: Loss of key seed dispersers, such as

ants (*disambiguation*) and salamanders (*Plethodon cinereus, Notophthalmus viridescens, viridescens),* can cause reproductive failure for specific species of plants.

Structures and/or Materials: Loss of structures and/or materials that affect habitat type and energy flow can cause the disappearance of species dependent on these particular resources.[4]

---

1. L. Scott Mills, Michael E. Soule and Daniel F. Doak "The Keystone-Species Concept in Ecology and Conservation," *BioScience* 43, April 1993, 219. Website: bio.research.ucsc.edu/people/doaklab/publications/1993mills_soule_doak.pdf.

2. Wikipedia, Keystone Species website: en.wikipedia.org/wiki/Keystone_species

3. Peter Bane in his article, "Keystones and Cops," suggests that the passenger pigeon was a keystone species for the entire Eastern Deciduous Forest. With the loss of the abundant pigeon dung, an impoverished forest soil may have weakened the American chestnut to the point where it was vulnerable to chestnut blight. Peter Bane, "Keystones and Cops," *Permaculture Activist,* May 2003.

4. Mills, Soule and Doak, "Keystone Species," *BioScience* 43, April 1993, 219.

Edge Effects

Forests have both edges and interiors. In the Middle Atlantic states, forest interiors are generally defined as the area of forest at least 300 feet in from the forest boundary. In a 1,000 feet wide forest, there are only 400 feet of interior, with 300 feet of edge on either side. These edges are subject to "edge effects." Whether adjacent to commercial and industrial uses, or to fields and gardens, edges tend to be noisier, sunnier, windier, drier and warmer during the day, and colder at night, than forest interiors.

The numbers and species of plants and animals are influenced by the edge effect. Some plants flourish and others decline. Increased numbers of trees are blown over, there is an influx of different seeds, there are often greater numbers of herbivores and an increase in predators, as well as a change in forest composition. In narrow or fragmented forests, where there is little interior and almost all edge, both plant and animal species can be inhibited or lost altogether.

Small forest patches lose species faster than those that are larger or less isolated. These patches do not support the same biodiversity as a single contiguous forest.[23] Perhaps the species most negatively impacted by extensive edges are the birds that live, feed and reproduce in the interior of the forest. Predation and parasitism appear to be higher along forest edges and in fragmented landscapes. Long, attenuated edges encourage attacks by "edge predators" and nest takeovers by "brood parasites."[24]

The extensive edges of a thin forest corridor can act like "travel lanes," providing cover for raccoons (*Procyon lotor*), skunks (*Mephitis mephitis*), rats (*Rattus norvegicus*),

Brown-headed cowbird
(*Molothrus ater*)
Source: Website:
lilibirds.com/gallery2/v/finches+and
+blackbirds/brown_headed_cowbir
d/brown_headed_cowbird.jpg.html

14:16

Loss of Bird Diversity | Brood Parasites

Brood parasites manipulate their own kind, or other species, into rearing their offspring. Because these parasitic parents do not invest resources in building nests or rearing their young, they have the advantage of extra time and energy and can feed better and produce more offspring. In the Eastern Deciduous Forest, the brown-headed cowbird (*Molothrus ater*) is the main brood parasite. This bird lays its eggs in the nests of over 100 species of small, perching birds.

The eggs of the brown cowbird

have a very short incubation period, and their chicks grow rapidly. In this way, the cowbird chick is given a head start over its nest mates, and can destroy or outcompete them.

In cases where the host nestlings are smaller than the cowbird chick, the original chicks will often starve to death. Cowbird chicks will push the other fledglings out of the nest shortly after they hatch, or kill them with their sharp beaks. Studies suggest that host parents do better when they accept the new egg. Cowbirds will return to check on their eggs, and later their young. Rejection of their

eggs may trigger a retaliatory action and cowbirds will destroy the offspring and nests of the hosts. If the hosts are compliant and accept the newcomer, they often have a second chance to breed and lay eggs after the cowbird chick has gone.[1]

Cowbirds prefer open fields and often travel in flocks, sometimes mixed with red-winged blackbirds (*Agelaius phoeniceus*) and bobolinks (*Dolichonyx oryzivorus*), as well as common grackles (*Quiscalus quiscula*) or European starlings (*Sturnus vulgaris*). They feed on the ground, eating seeds and insects.

snakes (*Elaphe obsoleta obsoleta, Agkistrodon contortrix mokasen, Lampropeltis trian-gulum, etc.*), cowbirds (*Molothrus ater*), as well as neighborhood pets and pets abandoned and gone wild. These edge predators can move under cover into the forest interior and take the eggs of birds that nest on the ground or in low shrubs. They can also wreck havoc on the small mammal population. Forest interior birds appear to be particularly vulnerable and increased forest edge could be partially responsible for recent population declines.[25]

The long, thin configuration of the forest in Wissahickon Park and the forest fragments above in the middle valley bring natural lands right up against developed areas. The extensive edge on both sides of the valley have meant that these natural lands are more vulnerable to assault.

Before European settlement, the cowbird followed bison herds across the prairies, feeding on the insects and seeds stirred up by these large animals. It appears that their parasitic nesting behavior complemented this nomadic lifestyle. Their numbers expanded when the forests were cleared and they followed cows and sheep instead of buffalo.

---

1. Jeffrey P. Hoover and Scott K. Robinson, "Retaliatory Mafia Behavior by a Parasitic Cowbird Favors Host Acceptance of Parasitic Eggs," *PNAS* 11, March 13, 2007, 4483.

Dickcissel nest (*Spiza americana*) with two brown-headed cowbird (*Molothrus ater*) eggs.
Source: Website: wiu.edu/biology/personnel/peer/pictures.html.
Photograph by Brain Peer

Loss of Bird Diversity | The Decline of Neotropical Migrant Song Birds

The last three decades have seen a sharp decline in songbirds that spend the summer in the temperate Eastern United States and the winter in the tropics. One of the best explanations can be found in a paper written by Patrick C. Burns. Selections from these writings have been combined and quoted below:

"Breeding Bird Surveys from 1947 through the 1970s, revealed that the yellow-billed cuckoo [(*Coccyzus americanus*)] and yellow-throated vireo [(*Vireo flavifrons*)]—as well as the northern parula [(*Parula americana*)], black-and-white warbler [(*Mniotilta varia*)], Kentucky warbler [(*Oporornis formosus*)], and hooded warbler [(*Wilsonia citrina*)]—were disappearing. Six other migrant song birds—Eastern wood-pewees [(*Contopus virens*)], Acadian flycatchers [(*Empidonax virescens*)], wood thrushes [(*Hylocichla mustelina*)], red-eyed vireos [(*Vireo olivaceus*)], ovenbirds [(*Seiurus aurocapillus*)], and scarlet tanagers [(*Piranga olivacea*)]—had declined by more than 50 percent ....

The decline of neotropical migratory song birds in the United States is closely linked to:

1. The Destruction of Tropical Forests: The population of Latin America and the Caribbean has doubled in the last 35 years, and with it has come unprecedented destruction of tropical rainforests. As populations have exploded, more landless peasants have colonized forest areas and cleared vegetation, with slash-and-burn cycles becoming progressively shorter. At the same time, logging over wide areas and the rapid expansion of commercial farming has accelerated the disappearance of forests and fueled the rapid destruction of once-lush bird habitat. In the Peten region of Guatemala, for example, 77 percent of the land was covered in dense forest in 1960. By 1990, that number had fallen to just 29 percent.

2. Pesticide Use in Central and South America and in the Caribbean: Neotropical migratory birds are being killed by the heavy use of insecticides, herbicides and fungicides, which are used to boost crop productivity to feed increasing numbers of people in the developing world. In some cases, birds are poisoned outright by chemical application, or by consuming grain and insects that have been sprayed. In other cases, the pesticides accumulate and concentrate within the birds, resulting in deformed chicks or eggshells that are so thin they break before hatching.

3. Forest Fragmentation by Suburban Sprawl: As the population of the United States has grown from 76 million in 1900 to over 300 million today, cities and suburbs have sprawled outward. Fairfax, Virginia, for example, a suburb of Washington, D.C., saw 69 percent of its forest converted to homes and businesses between 1980 and 1995. As human populations have risen, and forests have fallen, primary predators such as wolves [(*Canis lupus*)], bobcats [(*Lynx rufus*)], and cougars [(*Puma concolor*)]

have been wiped out, while the ecological niche of meso-predators has expanded. [These meso-predators] crows [(*Corvus brachyrhynchos*)], jays [(*Cyanocitta cristata*)], raccoons [(*Procyon lotor*)], possums [(*Didelphis virginiana*)], feral cats [(*Felis cattus*)] and fox [(*Vulpes vulpes, Urocyon cinereoargenteus*)] ...[now]... prey on once-secure migrant song bird nests. In addition, increasingly fragmented forests have enabled the brown-headed cow bird to colonize areas they once would have found unattractive....The result has been massive predation of Neotropical songbirds, which tend to nest in the open and near the ground rather than in tree cavities or higher up in the forest canopy. With forest fragmentation has come an invasion of native and non-native birds that compete with deep-forest species for food and nesting sites.

4. Intensive Agriculture: As American farmers make increasingly intensive use of their lands, bird populations suffer. Post-to-post cultivation has wiped out hedge-rows and thickets where many songbirds used to nest, while many farmers now cut hay three times a year where they used to cut just once. The result is that hedgerow and ground-nesting birds like the northern bobwhite [(*Colinus virginianus*)], the eastern meadowlark [(*Sturnella magna*)], the vesper sparrow [(*Pooecetes gramineus*)], and the grasshopper sparrow [(*Ammodramus savannarum*)] are in rapid decline."[1]

---

1. Blog and published article posted on "Terrierman's Daily Dose." Website: terrierman.com by Patrick C. Burns, (e-mail PBurns@erols.com).

Hooded Warbler (*Wilsonia citrina*), left.
Oven Bird (*Seiurus aurocapillus*), right.
Source: Photographs by Brian Small

Periodic Events

Periodic events were important in determining the landscape of the Wissahickon Valley. These recurring events included the visits of billions of passenger pigeons (*Ectopistes migratorius*), hurricanes and fires. With the extinction of the passenger pigeon, their dung no longer fertilized the soil. Hurricanes continue to shape the forest and are one periodic, natural event that will most likely play a greater role as the numbers and severity of these storms intensify with global warming.

Historically, fires almost certainly occurred at frequent intervals, but were suppressed as the valley developed. These fires perpetuated the white pines (*Pinus strobus*) on the hilltops and the mixed oak (*Quercus spp.*) forest on the plateaus, as well as the large grasslands, like the Houston and Monastery meadows. These meadows may have remained open for centuries, burned by lightening strikes, by the Lenni-Lenape and then by the early European settlers. The marshy wetlands of the middle valley probably burned in drier periods. Wherever these grasslands occurred, fire kept them from returning to forest. Removal of fire has probably had an important effect on the valley ecosystems and lack of fire may have contributed to the spread of pests and diseases.

14:18

Changes in Forest Composition

14:18

When the American chestnut (*Castenea dentata*) and the Canadian hemlock (*Tsuga Canadensis*) were no longer an important presence in the Wissahickon Valley, opportunistic natives gradually took their place. Red maple (*Acer rubrum*) was probably once confined to floodplains and swampy meadows.[1] It could also occasionally be found on high, dry ridges. In an article in the *Journal of the Chestnut Foundation*, William Lord points out that red maple was not a major part of most Eastern Deciduous Forests before European settlement.[2] However, it is a tree with very flexible requirements. With roots that are capable of developing differently in response to a variety of conditions, it is able to adapt to many soils, eleva-

tions and moisture regimens. It seeds early and prolifically (when the tree is only four years old). The seeds germinate almost immediately in early spring, giving it a head start over the competition. In addition, Gypsy moths (*Lymantria dispar*) will devour the leaves of the oaks (*Quercus spp.*) but the alkaloids in the leaves of the red maple repel them.[3] Perhaps most importantly, the red maple is less sensitive to disturbance and to soil acidification than other native canopy species and can grow and multiply under these new forest stresses.

Suppression of fire is another important factor in favoring the red maple. Maples, in general, (*Acer spp.*) have a thin bark and a surface root system. They were easily killed by the

regular fires in the forest of the Lenni-Lenape. Frequent fires favored the thick barked oaks (*Quercus spp.*) and hickories (*Carya spp.*) with their deep root systems. In the absence of heavy litter removed by the fire and in the increased sunlight created by the thinning of the understory, acorns and hickory nuts germinated more frequently.[4]

For all these reasons, two native maples, red and sugar (*Acer saccharinum*), the exotic invasive Norway maple (*Acer platanoides*) as well as the native tulip poplar (*Liriodendron tulipifera*), have taken over where the chestnut and the hemlock have left empty spaces. Cucumber magnolia (*Magnolia acuminata*), which previously occurred in the Wissahickon forest only

Acid Rain

Acid rain is precipitation (rain, snow and fog) with a pH of 5.6 or lower. It is caused by human emissions of sulfur and nitrogen compounds—sulfur dioxide (SO2) and nitrogen oxides (NOX)—which react in the atmosphere with water, oxygen and other chemicals to form a solution of sulfuric and nitric acid. Sunlight increases the rate of most of these reactions. Sulfur dioxide is a colorless gas released as a by-product of burning fossil fuels containing sulfur. A major source of these chemicals in the Northeastern United States is the emissions of Midwestern coal-burning power plants, blown east by the prevailing winds. The production of iron and steel and the processing of crude oil also generates this gas. Oxidation by ozone, photo-oxidation of sulfuric dioxide by ultraviolet light and the reaction of sulfur dioxide with moisture in the atmosphere, all produce sulfuric acid.

Nitrogen monoxide and nitrogen dioxide are both oxides of nitrogen. These gases are the by-products of firing processes at extremely high temperatures in engines of all sorts—cars, boats and lawnmowers. Nitrogen oxide is a dangerous gas by itself. It attacks the membranes of the respiratory organs, damages the ozone layer and contributes to smog.[26]

Forest floor in Wissahickon Park with Norway (*Acer platanoides*) and red maple (*Acer rubrum*) seedlings.
Source: Photograph by CLF

as scattered specimens, is also proliferating in Fort Washington State Park and in remnant forest areas throughout the middle valley. A wide range of birds, small mammals and insects dependent on oaks and hickories could suffer from this change in forest species composition.

1. Marc Abrams, Professor of Forest Ecology and Physiology, Pennsylvania State. "Fire and the Development of Oak Forests," *BioScience, 42,* 1992, 346-53.

2. "The Red Maple, An Important Rival of the Chestnut," *Journal of the American Chestnut Foundation,* Spring 2004, 42.

3. William K. Stevens, "Eastern Forests Change Color As Red Maples Proliferate," *New York Times,* Science Section, April 27, 1999.

4. Ibid.

Nitrogen oxides rise into the atmosphere where they react with water to form nitric or nitrous acid.

Chemicals can be deposited by acid rain or dust, washed from trees and other surfaces, increasing the acidity of the soil and the stormwater runoff. These acids have been shown to slow the growth of vulnerable forests and cause leaves and needles to turn brown and fall off. High altitude forests surrounded by clouds and fog are especially susceptible, since this precipitation is more acidic than rain. Acid rain has significantly contributed to the deforestation in Western, Central and Northern Europe, and in the Eastern United States, particularly in the Appalachian Mountains.

Acid rain dissolves calcium and other alkaline nutrients in the soil and washes them away. It can also trigger the release of toxic substances, such as aluminum, into the soil. In New England, the Hubbard Brook Study showed that forests, where the soil chemistry had been altered by acid rain, had essentially stopped growing.[26]

The soil on the forest floor can neutralize some or all of the acidity of rainwater. This process is called "buffering capacity." The ability of forest soils to buffer acidity depends on the thickness and composition of the soil, as well as the type of bedrock. Wissahickon schist, an acidic bedrock, weathers to form acidic soils that have a low buffering capacity. The thicker, more circum-neutral soils of the middle valley, which have developed over limestone substrata, have a higher buffering capacity.

Since there has been no comprehensive study of soil chemistry in the Wissahickon corridor, it is impossible to pinpoint the impacts of acid rain and to identify the specific ways this forest ecosystem has been damaged. However, scientists now believe that even in nitrogen poor forest soils (like those of the lower valley), the added nitrogen from acid rain greatly exceeds the capacity of the system to utilize this nutrient. Trees like the Canadian hemlock (*Tsuga canadensis*), which have adapted over millennia to nitrogen poor soils, are apparently "choking" on excess nitrogen that they are unable to use. As a result, hemlocks may have an increased susceptibility to wooly adelgid (*Adelges piceae*) and scale (*Cerya purchasi*). Diseases and pests in other native canopy trees—ash dieback (*Cytophoma pruinosa*), oak wilt (*Ceratocystis fagacearum*) and beech nectria (*Nectriaceae*)—may also be related to "soil nitrification." Because native species are less able to process these high levels of nitrogen, acid rain also favors the proliferation of invasive, exotic vegetation. New evidence suggests that the ability of fungi to break down lignan is also negatively affected by acid rain.[27]

A Radically Different Forest—Global Climate change

Perhaps the most insidious long-term threat to the forest of the Wissahickon is climate change. According to the Intergovernmental Panel on Climate Change (IPCC), a group established by the World Meteorological Organization (WMO) and the United Nations Environment Programme (UNEP), the average global air temperature near the earth's surface has increased 1.33 ± 0.32 degrees Fahrenheit during the 100 years ending in 2005. In the tropics, the Indian Ocean has warmed 2 degrees Fahrenheit over the last 40 years. In the Arctic and the Antarctic, this warming is greater. World temperatures could rise by between 2.0 and 11.5 degrees Fahrenheit during the 21st century.[28]

14:19

The Greatest Crisis | Climate Change

Local Trends (Wetter and Hotter)

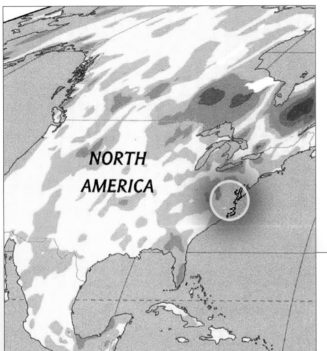

PERCENT CHANGE IN AVERAGE ANNUAL PRECIPITATION, 1976-2005

-15 -10 -5 -2 2 5 10 15

Percent precipitation change over a 30-year period—1976-2006, showing that the Wissahickon Valley is becoming wetter.

The planet could warm by 4°C as early as 2060 if greenhouse-gas emissions are not curbed quickly.[1]

1.Richard Betts, Met Office Hadley Centre,
  nature.com/news/2009/090929/full/news.2009.959.html

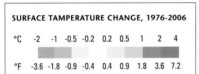

SURFACE TAMPERATURE CHANGE, 1976-2006

°C	-2	-1	-0.5	-0.2	0.2	0.5	1	2	4
°F	-3.6	-1.8	-0.9	-0.4	0.4	0.9	1.8	3.6	7.2

Surface temperature change over a 30-year period—1976-2006, showing that the Wissahickon Valley is also becoming hotter.

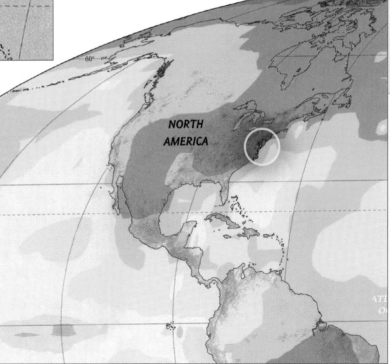

Source: *National Geographic Magazine*, August 2007, Map insert.

Anthropogenic global warming is caused by the discharge into the atmosphere of green-house gases—mainly carbon dioxide (CO_2) and methane (CH_4). For centuries human beings have been clearing forests and burning fossil fuels (coal, oil and gas) that release carbon dioxide into the atmosphere. Electricity generation is the biggest single source of this pollution, amounting to 37 percent of global CO_2 emissions.

The level of CO_2 in the atmosphere is now higher than it has been for hundreds of thousands of years. These gases have an effect similar to the glass panes covering a greenhouse, trapping and holding the heat inside. A three-degree temperature rise in Southeastern Pennsylvania would mean that, in less than a century, summers in Philadelphia would feel like those in Jacksonville, Florida. Experts now fear that "the projected warming may not be gradual, but could accelerate into a devastating climate lurch.... Already, we've pumped enough greenhouse gases to warm the planet for many decades to come."[29]

Temperature changes alter the seasons. Already Southeastern Pennsylvania is experiencing shorter winters and earlier springs. This shift in seasons affects plant and animal behavior. Buds break earlier, birds (neo-tropical migrants) arrive earlier and both migrants and over-wintering birds breed earlier. The cycles of interdependent creatures could fall out of sync.[30]

14:20

Climate Change | Effects on Plants

Global warming will influence all life on earth—from individual organisms to populations, species, communities and ecosystems. It will change behavior, population size, species distribution, the composition of plant and animal communities and the function and stability of ecosystems.[1]

How strongly different species will be affected will vary. Species with small population sizes, restricted ranges and a limited ability to move will be at greatest risk. Different habitats and ecosystems will change in various ways. It is possible that the mid-latitudes, the Philadelphia region and the Wissahickon Valley (unlike coastal, high-latitude and high-altitude regions), will be least impacted.[2]

The Audubon Society suggests four areas where the impacts of global warming would be most strongly felt:
1. Geographic range
2. Reproduction timing
3. Migration timing and patterns
4. Frequency and intensity of pest outbreaks.[3]

PRESENT RANGE

FUTURE RANGE

OVERLAP

Geographic range: the possible future range of the American beech.
Source: Margaret B. Davis and Catherine Zabinski. Changes in Geographical Range Resulting from "Greenhouse Warming: Effects on Biodiveristy in Forests," in Robert L. Peters, and Thomas E. Lovejoy, *Global Warming and Biological Diversity* (New Haven, 1992)

Although temperature changes are not taking place as rapidly in temperate regions, "global warming" will have grave consequences for the entire Wissahickon Valley, altering all levels of ecological organization, creating shifts in populations, changes in species composition and range, species extinctions and increased pests and diseases. Higher temperatures are expected to increase the intensity of storms and hurricanes and change the amount and pattern of rain and snowfall and the timing of the seasons. Recent studies project that the mid-latitudes of the northern hemisphere will become wetter.[31] Most importantly, global climate change adds another stress to an ecosystem already compromised.

The decline of the Canadian hemlock (*Tsuga canadensis*) in the Wissahickon, a species already at the extreme end of its range and confined largely to steep rocky outcrops in the Piedmont, is probably tied to climate change. As the cool, moist ravines where hemlocks grow become warmer and drier in the summers, these trees are increasingly stressed and susceptible to pests and diseases. Many other forest plants will be affected by climate change. Increasing temperatures could push the range of the American beech (*Fagus americana*) northward by as much as 500 miles. This would mean no beeches in the Wissahickon Valley, and potentially, the extinction of all beeches south of Maine.[32]

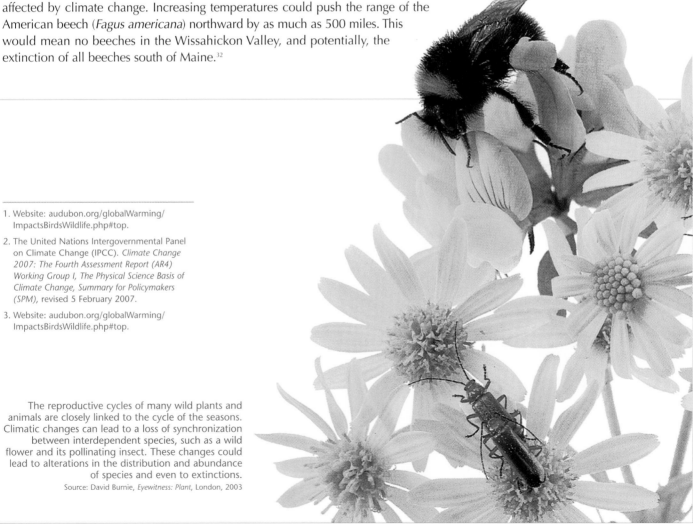

1. Website: audubon.org/globalWarming/ ImpactsBirdsWildlife.php#top.

2. The United Nations Intergovernmental Panel on Climate Change (IPCC). *Climate Change 2007: The Fourth Assessment Report (AR4) Working Group I, The Physical Science Basis of Climate Change, Summary for Policymakers (SPM)*, revised 5 February 2007.

3. Website: audubon.org/globalWarming/ ImpactsBirdsWildlife.php#top.

The reproductive cycles of many wild plants and animals are closely linked to the cycle of the seasons. Climatic changes can lead to a loss of synchronization between interdependent species, such as a wild flower and its pollinating insect. These changes could lead to alterations in the distribution and abundance of species and even to extinctions.
Source: David Burnie, *Eyewitness: Plant*, London, 2003

The Wissahickon in Crisis

A growing number of overlapping pressures transformed the relatively healthy forest of the Wissahickon Valley into an ecosystem in decay. By the early 1970s, the forest was radically different in structure, species composition and processes from the forest of the Lenni-Lenape.

At first, many of these problems went unrecognized, and the few who tried to call attention to this collapse were ignored. Gradually the magnitude of the problems—the dead and dying trees, the huge eroded gullies, the bare, exposed mineral soil, the loss of woodland wildflowers and the heaps of vines— began to seep into the everyday awareness of park users.

This recognition would fuel new partnerships and a major escalation in the number of devoted individuals and organizations willing to tackle repair of Wissahickon Park. These efforts would strengthen and professionalize the FOW. This organization would greatly extend its reach and expertise, becoming a leader in the growing renewal of the entire Wissahickon corridor.

Rebuilding Natural and Social Capital

1985-2010

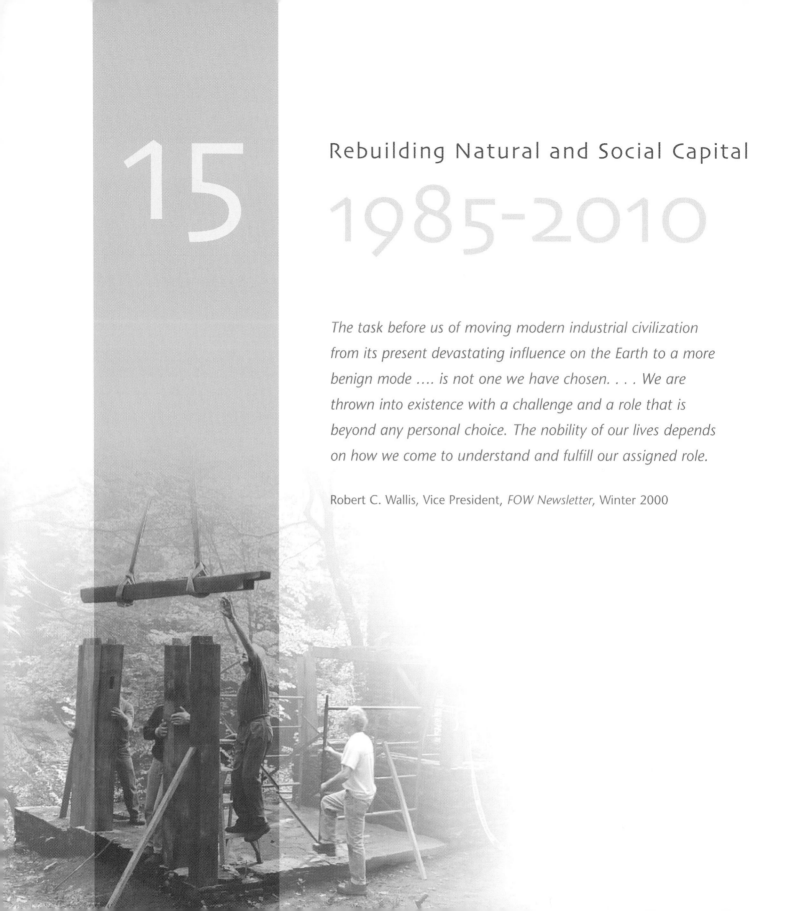

15

Rebuilding Natural and Social Capital

1985-2010

The task before us of moving modern industrial civilization from its present devastating influence on the Earth to a more benign mode …. is not one we have chosen. . . . We are thrown into existence with a challenge and a role that is beyond any personal choice. The nobility of our lives depends on how we come to understand and fulfill our assigned role.

Robert C. Wallis, Vice President, *FOW Newsletter*, Winter 2000

B y the 1960s and early 1970s, the FOW had participated in a number of important regional initiatives to preserve the valley. Although this was a period of enlightened leadership, most members came from Chestnut Hill, and there were few efforts to reach out to surrounding communities. During the next decade, with a different leadership, the FOW turned inward, keeping a low profile and focusing mainly on the operations of the Valley Green Inn. During this period, the organization failed to build the bridges essential to realizing the potential of its social capital. Partnerships with the Fairmount Park Commission and with other non-profits were not pursued, and, as in the recent past, membership continued to be largely white Anglo-Saxon Protestants from Chestnut Hill.

Filling the vacuum left by both Fairmount Park and the FOW were a number of individuals, volunteer groups, non-profit organizations and private foundations. They woke up to the realization that the Wissahickon—like any household—must be actively cared for and maintained. Initial efforts at "hands-on repair" led to a revitalization and increasing professionalization of the FOW, as well as to a restructuring of Fairmount Park operations. For the first time, a private non-profit organization, the William Penn Foundation, provided a very large grant for the study and repair of the natural lands in Fairmount Park. As with the Philadelphia and Chestnut Hill Renaissances in the 1950s, organizational reform was the foundation and the catalyst for sustainable physical change.

The Wissahickon Rebuilding Project

With the disbanding of the Fairmount Park Guards, the WPA guardhouses and picnic shelters were no longer monitored. Without surveillance, these buildings were quickly vandalized. Fairmount Park, with a reduced budget and staff, was stretched too thin to do more than essential park maintenance. There were neither resources nor staff to repair these buildings.

To fill the gap, a few individuals and non-profit groups outside the FOW began to make experimental repairs in Wissahickon Park. One of the earliest of these organizations was the Wissahickon Rebuilding Project (WRP), formed in 1977 by Dustin Del Grande, a

Claire Billet and Joseph Dlugach discussing stormwater problems at Gorgas Lane. Source: Photograph by CLF

professional photographer from Mt. Airy. At its height, in the early 1980s, there were more than 100 dues-paying members.[1] The WRP board was a small group (10-12 people) who came together to do volunteer work and coordinate designated projects with Fairmount Park staff. They were also an advocacy group, and lobbied city council for increased park budgets and for additional park employees. Members included representatives from local conservation organizations—chiefly the FOW and the Wissahickon Valley Watershed Association (WVWA), a conservancy group in the middle valley.[2] The WRP met in private homes to decide on projects with Fairmount Park director Peter Hoskins and later with his successor, William Mifflin.

At first, park staff were tentative about permitting volunteers to work—worried that these amateurs would be unskilled and damage the park. Park staff were also concerned about insurance liability for these non-city workers and feared union opposition to

15:1

Joseph Dlugach (1921–2004)

A semi-retired veterinarian from Northeast Philadelphia, Joe Dlugach was one of the first people to initiate programs in the hands-on repair of the Wissahickon in the late 1970s. Dlugach was also one of the earliest FOW members to bring attention to the need for care and repair in a park in crisis. From the early 1980s to the mid-1990s, he was unquestionably the most organized and most vocal force for change, identifying and tackling critical park problems and recognizing—as few others did at the time—that trail deterioration and misuse, stormwater mismanagement, takeover by invasive exotic species, and deer overpopulation were all interlinked. He saw the larger picture and acted, undaunted by either the size of the challenge or by the fact that he had no special training in trail repair, urban forestry or conservation biology.

Dlugash was also a critical force in the revitalization of the FOW.

Unhappy with the leadership he spearheaded the drive for change in the late 1980s and early 1990s. As a board member, he created the trails committee, and when the FOW reorganized, he helped this committee to metamorphose into the far more powerful and comprehensive conservation committee. Five "field" subcommittees tackled problems of trash and vandalism, stormwater, wildlife, trails and vegetation. These sub-committees grew out of those begun under the trails committee.

Direct, hands-on participation was central to Dlugach's ideas. Throughout its previous history, the FOW had never officially used its members to work in the park. Dlugach initiated projects, raised money and mobilized cadres of volunteers, year after year, who came from all over the region and from all walks of life. In many ways, he began the democratization of the FOW and

helped to prod the organization into what has become its most far-reaching and sophisticated period of activism.

Dlugach recruited Sam Tucker, a pediatric neurologist and faculty member at the University of Pennsylvania Medical School, to join the FOW and head the wildlife sub-committee. Tucker persuaded the FOW to hire wildlife expert Brian Shissler, and Shissler's report on deer in the Wissahickon was the impetus for one of the FOW's most successful initiatives. In his continuing efforts to reach out to professional advice in the work of the conservation committee (bringing in experts on vegetation management, deer control and trail construction), Dlugach began an important tradition—one that has served the FOW well.

Dlugach was a complex and contradictory person. On the one hand, his commitment to the use of volunteers for restoration projects

volunteers who appeared to be taking their jobs. This fear was groundless because the park staff had a backlog of new projects and deferred maintenance that would take them years to complete.

Once it was shown that the volunteers would do a competent job, the FPC supported the idea. Hoskins was a sympathetic park director who recognized the potential contributions of volunteers and opened the door to their participation. During the dozen years of their operation, the group rebuilt WPA guard houses and shelters, replaced broken and fallen concrete fence posts along Forbidden Drive, reset the stepping stones below the Livezey dam and repaired a stone retaining wall at the site of the former Livezey Mill.[3]

Among the members, Joseph Dlugach, a veterinarian from Northeast Philadelphia, was powerful, outspoken and a very hard worker. During his tenure with the WRP, he focused primarily on deteriorating trails. President of the organization for one year,

15:1

kept him from hiring professionals and fully exploiting their recommendations. On the other hand, he was one of the first board members to advocate for the professional management of volunteers by a paid FOW staff member.

Dlugach joined the FOW as a regular member and then became a member of the board. As a lower middle-class Jew from Northeast Philadelphia, he was considered an outsider by the almost entirely upper-middle-class WASP community who made up the FOW. This status worked both for and against him. In this sense he was not unlike Lloyd Wells, another outsider, who had shaken up the commercial district of Chestnut Hill a generation earlier. Both men were passionate believers in democracy—at least in theory. In practice, they were often authoritarian in their dealings with others. In their far-reaching visions, these men could be impatient, single-minded, abrasive

and even very wrong. They did not suffer fools gladly. But the changes they began were far-sighted and far-reaching.

Dlugach's difficult character traits and a strong need to run his own show, along with impatience with what he saw as insufficient financial and emotional support from the FOW, led to personal conflicts with various members of the board. This pattern was a repeat of his relationship with the Wissahickon Rebuilding Project (WRP), and may have characterized even earlier relationships with community groups. Eventually, Dlugach broke with the FOW and formed his own organization—the Wissahickon Restoration Volunteers (WRP). This organization, established in 1997, continues to orchestrate hands-on, volunteer reforestation efforts in Wissahickon Park, and now frequently partners with the FOW and with the Fairmount Park Volunteer Coordinator, David Bower.

After leaving the FOW, Dlugach continued to explore numerous creative ideas for restoration in the valley. These ideas included harvesting the princess tree (*Paulownia tomentosa*), an oriental, invasive exotic tree for veneer for the Japanese lumber market. It also included establishing a native plant nursery jointly with Saul School and the Schuykill Environmental Education Center called the "Seed to Tree" project. This project was fleshed out by Wayne Lee and Jason Lubar. Dlugach created an exhibit with other organizations to showcase the Wissahickon watershed at the main branch of the Philadelphia Free Library.[1]

1. Interviews by Franklin, February 22, 2002, April 18, 2003, telephone interview by Contosta, January 29, 2004. Profile of Joe Dulgach, by William Hengst, *FOW Newsletter*, Winter 1993-94.

he eventually quarreled with the leadership over two fundamental issues. Dlugach believed strongly that Wissahickon Park was a "nature preserve" and that any buildings were an intrusion and should be torn down—including the WPA structures the rest of the organization was trying to rebuild.[4] Impatient with political and educational activities, Dlugach simply wanted to go out and "do things." Increasingly frustrated, he drifted away from the WRP in the early 1980s.

Gathering some of his own friends, Dlugach formed an independent trail repair group in 1983. He became a member of the FOW and was then elected to the board. In 1985, he convinced the board to create a trails committee and to provide money and supplies for trail maintenance and repair.

Over the next decade, the WRP gradually faded away, and in 1996, Steve Kurtz, a local roofing contractor and long-time member, turned over their remaining monies ($1,200) to the FOW.[5] Although no longer active, the clean-ups, rebuilding park structures and trail repair pioneered by this organization would become central activities of the FOW—first through a new trails committee and later through the conservation committee.

15:2 Early Infrastructure Repairs | Fingerspan

The Fingerspan is a sculpture by Jody Pinto that is also a pedestrian bridge across a little tributary in Wissahickon Park, along the Orange Trail. The sculpture is a 59-foot-long covered bridge in the form of a slightly bent finger—a work of art, which also has a utilitarian function.

Samuel Harris of Kieran Timberlake and Harris (now KieranTimberlake Associates) collaborated in developing the concept into a practical work and served as architect, engineer and construction manager for the project.

The bridge, installed in 1987, is made entirely of "weathering steel" (Cor-ten), a material that gradually develops a self-protective coating of dark brown rust, when exposed to the weather.

To protect the landscape from construction vehicles, the work was fabricated in sections and brought to the site by helicopter. The brown weathered steel is durable, low maintenance and blends into the surrounding forest. At the same time, this sculpture is a startling discovery along the trail.[1]

The Fairmount Park Art Association was founded in 1872 to bring sculpture to Fairmount Park. Later, this organization expanded beyond the park to the city as a whole (supporting planning projects such as the design of the Benjamin Franklin Parkway). Members are dedicated to the integration of public art with architecture, landscape architecture and urban planning.

In the early 1980s, they developed a new program—Form and Function— "to bridge the gap between public art and daily life ....Each artist was asked to give meaning or identity to a place, to probe for the genius loci, or the 'spirit of the place.'"

Fingerspan was developed as a part of this program. It was funded primarily by a grant from the Art In Public Places program of the National Endowment for the Arts and supplemented with funds from the Fairmount Park Art Association. The work was donated to the city of Philadelphia.

1. Fairmount Park Art Association Website: fpaa.org/other_prog.html#form and /about_rece_comm

2. Website: wissahickondiary.blogspot.com/2008/07/shape-of-finger

Experiments in Trail Repair

Historically, FOW members had not done hands-on work in the park. They had confined the organization to providing money for improvements (acquiring parkland, repairs to Valley Green, rebuilding park infrastructure and replanting forest gaps).

By the 1980s, it was increasingly clear that the 57-mile system of trails in Wissahickon Park were seriously degraded. Stormwater runoff had eroded deep gullies in some trails. Park users of all kinds—hikers, equestrians and mountain bikers—were creating new "rogue" trails, in many cases to get around the badly damaged or impassable official trails. The deteriorating trail system exacerbated damage to the forest ecosystem.

Some large-scale infrastructure projects were undertaken—the Fingerspan Bridge, sponsored by the Fairmount Park Art association, and three new bridges at Devil's Pool, sponsored by the FOW. These projects were developed in concert with the Fairmount Park Commission, but not initiated by them.

The artist's provocative conception of a slightly bent finger did not compromise park user safety or security. The perforated steel covering prevents people from falling or climbing over the edge, but also allows dramatic views to the gorge below.
Source: Fairmount Park Art Commission

Judy Pinto describes the impulse that led her to this solution: "When I think of a bridge, I think of a reaching, a touching, a connection. So I decided to use a finger, the shape of a finger, for the bridge"[2]
Source: Fairmount Park Art Commission

In the spring of 1994, the trails subcommittee of the FOW conservation committee under Dlugach began a major repair project, on a 2,000-foot section of the Yellow Trail. This section of trail is located above Forbidden Drive and opposite the Indian statue, on the Roxborough side of the creek in Wissahickon Park. The FOW and FPC staff from District #3 cooperated closely throughout the project. Funds were raised from Pennsylvania Initiative Grants obtained by state representatives Chaka Fattah and Allyson Schwartz.

To repair the trails, the gullies were filled and the trail surface leveled. Many truckloads of fill were donated by D'Angelo Brothers and by the Conduit & Foundation Corporation. Improvements were made to the trail alignment and to the trail surface and edges to ensure that problems would not reoccur. Drainage ditches were dug to pull stormwater off the path, rolling dips were created to provide shorter drainage areas, retaining walls were built to support a level path and the trail edges were reforested. This project took until the fall of 1995 to complete.

Source: *FOW Newsletter* (Spring, 1996)
Photograph by Joseph Dlugach

The Wissahickon Rebuilding Project set a precedent and a new generation was eager to roll up their sleeves and participate actively in park repair. Dlugach organized volunteers in small work groups and sought out experienced people to help orchestrate the projects and manage the volunteers. Despite later opposition to mountain bikes in the park, he even initiated partnerships with bicycle organizations, using club members to repair trails. The early trails committee closed rogue trails, filled gullies and washouts, built bars to divert water off the pathways and engineered rolling dips to shorten the drainage areas.

Dlugach raised outside funds for specific trail repair projects, established a variety of partnerships with other non-profits and encouraged close working relationships with Fairmount Park staff. As early as 1986, he had already procured several large grants, including $20,000 from a Chestnut Hill "angel," and was talking to the park director, William Mifflin, about multiple agency projects.[6]

To make trail work easier to locate, Dlugach organized park trails by color, identifying the trails with colored blazes. This legacy has left a romantic park with white, yellow, orange, brown and purple trails. Because these names were useful they have unfortunately lingered.

At the request of the trails committee, new barriers were installed where park trails met public roads.
Source: Photograph by CLF

Two Adirondack-style bridges spanned Devil's Pool in the late 19th century, connecting the trail along the east side of Wissahickon Creek (later called the Orange Trail) across Cresheim Creek at Devil's Pool. These bridges were replaced several times. In the late 1970s, a severe storm wrecked the single wooden span that remained. For the next decade there was no way to cross the mouth of Cresheim Creek safely and easily.

In the late 1980s, F. Markoe "Koey" Rivinus, then president of the FOW, decided that this important connection should be restored. The Woodward family donated the funds for a set of three bridges—one across Cresheim Creek and the others across nearby difficult rocky chasms along the Orange Trail.

Fairmount Park staff chose the new bridge locations. Fearful that people would dive off a high bridge, they specified that the main span should be low and far from Devil's Pool. The new bridge crossed Cresheim Creek about 50 yards upstream of the confluence with Wissahickon Creek.

FOW board member David Pope, a professor at the University of Pennsylvania's school of engineering and applied science, asked E.T. Techtonics (a small company run by an associate professor in his department, G. Eric Johansen) to design the three bridges.

For their senior project, students helped design the bridges. The trusses were made of composite material—fiber-reinforced plastic on the top, with a steel cable on the bottom. The first of these bridges was installed in the spring of 1991. These elegant, modern bridges were intentionally very light-weight. They could be hand-carried to the site and their installation would cause minimal disturbance. In September 1999, Hurricane Floyd wiped out the new main bridge in a storm of biblical proportions. Masses of Japanese knotweed (*Polygonum cuspidatum*) washed down Cresheim Creek and formed a dam against the bridge. The force of the water dislodged the bridge and wrecked it. The bridge was not replaced out of concern that it would be washed away in another heavy storm.

Instead, FOW volunteers placed massive stepping stones in the creek. Over time, these stones have been dislodged, and there is again no safe and easy way to cross Cresheim Creek. People clambering down the slopes to cross the creek have caused massive soil erosion and damage to vegetation. Devil's Pool has become a dead-end. Its isolation invites bad behavior—drinking, trashing and vandalizing the area, and also jumping into Devil's Pool from the adjacent rock cliffs and from the sewer aqueduct.[1]

1. David Pope, Telephone interview by authors, July 11, 2008; F. Markoe Rivinus to William Mifflin, April 12, 1991; David Pope, memorandum to authors, June 29, 2008.

Devil's Pool has always attracted swimmers who want to dive off the rocks and the bridge into the pool, although it is only about eight feet deep. Fairmount Park is afraid of accidents with the attendant lawsuits, but no measures have stopped the swimming and diving.
Source: David Pope, photographer unknown, c. 1970

University of Pennsylvania engineering students carry light-weight sections of their bridge to Devil's Pool for assembly.
Source: Photograph by David Pope

View of the third bridge, crossing a small chasm to the north of the pool itself.
Source: Photograph by David Pope

Experiments in Forest Repair

Actively working in the park, Dlugach saw that something was badly wrong with the forest vegetation. Knowing almost nothing about local ecology and the native plants of the area, he sought expert advice. In 1986, he joined forces with Andropogon, an ecological landscape architecture firm in Philadelphia. Leslie Sauer, a partner at this firm, was then working with New York's Central Park Conservancy to restore the northern end of Central Park—the "Ramble" and the "North Woods."

Andropogon, providing services pro bono, suggested a demonstration area in Wissahickon Park where Dlugach's volunteers could define and test a set of management and restoration techniques. The work in this area would serve as models for other parts of the Wissahickon—and ultimately for any deteriorating urban wildlands in the region.

The area selected was a 40-acre section of the park on the Roxborough side of Wissahickon Creek. It was a highly disturbed tributary valley along Oil Mill Run, the site of the old Gorgas Mill. This little valley was particularly appropriate for a demonstration site because it was a single, coherent piece of land, with a multitude of problems typical of the gorge as a whole. The FOW repair efforts at Gorgas Lane continued for five years, from 1986 to 1991, with a new project each year. Each project explored a new restoration technique, and over five years tackled a variety of prototypical problems in Wissahickon Park. Each experiment was a revealing mix of successes and failures. The Gorgas Lane projects were the FOW's first efforts in ecological forest management and set precedents that have continued to the present day.

After World War II, this tributary valley had suffered a litany of assaults. The Henry Avenue arterial had included a major bridge over the mini-gorge at Gorgas Lane. Dense duplexes were built that lined the park boundary, coming right up to the edge of the valley slopes. A concrete channel built to carry runoff from the new residential development into Oil Mill Run fell apart, allowing water to cascade down the hillside and tear out a deep gully.

Above the park, on the steep hillsides of Lower Roxborough, Gorgas Lane, an old mill road, had been repaved and widened. Where this road met the park, it became a trail running straight down the hillside to meet Forbidden Drive. Road and park trail acted as a conduit, carrying massive amounts of stormwater into Oil Mill Run and gouging out its banks. Water flowed down the trail, eroding its soft surface. Additional stormwater also poured off the highway bridge, blowing out the opposite hillside and undermining the channel of the run. In the early 1970s, Hurricane Agnes eroded the stream banks and trail still further and swept away the last remnants of the millponds and the walled millrace from the old Gorgas Mill. Fairmount Park staff then cleared a large area of forest to reconstruct a footbridge that had been washed away.

Invasive, non-native plants quickly took root on the exposed ground. Japanese honeysuckle (*Lonicera japonica*) hung over the trees in thick mats. Japanese knotweed *Polygonum cuspidatum*, (now renamed *Reynoutria japonica*), and multiflora rose (*Rosa multiflora*) grew in dense stands where the floodplain widened out. Norway maples (*Acer platanoides*) seeded into the scoured areas on the hillsides. In addition to the invasive

Central Park |
Restoration Model

Wissahickon and Central Parks have a long history of reciprocal influence. In the late 1860s Olmsted and Vaux advised the Fairmount Park Commission on the aquisition of the Wissahickon gorge. That relationship was revived in the 1970s when Andropogon advised the Central Park Conservancy on the restoration of the "North Woods" and the "Ramble." Many of the techniques initiated in Central Park were first tested or later used in Wissahickon Park.

Maps showing ground disturbance at two different scales. At the largest scale, the entire north end of Central Park is mapped, showing areas of erosion and compaction.
Source: Central Park Conservancy

At the level of an individual project, this site mapping illustrates the pattern of stormwater damage, erosion, trampling and unauthorized "rogue" trails.
Source: Central Park Conservancy,
Map by Marianne Crammer

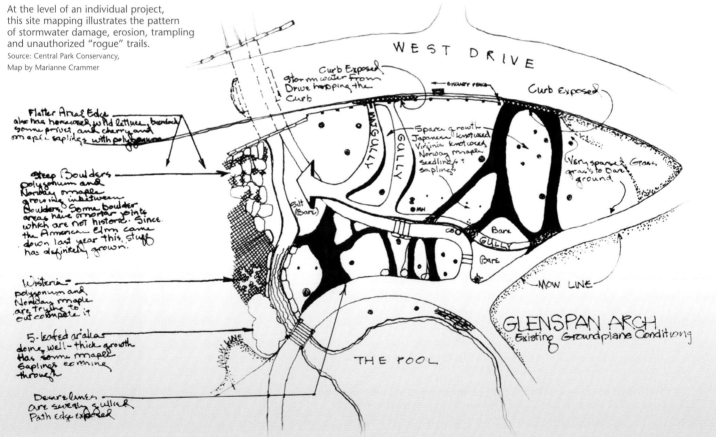

A Central Park Model

Hired by the Central Park Conservancy, Andropogon worked in the north end of Central Park—The "Ramble" and the North Woods"—from 1988 to 1992. A sequence of repairs and a set of techniques were developed there to tackle the problems of natural areas in a large, urban, park.

1.

2.

3.

4.

WHAT'S HAPPENING?

WOODLAND RESTORATION.

This part of the North Woods called the Ravine was designed over 130 years ago by Frederick Law Olmsted and Calvert Vaux to provide a little bit of the Adirondacks in the City. Now under restoration, the new woodland plantings will:

CONTROL EROSION.

Woodland plants help hold top soil in place. If top soil is allowed to erode, it will clog catch basins and fill in streams and lakes. Woodland plants are very fragile. If they are trampled, they will die. That is why new stone and gravel "Adventure Trails" have been added so you can enjoy the stream and cascades without trampling the woodland plants.

REPLACE INVASIVE PLANTS.

The new plantings contain species that traditionally grow in the deciduous forests and along stream banks of New York state. They include hay scented, New York and evergreen wood fern, yellow root, bluebells, iris, violets and Virginia creeper. Let them grow so that every Park visitor can enjoy their beauty.

PROVIDE WILDLIFE HABITAT.

Since Central Park is on the Atlantic flyway, it is host to migrating birds in the spring and fall. Park woodlands are favorite places for them to rest and refuel and you can find them here along with other woodland creatures. Now that this park landscape has been restored, we invite you to enjoy and care for its health and beauty.

YOU CAN HELP THE CONTINUING EFFORT TO RESTORE THE WOODLANDS! JOIN THE CENTRAL PARK CONSERVANCY'S WOODLAND RESTORATION VOLUNTEER PROGRAM. IT'S A GREAT WAY TO RECREATE IN THE WOODS. CONTACT DENNIS BURTON, WOODLANDS MANAGER AT (212) 360-2751.

Signs inform park users about restoration efforts and the meaning of the project.
Source: Central Park Conservancy

1. Repair of the drainage structures to mitigate erosion from uncontrolled stormwater.
   Source: Central Park Conservancy

2. Repair of the highly eroded ground. Here gullies were filled, then stabilized with "Dutch burlap,"a wide weave, coarse jute matting.
   Source: Andropogon, photograph by Rolf Sauer

3. Where necessary, new paths were built to provide direct connections and to discourage "rogue" trails. Source: Andropogon, photograph by Colin Franklin

4. Bridges were repaired or rebuilt to ensure that park visitors would stay on the paths and out of the forest and off the streambanks. Source: Andropogon, photograph by Rolf Sauer

Students from the Manhatten School of Science study soil fungae in urban wildlands.
Source: Central Park Conservancy, Photograph by Sara Miller

Volunteers with Dennis Burton (back row center, with weed-wrench), Central Park Woodland Manager and Volunteer Coordinator. This position was the brainchild of Leslie Sauer and became the model for the volunteer coordinator hired by the FOW and later for the job at Fairmount Park. Burton is now the Director of the Schuylkill Environmental Education Center in Philadelphia, an institution that works closely with the FPC and the FOW.
Source: Central Park Conservancy

Before: Trampled and eroded slope. After the repair of the other problems, the forest layers could be replanted. Highly imaginative solutions were tried to prevent new compaction of the soil and to recreate a living soil.

During: Short branches are collected and pounded into the slope. The stakes discourage rogue access. They pull water down into the soil and as they rot, they encourage forest fungal mats to grow.

After: Two years later a continuous ground layer of ferns, native ginger (*Asarum canadense*) and white woodland aster (*Aster divaricatus,* now reclassified as *Eurybia divaricata*) have covered the slope.
Source: Photographs by Leslie Sauer

The Gorgas Lane Projects 1986-1991 | Project #1

Replanting Native Canopy Trees

Gorgas Lane was a 40-acre site in Wissahickon Park in the lower watershed of a small tributary valley along Oil Mill Run. This valley was the location of the old Gorgas Mill. The terraces for the vineyard could be seen on the hillside and the stream had been dammed to create a series of millponds.

Throughout these projects Neil Korostoff and then Claire Billet, both of whom worked at Andropogon, acted as defacto "volunteer coordinators," organizing the project for Dlugach and defining the many roles of the job, including mobilizing support from city and state agencies. Korostoff is now a professor of landscape architecture at Penn State University. Since leaving Andropogon, Billet has worked for several land trusts. All the activities were approved and permits obtained from William Mifflin, the Fairmount Park Director of Operations and Management at that time.

Volunteers unload "bareroot" trees, purchased and transported from Princeton Nurseries. Korostoff organized the trail committee volunteers, including several FOW board members (David Pope, Robert Wallis and Robert Lukens) and taught them the special techniques necessary for bareroot planting.

The first project began in the spring of 1986. The trees were purchased with funds provided by the FOW. Fairmount Park staff provided mulch and took away debris. The publicity following this event inspired a local benefactor to make a very generous grant to continue reforestation activities. Source: Photograph by CLF

The bareroot trees were dipped in a bucket of "hydrogel," or water-storing granules (a starch-polyacrylonitrile graft co-polymer). This solution coated the roots and allowed the soil to increase its water-holding capacity by 50 times.

There are adverse side effects to the environment with hydrophilic polymers and this method should be used sparingly. Hydrogel was used in this restoration project to help the plants establish and avoid desiccation, in a situation where there was little opportunity for later watering. Source: Photograph by CLF

Gorgas Lane before. Where the bridge had washed out and been repaired, construction had left a large "canopy gap."

Gorgas Lane after planting 120 "bareroot" trees—white ash, (*Fraxinus americana*), red oak (*Quercus rubra*) and red maple (*Acer rubrum*). Small groves now filled the canopy gap. Source: Photograph by CLF

The Gorgas Lane Projects 1986-1991 | Project #2

Eradication of Japanese Knotweed

Over time, the old Gorgas dam was breeched and the millpond filled with sediment. The millpond became a grassy meadow in a broad flood-plain. This highly disturbed area was overtaken by Japanese knotweed (*Polygonum cuspidata*, later renamed *Reynoutria japonica*).

In a courageous attempt to remove huge, old stands of Japanese knotweed and reestablish a grove of walnut trees in the old millpond (now filled with sediment), volunteers experimented with different ways to remove this tough, deeply rooted plant. They tried to dig up individual plants, but like the legendary hydra, every root that remained in place generated new plants. Next they tried the old gardening trick of smothering weeds with a plastic mulch. This technique failed miserably.

In the end, the knotweed was recut to the ground. Turney Hernandez of Hernandez Beautification and Vegetation Management Company, in Centerville, Delaware, a nationally known expert in the responsible use of herbicides, was asked to help. Hernadez volunteered to apply herbicides selectively to the freshly resprouting knotweed, and this persistent plant was finally much reduced in extent.

Volunteers chop down the stalks of Japanese knotweed in late winter in preparation for covering the ground with sheets of plastic.
Source: Photograph by CLF

In a misguided experiment, volunteers covered the cleared ground with transparent plastic sheets hoping to smother the plants. Instead, by spring, the incredibly strong stalks of the Japanese knotweed (*Reynoutria japonica*) pushed up through the plastic, undeterred. By mid-summer, the sun had shattered the plastic into a thousand tiny shards, creating an environmental mess.

Hoping to shade out the knotweed, and in an attempt to recreate a walnut grove, dozens of tiny black walnut trees (*Juglans nigra*), purchased from nut growers, were planted through the plastic. Only a few walnut trees survived and the knotweed grew back as thick as ever.

The Gorgas Lane Projects 1986-1991 | Project #3

Floodplain Meadow

At the entrance to the park Gorgas Lane becomes a park trail. Runoff from the road poured into the park and down this trail. Dlugash wanted a solution that would stop water running down the trail. He asked Fairmount Park staff to build a small berm where the road met the park path. Park staff contributed several very ugly "Jersey barriers" to block the road.

The goal of this project was to manage stormwater by creating a surface channel where the run was buried. Volunteers dug a long, sinuous swale and diverted the runoff from the path into this channel. Along the channel a series of small depressions were dug in the broad floodplain to capture and hold stormwater in heavy rains. The channel and the small depressions slowed the water and allowed it to infiltrate gradually into the soil.

Volunteers planted the edges of the swale and the little ephemeral ponds with native wetland vegetation. However, without monitoring and ongoing maintenance, the entire swale and pond system was soon choked by sediment and the return of invasive exotics.

Park trail at the entrance to Wissahickon Park at Gorgas Lane. Stormwater pours down off this path into Oil Mill Run.

Volunteers dug a long sinuous swale to capture stormwater and bring it into the broad floodplain meadow beside the path. In this meadow, water could infiltrate slowly into the ground. The swale and small ephemeral ponds were planted with native wetland vegetation. Source: Photographs by CLF

The Gorgas Lane Projects 1986-1991 | Project #4

Hemlock Replanting

A large grove of debilitated hemlocks stood at the bottom of the hill near the intersection of Gorgas Lane and Forbidden Drive. These hemlocks, like the others in the park, were suffering from a multi-year attack of wooly adelgid (*Adelges piceae*) and scale (*Fiorinia externa ferris*). The park had discontinued aerial spraying of dormant oil after protests by residents. It was now too late to save this once beautiful grove.

Volunteers planted one thousand hemlock seedlings and 20 five-to-six- foot high balled and bagged trees, to determine if either of these methods could help to reestablish hemlock in the Wissahickon.

The deer ate the seedlings as soon as they were planted. During the winter they stripped the bark from the balled and bagged trees by rubbing their antlers on the trunks. This experiment was a case of "everyone should have known better." Nonetheless, it was worth while to see if hemlocks could be returned to key areas where important historic groves had once stood.

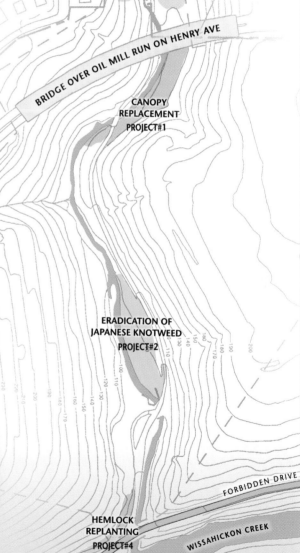

FLOODPLAIN MEADOW PROJECT#3

REPLACING SHRUB AND GROUNG LAYER PROJECT#5

BRIDGE OVER OIL MILL RUN ON HENRY AVE

CANOPY REPLACEMENT PROJECT#1

ERADICATION OF JAPANESE KNOTWEED PROJECT#2

FORBIDDEN DRIVE

HEMLOCK REPLANTING PROJECT#4

WISSAHICKON CREEK

Newly planted grove of hemlocks at the bridge over Oil Mill Run.
Source: Photograph by CLF

Source: Topographic survey of Wissahickon Park, FPC, 1987

The Gorgas Lane Projects 1986-1991 | Project #5

Replacing Shrub and Ground Layers

The steep eroded slopes at the top of the valley of Oil Mill Run had remained oak (*Quercus spp.*) and beech (*Fagus americana*). Stormwater from the houses above the park had stripped the topsoil from these steep slopes and only a few straggly mountain laurels (*Kalmia latifolia*) remained. This project was an attempt to re-create the historical plant community. One technique used was to replace the forest layers under the canopy trees. The adjacent healthy forest was used as the model to determine what plants should be planted—and in what relationship to the land and to other plants.

With help from students from the landscape department of the University of Pennsylvania, School of Design, large numbers of mountain laurels (*Kalmia latifolia*), Christmas ferns (*Polystichum acrostichoides*), marginal wood fern (*Dryopteris marginalis*) and white woodland asters (*Aster divaricatus*, renamed *Eurybia divaricata*) were planted to replace these missing layers. Within two years, for reasons that are still not well-understood, these new plants had completely disappeared. After planting, however, the slope no longer eroded and supported tough, native wildflowers.

The slope was stabilized with burlap laid over straw. A layer of leaves was used as mulch and covered the burlap. Over the time, it became apparent that neither straw nor burlap was appropriate. In subsequent projects, only local leaves and coarse open weave "Dutch burlap" were used.

Volunteers plant mountain laurel (*Kalmia latifolia*) and evergreen ferns through the burlap.
Source: Photographs by CLF

Source: Photograph by CLF

Repair of Storm Water Infrastructure

The last project at Gorgas Lane was the repair of the broken stormwater conduit that ran under the bridge on Henry Avenue—from the road on the plateau to Oil Mill Run.

Once the conduit was repaired, water would again be directed into this channel, and from there dumped directly into the run. While this circumstance was far from ideal, the deep gullies in the steep hillside could be filled and stabilized.

Since Henry Avenue was a state road, Dlugach asked the Philadelphia Water Department to fix the channel and Penn DOT (the state highway department) to repair drainage from the bridge.[1] After considerable time, both agencies responded. Penn DOT repaired the stormwater pipes on the bridge and the Water department filled the adjacent gully and repaired the concrete channel. It was the first time that the FOW had reached beyond the Fairmount Park Commission to city and state agencies, called their attention to problems in the park and persuaded them to do actual repairs.

1. Neil Korostoff to Robert Wright, Penn Dot Project Design Engineer, February 26, 1991.

takeover, increasing numbers of white tailed-deer (*Odocoileus virginianus*) were eating all plants up to a height of five to six feet. Only a few patches of beech (*Fagus americana*), oak (*Quercus spp.*) and mountain laurel (*Kalmia latifolia*) remained.

Among the most important lessons learned was that it was not possible to go in and simply replant bare areas in the forest. In these highly disturbed places, extensive preparation was needed for successful planting. During this project, the FOW had to confront and resolve issues originating beyond park boundaries—stormwater run-off, erosion, takeover by invasive exotics and unchecked deer. Then it would be possible to stabilize eroding soil and remove invasive exotics. Only then, would it be possible to plant successfully.

By the early 1990s, Dlugach had attracted Edgar David and Clare Billett, landscape architects, and their friends Wayne Lee and Jason Lubar, to the newly formed conservation committee. They brought a wider ecological understanding and a stronger organizational framework that allowed Dlugach to develop the replanting projects begun at Gorgas Lane. In 1994, this group created a community-based natural resource management program that became known as the "Wissahickon Stewardship Project" (WiSP). One of the most important initiatives of the WiSP program was the 1996 Canopy Gap Study.

The Gorgas Lane projects mobilized a remarkable number of volunteers and raised private funds to address the interrelated problems of soil, water and vegetation. These projects would set the pattern for forest repair in Wissahickon Park for the next decades.

With a major grant from the William Penn Foundation, the ideas originally explored at Gorgas Lane and later by the FOW conservation committee, as well as in Wisp and in the Canopy Gap Study, would evolve into a recognition of "natural lands" as park areas with their own unique problems. Recognition of the idea of natural lands would lead to the reorganization of the Fairmount Park Commission staff to address these areas specifically.

The grant allowed Fairmount Park staff to take over much of the vegetation management work. Money and new employees would achieve much needed, large-scale change, but Dlugach's quirky, imaginative explorations were abandoned. Forest repair would come to mean "invasive exotic removal" and "canopy replacement." The park commission and its staff lacked the expertise, the science and the will to guide genuine "ecological restoration." Later initiatives—the deer management program and the sustainable trails projects in Wissahickon Park, as well as the worm control experiments at the Schuylkill Center for Environmental Education (SCEE), would point to a more holistic approach to forest ecosystem repair.

Source: Hopkins, *Philadelphia Atlas, 21st Ward*, 1885

The Wissahickon Stewardship Project—WiSP

The "Wissahickon Stewardship Project" (WiSP) divided the park into mini-watersheds—39 in all. Members of each mini-watershed group would be the eyes and ears for their part of Wissahickon Park. They would develop repair projects of all kinds within their own area, map the locations of invasive plants, remove them and replace them with native vegetation. WiSP then searched for a willing "Watershed Manager" from each of these mini-watershed districts. It was hoped that by giving leadership to district managers, each group would feel a sense of "ownership." WiSP would provide training, support and resources. Managers were encouraged to involve friends, families, neighbors and local businesses in the restoration efforts.

The FOW conservation committee developed a training manual for the watershed managers. They solicited and screened candidates for the watershed manager positions and ran free training workshops. These workshops were actual projects that gave the new managers hands-on experience. WiSP hoped to teach volunteers to design and implement restoration projects. It also hoped to help volunteers understand key ecological processes and why the park's natural systems were in trouble.

In 1995, based on a model suggested by Leslie Sauer for Central Park, Jason Lubar was hired by the FOW to act as a part-time "woodland manager" and coordinator of the WiSP volunteers, becoming the FOW's second paid employee. Lubar's job as a volunteer coordinator was to discover and empower the watershed managers and to handle the logistics of each project. This job involved designing and supervising the work—purchasing plants and equipment and moving these, along with the volunteers, to the project site.

The conservation committee provided direction and oversight to WiSP. It raised an average of $25,000 annually through a variety of grants (Pennsylvania Department of Conservation and Natural Resources; America the Beautiful; National Federation of Wildlife; American Forests and the Philadelphia Urban Resources Partnership).

Despite its short lifespan, WiSP left a provocative model for the future involvement of local residents in restoration work. At its peak, it had 10-15 reliable and committed watershed managers. From 1993 to 1999, WiSP volunteers planted over 1,000 bare-root native canopy trees each year, using 4,500 man-hours of labor annually.[1]

---

1. The authors are indebted to Clare Billet and Jason Lubar for interviews and reviews of this manuscript, April-May, 2008.

Map showing Wissahickon Park, divided into 39 mini-watersheds.
Source: FOW, map by Claire Billet and Jason Lubar

Park Rangers

In 1987, in an attempt to fill the gap left by the loss of the park guards, Philadelphia's William Penn Foundation gave a $10-million grant to Fairmount Park to establish a ranger corps. The ranger program began in 1988. Park rangers were modeled after the National Park Service rangers. William Mifflin,

then director of operations and landscape management for the park, had written his Temple University master's thesis on park ranger programs. Alexander "Pete" Hoskins, former director of Fairmount Park (1980-88), had proposed a ranger program as early as 1981, but this program was not funded by the city.

Initially, the rangers, 40 each year, were recruited from seniors in Philadelphia high schools, students who probably would not have gone to college. The grant paid for two years of tuition at Temple University's leisure and recreation department. The trainees went to Temple full-time and worked part-time in the park on

Park rangers at Valley Green, c. 1988
Source: CHHS

weekends. If they graduated, they received a two-year degree. These trainees were encouraged to continue at Temple and could earn a full bachelor's degree at their own expense. They were also given field training at the Philadelphia Police Academy and at the National Park Service.[1]

The rangers wore a distinct uniform modeled on National Park Service rangers. Unlike the park police or the former park guards, the rangers could only issue citations, but could not arrest troublemakers. When park rules were broken, they could use friendly persuasion to change behavior.[2] Nonetheless, their presence helped to make the park feel friendly and safe. They offered information to the public, conducted tours and went out to schools to present programs. Many rangers helped with trail, structures and reforestation projects. After the first four years, the role of the ranger was reduced to helping to enforce park rules. Since 1992, when the Temple program ended, the ranger corps has recruited people with at least some college education, interested in environmental issues or with experience in law enforcement.

At their peak in 1992, there were 80 rangers working throughout the park system, with six full-time rangers assigned to Wissahickon Park, along with seven trainees. The ranger corps was very active—walking, riding bicycles or mounted on horseback. They helped the FOW conservation

committee with a wide range of projects.[3]

Three ranger stations were planned in Wissahickon Park: one at Cedar House (the old Andorra Nursery office), another at Valley Green and a third at Rittenhouse Town. When the grant ran out in 1994, the Board of the Philadelphia Ranger Corps eliminated administrative personnel and transferred the operational staff and the balance of the funding to the Fairmount Park Commission.

In addition to the original $10 million, William Penn donated another $9 million to the ranger program. Part of this money was invested. It is the main responsibility of the Board of the Philadelphia Ranger Corps to oversee these investments and manage the income for the program. The city now provides about $850,000 a year, as part of the FPC budget, to help fund the ranger program. The ranger board combines this annual appropriation with income from its investments to pay for the program.[4]

In 2004, there were 18 Fairmount Park Rangers, 16 in 2005, 18 in 2006 and 18 in 2007. By 2008, the number had grown to 24, and in June, the city adopted a budget that increased park funding by $2.5 million, some of this money earmarked to add park rangers. Hoskins currently chairs the ranger board.[5]

The Ranger Corps operates in three park districts, one of which is District #3, which covers Wissahickon

Park. Rangers in Wissahickon Park operate out of the Thomas mansion. They worked closely with the police from the 92nd district, then stationed at the old Gypsy Lane park guard headquarters (Wissahickon Hall). Rangers patrol Fairmount Park and provide visitor assistance, park education and emergency services.[6]

In January 2008, the FOW started a program called the Wissahickon Trail Ambassadors to supplement the work of the Ranger Corps. Ambassadors are interested volunteers trained in the natural and cultural history of Wissahickon Valley. They patrol the park three to four hours a week, helping visitors and providing a presence.

1. Tom Utescher, "Park Rangers to be Educated for the Job," *Chestnut Hill Local*, September 3, 1987; *FOW Newsletter*, Spring 1992.

2. *FOW Newsletter*, Winter 1992-1993.

3. Jamie Hazelton, Ranger Operations Manager, Fairmount Park Ranger Corps, telephone interview by Contosta, July 14, 2008.

4. Ibid.

5. Website: fairmountpark.org/RangerCorps.asp Website:philly.metro.us/metro/local/article/Fairmount_cant_keap_up/12519.html.

6. Jamie Hazelton, Ranger Operations Manager, Fairmount Park Ranger Corps, telephone interview by Contosta, July 14, 2008.

Canopy Gap Study

By the late 1980s and early 1990s, inappropriate construction projects, stormwater gullies, pests and diseases and deer browse had caused large gaps in the forest canopy. Contributing to this problem was an ever-increasing number of park visitors—mountain bikers, exploring children, rock climbers and general park wanderers—going off-trail into the forest, especially on steep slopes. These activities widened trails, created unauthorized new ("rogue") trails, tore away fragile vegetation and compacted forest soils.

One of the most important initiatives of the WiSP program was the 1996 Canopy Gap Report, made possible by the financial support of the Dolfinger-McMahon Foundation. A follow-up grant from the Philadelphia Urban Resources Partnership also supported this project. The study located all the large holes in the forest (canopy gaps) and measured their size. This mapping showed that within the 1,841 acres of Wissahickon Park, there were an astonishing 600 openings of different sizes, covering a total of 390 acres, or over one-fifth of the entire area of the park. Careful examination of these gaps provided evidence that natural processes were not enough to heal these holes in the forest. Natural regeneration could not occur because exploding numbers of deer were eating every tender seedling and invasive exotics quickly choked any openings.

The study estimated that it would take over 120,000 trees to close these openings. At a planting rate of 1,000 to 1,500 trees per year, it would take well over a century to fill existing holes—not counting any new holes that might develop.[1] It was clear that restoration efforts needed to be intensified.

1. Jason Lubar, Wayne Lee, Jr. and Clare Billett, Wissahickon Park, Canopy Gap Report, FOW, Fall 1997, 5.

Reorganizing and Revitalizing the FOW

In the late 1980s, a mixture of old and new FOW members became increasingly frustrated with the organization's failure to recognize and act on the crisis in the Wissahickon Valley. In early 1991, these reformers met with others in the community to discuss how to work effectively in the park—whether to form a new organization and if so what form this organization might take. Many of those who would become the new FOW leadership were participants in this group, including David Pope, Robert Wallis, William Hengst and Joesph Dlugach. They considered a number of models, the newly formed Central Park Conservancy among them. After much discussion, they agreed that more could be achieved by reorganizing the existing FOW—building on its reputation, longevity and previous accomplishments—than by establishing a new organization.

At the end of 1991, as part of this reorganization effort, a number of board members asked the FOW to create a new standing committee—the conservation committee—to replace the older trails committee. This committee took over the previous programs—trash removal, trail repair and reforestation. New Committees—wildlife and hydrology, as well as outreach, membership, development and publications, were added to support the growing organization.[7]

Modern Heavy Hitters

Previous heavy hitters, the early leadership of the FOW, tended to be men of great wealth, who did not consider "hands-on" work in the Wissahickon to be a part of their mission. They had been shaped by the early 20th-century Conservation Movement. A group of amateur enthusiasts in the English aristocratic mold, they did not reach out to expert advice on troubling problems in the park.

Coming out of the paradigm of the 1960s, the new leadership in the 1990s and early 2000s were working professionals, who understood the need for activism, consensus-building and public–private partnerships. These individuals led the FOW at a time of a growing understanding of ecological ideas and the complexity of problems facing the park.

Their vision and their organizational and practical skills

complemented each other. They shared, in different proportions, a combination of large ideas and an enthusiasm for hands-on solutions. Without this extraordinary group of people, the FOW could not have evolved into the important and effective organization that it has become.

The publications committee began issuing a quarterly newsletter, edited and often largely written by board member William Hengst. The newsletter was an extraordinary labor of love and has continued to be a careful record of expanding FOW activities. Like the *Chestnut Hill Local* at its height, the *FOW Newsletter* has been a paper of extraordinary quality that focused member concerns and brought the cohesiveness of the organization and the significance of its topics to regional attention. While the hydrology subcommittee would not realize its potential, the wildlife committee would lead the FOW to a deeper engagement in critical park issues. It would expand FOW expertise and take the organization into political advocacy and broad community outreach.

During this time of transition, both Dlugach and Pope served as co-chairs of the conservation committee. These two very different men both wanted to be the new president of the FOW and to control the direction of the organization. The next two years were a time of important administrative changes. This evolution was marred by their implacable dislike for each other, and by the ensuing personality struggles. The conflict nearly destroyed the organization. The core of their disagreement was how to approach FOW goals. Dlugach preferred the organization to be a loosely run cadre of volunteers with modest financial support. Pope wanted a more professional structure backed by serious fundraising, so that projects could be undertaken not only by volunteers but also by paid experts.[8]

Pope, Professor of Materials Science and Engineering at the University of Pennsylvania and a university ombudsman, had the support of both the old and new leadership. He was an eloquent spokesman for the new directions and had a gift for fundraising and managing organizations. Dlugach was the originator of many key changes. Without Dlugach, a new FOW would have taken far longer to emerge, but he would have made a disastrous president.[9]

15:16

David Pope (1939–)

A native of Wisconsin, David Pope moved to Philadelphia in the late 1960s. Pope has served as associate dean at the University of Pennsylvania's School of Engineering and Applied Science, has been chair of the mechanical engineering department, and is professor and chair of the department of materials science and engineering. He believes that his role as university ombudsman, the official mediator for students and faculty at Penn, helped him to lead a fractious FOW.

Pope joined the FOW in 1988 and was one of the board volunteers who worked on Dlugach's reforestation projects at Gorgas Lane. In 1991, recognizing Pope's talents as an engineer, F. Markoe "Koey" Rivinus, then president, asked him to take charge of building three new bridges near the mouth of Cresheim Creek—one just upstream from Devil's Pool and the other two across deep, rocky chasms along the Orange Trail. Pope

was now fully involved in the physical renovation of the park.

As the first president of the FOW after the reorganization, Pope orchestrated a seamless transition from a comfortable group of Chestnut Hill neighbors to an active, professional non-profit. He used his organizational and "people" skills to enable the FOW to hire professional management consultants to write the FOW's first strategic plan. He was a dynamic force in seeing this plan realized, pushing to find a headquarters and hire staff. One of his most important contributions was pushing the board to raise the money needed to fund large-scale change.

As co-chair of the conservation committee, with Dlugach, Pope gradually understood the depth of the threats facing the valley. He became an ardent spokesman for the two major stewardship initiatives of the FOW—deer management and trail design and repair. He is one of the

longest serving board members and continues to contribute both time and money. He and his wife Myrna have also donated a conservation easement on their property adjacent to a small Wissahickon tributary.[1]

1. *FOW Newsletter*, Winter 1992-93; David Pope to authors, June 29, 2008. On the Pope's conservation easement see *FOW Newsletter*, Spring 2007.

David Pope camping in western United States. Source: David Pope

F. Markoe "Koey" Rivinus, then FOW president, designated Pope as his successor and graciously stepped down, sensing the need for a new generation of leaders.[10] The board ratified this choice. Pope, with his skills at bringing different sides together, could unite the various factions.

Pope was able to replace the previous governance, while continuing to honor their contributions. Dlugach, on the other hand, wanted a clean sweep of the people with whom he had frequently disagreed. Pope's election achieved a "bloodless coup" with minimum upheaval.

As president, Pope created an executive committee of people with strong complementary skills. This group included Charles Dilks, William Hengst, Robert Lukens, Edward Stainton, Ella Torrey and Robert Wallis. They steered a rapidly evolving non-profit into a large, professionally run organization with major projects throughout the park and a renewed regional emphasis.

The executive committee restructured old committees and established a new standing committee for fund-raising. A good fundraiser himself, Pope helped establish the Society of Generous Friends (under the presidency of Charles Dilks), which spurred donors, old and new, to make substantial contributions. A measure of this success was the increase in the annual FOW budget from approximately $30,000 in the early 1990s to over $1.2 million two decades later.[11]

The revitalized organization had new clout and the skills and vision to carry the institution forward. The leadership of the FOW was now dedicated to understanding and tackling environmental problems in the lower valley. A reenergized FOW recruited and attracted new members from a broader segment of the community. The conservation committee, supported by the larger organization, spearheaded key FOW initiatives in the park.

The personal conflict with Pope eventually led Dlugach to leave the FOW and found his own organization in 1999—the Wissahickon Restoration Volunteers (WRV). Pope appointed Wallis as chair of the conservation committee, with Robert "Bob" Lukens as co-chair. Under this leadership, the committee broadened its expertise and scope. It would continue to confront, with increasing sophistication, the problems of reforestation, invasive exotics, an exploding deer population, stormwater mismanagement, mountain bikes, littering and vandalism, signage, repair of trails and structures, the modernization of Valley Green Inn and the rehabilitation of the Valley Green landscape.

Professionalizing the FOW

To sustain the renewed purpose of the organization, the FOW began the critical task of transforming a non-profit run by volunteers (no matter how talented and dedicated) into a professionally managed association. This evolution was undertaken in several steps.

The first step was to find a stable home and a paid director. By the mid-1980s, the Chestnut Hill Historical Society (CHHS) had been reinvigorated. In 1987, its president, long-time civic leader and Philadelphia attorney J. Pennington Strauss, convinced the society to buy the former Presbyterian Church "manse" (or minister's house) near the corner of Germantown and Rex Avenues. Richard Snowden's family donated a good portion of the money for this property. Although founded two decades earlier, the CHHS had not had a permanent headquarters or space for offices, meetings and archives.

Joint headquarters of the CHHS and the FOW, on Germantown Avenue, the main commercial street.
Source: Photograph by CLF

The FOW was in similar straits. They had no official telephone number, no regular board meetings and no readily accessible way for people to join the organization. These circumstances reinforced the perception that the FOW was an elite club of West Chestnut Hillers. The budget at the time was only 30 thousand dollars.[12]

In 1993, Snowden suggested Howard Kittell as a potential executive director for the CHHS. The FOW collaborated with the CHHS to share their new building and to hire Kittell as a joint director. Later, the FOW would hire its own full-time director, while continuing to share the building and archival collections with the CHHS. With a professional director and the use of the historical society's building and archives, the FOW could turn to basic issues of membership and governance.[13]

FOW Presents Since Reorganization

FOW Presidents since F. Markoe "Koey" Rivinus retired in 1992:

David Pope 1992-1998
Edward Stainton 1998-2004
Charles Dilks 2004-2005
Robert Lukens 2005-2007
Cindy Affleck 2007-

A second step was to generate a Strategic Plan. In 1993, Ella Torrey, an FOW executive committee member, convinced John Austin, of the Executive Service Corps of the Delaware Valley and past president of PECO, to volunteer to develop a plan. This plan clarified and focused the organization's direction and outlined several ambitious goals: the FOW should be the "leading voice" on public policy and private actions that directly or indirectly affect the Wissahickon; the organization should actively undertake physical improvements that would preserve and restore both the natural environment and the cultural landscape; and these projects should enhance the beauty of the valley and promote the appropriate use of a wilderness park.[14]

The strategic plan committed the FOW board to move from being a group enmeshed in day-to-day activities—with no staff—to a "governance" board where members shape policy and programs and raise money. These changes required increasing and diversifying the revenue base, putting in place a full-time staff, and building an active and engaged board to bring "wealth, wisdom and willingness to work."[15] This plan was supported and gradually realized by a series of able presidents—a reminder that an organization cannot go forward without strong leadership.

A third step was a further reorganization of the committee structure. The conservation committee continued to address previous concerns and added the Valley Green committee to oversee the FOW's first large scale improvement project in decades.

The communications committee took over producing the trail map, the newsletter and eventually the website. Professional staff gradually reinforced the development, membership, finance and nominating committees. A newly created advocacy committee recognized the need for a pro-active public policy stance. The FOW continued its new partnership with the CHHS by participating in two shared committees—easements and archives. The FOW archives became a separate collection donated by their members, but housed in a joint library overseen by joint staff.[16]

The FOW used the strategic plan as the basis for an application to the William Penn Foundation for a grant. In 2004, the foundation funded a three-year grant of $275,000 to the FOW. The funds were used to hire a full-time executive director and additional development staff. The grant required the FOW to raise an additional $100,000 each year before the funds would be released.[17]

Two controversial initiatives brought the FOW to maturity and boldly into the 21st century—deer management and trail repair. Many FOW members wanted to replant the declining forest, but began to realize that this could never be achieved without reducing deer numbers. They also wanted to address the deteriorating trails, but discovered that they must first tackle concerns about mountain bikes. These divisive issues threatened to tear the organization apart—both from within and without. The ability to resolve these concerns, based on a dispassionate examination of the evidence, allowed the FOW to gain credibility and to achieve consensus. In dealing with both deer and mountain bikes, the organization came out stronger, more confident and more sophisticated.[18]

FOW Initiatives: Managing Deer

During the initial reorganization period, the most significant accomplishment of the revitalized FOW was its leadership on the deer problem. It took the entire decade of the 1980s for the FOW to recognize the impact of the deer in Wissahickon Park, and much of the early 1990s to tackle the problem. Nonetheless, the FOW was among the first conservation organizations in the country to identify this problem, courageously explore solutions and implement a successful program to control deer.

With the direction of a number of very hard working, responsible members of the board, the FOW came to accept that the impact of white tailed deer (*Odocoileus virginianus*) on the forest is a regional as well as a national problem, and that the survival of urban parks depended on management of an excess deer population. After a great deal of careful research, consultation with regional experts and public debate, the FOW agreed to advocate for and to finance deer management by culling. Some board members were so upset with this position that they resigned in protest. Deer management remains one of the most important projects ever undertaken by the FOW, in part because this issue was so difficult and so emotionally charged.[19]

FOW Committees Present Structure

15:17

In 2003, the Executive Committee of the FOW fine-tuned the administrative structure of the organization. The proliferating existing committees were consolidated into a more logical system.

Standing Executive Committee

Advocacy
    Subcommittee: Park Uses

Conservation
    Subcommittees:
      Deer, Wildlife, Structures
      Valley Green Inn
      Landscaping, Forestry and Plantings
      Water Resources and Trails

Valley Green Oversight

Communications and Education
    Subcommittees:
      Maps, Newsletter and
      Education and Programs

Development

Membership

Finance, Budget and Audit

Nominating

The FOW participates with the CHHS in two joint committees

Easements

Collections[1]

1. *FOW Newsletter* Fall 2003, 4.

Beginning in 1992, a wildlife committee (a subcommittee of the FOW conservation committee), of unusual competence and concentrated focus, explored the deer problem in depth. Gradually this subcommittee brought the larger organization to the recognition that deer management was central to nearly every problem in a deteriorating Wissahickon ecosystem—from loss of habitat for birds, butterflies and small mammals, to the difficulty of reestablishing natural forest vegetation, particularly wildflowers, shrubs and small trees. Tackling this explosive issue led the FOW board and ultimately the entire membership into political advocacy, including complex negotiations with relevant state authorities and the formation of a number of successful partnerships with other conservation non-profits.

In undertaking this controversial issue, the organization needed to move beyond anecdotal evidence and piecemeal solutions, to consultations with the best scientific experts in the field. These experts had experience in the multifaceted problems of deer management and could provide a program that would be ecologically sound and widely respected.

Samuel H. "Sam" Tucker joined the conservation committee because deer were eating the ornamental plants in his garden at the edge of Wissahickon Park in East Falls, not far from Philadelphia University. Tucker, a pediatric neurologist at Children's Hospital in Philadelphia and a faculty member at the University of Pennsylvania Medical School, eventually agreed to head the wildlife subcommittee. Both a scientist and medical doctor, he required unassailable data before making recommendations. Realizing that personal testimonials about an overabundance of deer in the valley and their impacts on forest vegetation would not convince the Fairmount Park Commission or the Pennsylvania Game Commission, Tucker cast a wide net to discover the right person to document the problem. Eventually he found wildlife biologist Bryon Shissler and his firm, Natural Resource Consultants (NRC), in Conestoga, Pennsylvania. Shissler had done the 1989 deer study for the Schuylkill Center for Environmental Education (SCEE) and was well respected in both scientific and political circles. Tucker invited Shissler to speak at the October 1992 meeting of the conservation committee.[20]

Shissler pointed out the need for a professional deer count and documentation of the effects of these animals on vegetation and other wildlife, before any action was recommended.[21] Tucker and Dlugach pressed the board to back a deer study, but interestingly, those who later became the greatest supporters of deer management were not originally convinced of its merit.

After considerable discussion about the need for a study and possible ways to fund it, the board agreed to poll the membership to see if they would be willing to contribute the $35,000 to hire Shissler's firm. Membership response was overwhelmingly positive and the money was raised from within the organization, as well as from the members of the Morris Arboretum and the Wissahickon Valley Watershed Association (WVWA). In 1994, the FOW retained NRC to prepare an in-depth study of the deer impact on the forest in Wissahickon Park, to evaluate alternatives and recommend action.[22]

Completed in the spring of 1996, NRC's report estimated the white-tailed deer (*Odocoileus virginianus*) population at around 200. With 1,841 acres in Wissahickon Park, or approximately three square miles, this meant nearly 69 deer per square mile. Evidence from other forests in the region showed that more than 20 animals per square mile posed a serious threat to the biodiversity of the ecosystem. In researching the historic forest, Shissler found that eight to ten deer per square mile were the number that had been supported in the forest of the Lenni-Lenape. The optimal number of deer in the entire park should be 24 to 30 animals.

Scientific studies have shown that with numbers of deer greater than 22 per square mile, the number and diversity of other animals, particularly forest interior birds, decline. The NRC study found evidence of heavy deer browsing on tree seedlings, shrubs and wildflowers throughout the park. Wildflowers had all but disappeared in most of the lower valley, and low shrubs and the seedlings of native canopy trees were difficult to find. Without these forest components, there was little food or shelter for butterflies, birds and small mammals, as well as amphibians such as salamanders, on which important functions of the forest ecosystem depended. Without seedlings, the forest no longer had the capacity to reproduce and would become an "old age home for trees."[23]

Return to a balanced population of 24-30 deer in the entire park came down to three possible solutions: culling by professional sharp shooters, relocation and birth control. Animal rights groups were vehemently opposed to culling. Relocation was not acceptable. Evidence showed that deer nearly always died when relocated. Most nearby regions had deer problems of their own and would not accept new deer. Birth control was expensive and ineffective. For birth control to be successful, all or nearly all the does would have to be injected twice yearly by darts with a chemical contraceptive that would be good for only 6 months. Does would have to be lured with food and trapped in an enclosure to put them within a darting range of 30 to 40 feet. After extensive research into birth control, the wildlife committee rejected this solution as impractical and prohibitively expensive. Birth control for deer is also not currently permitted under Pennsylvania law.[24]

When Tucker retired and left the area, Robert Wallis and Antoinette "Tony" Seymour became co-chairs of the wildife committee. They renamed it the deer committee and focused entirely on the deer problem in the park. Aware of the many currents of opinion in the community, the committee under this new leadership initiated an educational campaign with brochures and public meetings. In March 1998, Wallis and Seymour organized a public forum at a Chestnut Hill school (Springside) to bring together a number of experts to speak on the deer issue.[25] At this meeting, an overwhelming number of scientists and wildlife management experts spoke about the urgent need to bring the numbers of deer back into balance with the capacity of the forest to shelter and feed them.[26]

Those emotionally attached to deer as a beautiful and "natural" part of the Wissahickon Valley found it difficult to understand the threat posed by deer to other animals and to the forest itself.

A Japanese forest where 40 years of unmanaged deer population (*Cervus nippon*) have reduced the forest to a "moonscape." In desperation, ecologists have tried to protect the bark on the tree trunks from being eaten by circling the trunks with chain link fence (not shown in photograph).
Source: Photograph by CLF

Robert C. Wallis (1943–)

Bob Wallis in the field.
Source: Photograph by CLF

Robert "Bob" Wallis is a "can-do guy." With his energy, enthusiasm and drive, projects move ahead. With his broad vision of environmental issues, he inspires others with a sense of larger purpose.

Wallis is inclusive and has a gift for bringing new people to the table and for delegating responsibility. He also has the ability to pick good, dedicated people to join with him in implementing projects.

As a professional fund-raiser for non-profits, he has been very effective in identifying potential grants and structuring gift-giving for the FOW.

Wallis became a board member of the FOW in 1991, and was a central figure in the reorganization. When David Pope became president, he named Wallis head of the conservation committee, which Wallis then co-chaired with Robert "Bob"Lukens. Lukens organized committee operations. Shortly afterwards, Wallis assumed the leadership of the deer committee with Antoinette Seymour.

Of all Wallis's accomplishments for the FOW, he is proudest of his leadership of the deer committee and the successful reduction of deer population in Wissahickon Park. This task required strategy, tenacity, political sensitivity, good "people skills" and a broad ecological perspective.

Homeowner struggling to move a deer (*Odocoileus virginianus*) killed by an automobile on a residential road next to Wissahickon Park.
Source: Photograph by CLF

Their attachment was to the individual animal and not to the survival of the system itself. Animal rights groups continued to protest and would later bring legal action to stop the culls.

FOW members were reluctant to kill deer and certainly did not want to eliminate deer in the park. They made it clear that their commitment was to reduce the deer population to their historical numbers and to restore nature's balance.[27] Following the meeting, the FOW board passed a resolution supporting a deer cull as the best possible solution at the time. The resolution, written by Hengst, read: "WHEREAS the overpopulation of deer threatens the survival of the Wissahickon forest of Fairmount Park, THEREFORE BE IT RESOLVED THAT we support and will facilitate culling of the deer population in the Wissahickon to achieve a deer population in balance with the natural environment."[28]

In Pennsylvania, the state game commission owns all wildlife. It was necessary to apply for a permit to the commission to cull the deer using professional sharpshooters. In April 1998, the FOW requested that the Fairmount Park Commission apply for this permit. An impressive list of conservation organizations, also

Animal Rights protesters outside the Chestnut Hill Branch of the Free Library of Philadelphia, opposite the headquarters of the FOW, March, 1999.
Source: Photograph by David Pope

troubled by deer problems, formally backed this resolution. Supporting non-profits included the Morris Arboretum, the Friends of Philadelphia Parks, the Schuylkill Center for Environmental Education (SCEE), the Natural Lands Trust (NLT), the Academy of Natural Sciences of Philadelphia, and the American Lyme Disease Foundation.[29] With this widespread collaboration, the FOW board formally asked the Fairmount Park Commission to sanction a cull to thin the herd. Two public hearings were held in the summer of 1998 by the park commission, and a parade of individuals testified both for and against the proposal. The commission, convinced by cogent arguments and the broad consensus for reducing the number of deer, agreed to get permission from the city to request a permit from the state.[30]

Because of difficulties in obtaining a permit from the Pennsylvania Game Commission, the first cull did not begin until late March 1999 and only 43 deer were killed the first year. Before a second cull, scheduled for the winter of 2000, could take place, animal rights groups filed suit and obtained a judge's temporary restraining order to stop it. At the same time, the Pennsylvania Game Commission demanded that park authorities include amateur hunters in any plan to reduce deer populations in the park.[31]

It was essential to break this deadlock and prevent frustrating delays. The FOW hired a communications expert and went directly to the state legislature. A rider to an omnibus bill was drafted after two members of the deer committee, Edward "Ed" Stainton and Ernesta Ballard (who was also a Fairmount Park Commissioner), met with a key state senator and persuaded him to push forward the legislation.[32] This rider required the game commission to issue a sharpshooter permit within 30 days after application from "cities of the first class." (Philadelphia is the only city of the first class in Pennsylvania.) Interference in the cull was declared a felony and the requirement that amateur hunters be allowed to participate was dropped. Meanwhile, the park commission won all the suits brought by animal rights groups. With the legal obstacles cleared, a well-organized and unimpeded cull took place in early winter 2001, through early spring 2002.

The U.S. Department of Agricultural (USDA) was asked to manage the cull but would not take the contract until all private approaches had failed. The first cull was contracted to a private organization (White Buffalo), who were harassed by animal rights advocates and withdrew. As a result, all culls have been carried out by sharpshooters hired by the USDA, in concert with the FPC.[33] The meat was cut up into small packages and delivered to charity organizations for distribution to the needy. Money for the entire process has been raised by the FOW. Special appeals and other private funding sources have helped pay for the more recent culls. In this way, the park commission, a public agency, remained free of controversy. Pope, president of the FOW at the time, was an eloquent spokesman for this groundbreaking program and persevered despite harassment. The FOW initiative was strengthened by an alliance with Barry Bessler from the managing director's office at Fairmount Park, the Friends of Pennypack Park, who joined in the cull, and Ernesta Ballard, a Fairmount Park Commissioner, who worked ceaselessly to convince her fellow commissioners of the need to reduce deer in the park.[34]

In the 2001-02 cull, 177 deer were taken in Wissahickon Park, including 170 does bearing fawns. At this time, a count showed an estimated 300 deer in the park—100 more than the earlier survey six years before. In 2002-03, 177 deer were again taken. The 2003-04 cull was less successful because of high winds and other weather-related difficulties, with only 46 deer taken. In 2004-05, 82 deer were taken, 42 deer in 2005-06, 52 in 2006-07 and 45 in 2007-08.[35]

Although culling has eliminated a significant number of animals (703 deer over eight years), deer have continued to reproduce in high numbers. A third census, taken January 2004 (from an airplane using infrared cameras), showed more than 170 deer remaining in Wissahickon Park. After four successive years of culling, the deer population, though slightly smaller, was nowhere near the 24 to 30 animals recommended. Residents living close to the park still found deer eating their plants and sleeping in their gardens.[36]

After eight years, however, the cull has significantly reduced the deer population and a great change can be seen in the forest of Wissahickon Park. There has been no recent survey of deer numbers, but by 2008, deer were seen only rarely and a glimpse of one or two animals, flashing through the forest, was once again a special event. However, despite hopes that a cull could be a one-time effort, continuous culls will be required to achieve a long-term and sustainable forest recovery.[37]

There has been no vegetation study of Wissahickon Park as a whole, but anecdotal evidence suggests that throughout the lower valley, there has been a significant recovery of the forest vegetation. Wildflowers have returned to the ground layer and the seedlings of oak (*Quercus spp.*), ash (*Fraxinus spp.*), hickory (*Carya spp.*), tulip poplar (*Liriodendron tulipifera*), beech (*Fagus americana*) and hemlock (*Tsuga canadensis*) —the major canopy trees—can be found on the forest floor for the first time in decades.

In the fall of 2002, the FOW, with the assistance of Ann Rhoads and Timothy Block, botanists from the Morris Arboretum, and David Bower of the park staff, began a scientific study of plant recovery to measure the results of the cull. Six sites were chosen in Wissahickon Park. At each site two 10 x 10 meter plots were staked out—one surrounded by deer-proof fencing and the other laid out, but left open. Tree species and their diameter (at breast height) have been recorded for both fenced and open plots. To date, this study has yielded no conclusive data. Initially, the fenced plots were slow to recover since so much damage had been done. Then, with a continued reduction in the numbers of deer, both the control plots and the fenced plots are recovering.[38]

Progress in returning the forest to a healthy ecosystem depends on continued management of deer. Remaining deer have bred prolifically and new deer have entered the park from the Schuylkill River watershed, as well as from Montgomery County to the north. Public and private lands in the middle valley are overrun with deer and the condition of almost all natural lands is very poor. While some deer are harvested by private bow-hunting clubs, there has been no initiative to manage deer by public agencies. The FOW deer committee has begun talks with Fort Washington State Park, managed by the Pennsylvania Department of Conservation and Natural Resoures (PA DCNR) and with the Wissahickon Valley Watershed Association (WVWA) to sponsor a joint deer survey and manage deer on public lands in the middle valley.

Wissachickon Park forest floor with mayapple (*Podophyllum peltatum*), wild ginger (*Asarum canadense*), and ash (*Fraxinus americana*) seedlings, along upper Forbidden Drive, May, 2008.
Source: Photograph by CLF

FOW Initiatives: Sustainable Trails

By the mid-1990s, the FOW urged the FPC to undertake a comprehensive trail plan as a basis for raising money for trail repair. Increasing trail use, volunteer trail repair and the growing influence of the FOW conservation committee ultimately pushed then Fairmount Park director, William Mifflin, to commission a Wissahickon Trails Master Plan.

In 1996, the firm of Simone and Jaffe (later Simone Collins, Landscape Architects) developed a Wissahickon Trails Master Plan, with significant input from the FOW conservation committee. The report made a number of important recommendations: closing dangerous or unmanageable trails; improving deteriorated trails, bridges, and structures; monitoring trail, bridge, and structure conditions; and maintaining trails, bridges, and park structures in safe condition.[39]

To resolve user conflicts, the master plan recommended: segregating uses on the hillside trails; designating one trail on each side of the creek for shared use by bikers, horseback riders, walkers and joggers; purchase of permits for bike and horseback riders; the reestablishment of volunteer bike patrols; easier access to information about proper trail etiquette and the improvement of trail signage.[40] After two long and difficult public meetings, the FPC accepted these proposals.

The conservation committee monitored implementation of the recommendations. Bringing in experts from the outside, they educated themselves on the latest/best approaches to trail design and repair and kept up pressure on park staff to follow through with the recommendations. Following the plan, a number of policies were put in place—designated trails for shared use, annual registration of bikers and prohibition of bike riding in muddy conditions. These policies were insufficient and ineffective. Worse, they were rarely enforced. By 2001, the FOW was receiving increasing complaints. Bikers were neither registering nor riding only on designated trails.

In response to these problems, the FOW formed a mountain bike committee (a sub-committee of the conservation committee) to review the current bicycle policy. The underlying assumption was that this committee would recommend banning mountain bikes from the park. Members of this committee were David Dannenberg, David Pope and Louise Johnston. Dannenberg was considered pro-bike, Pope neutral and Johnson anti-bike, allowing all points of view to be represented.

The committee report, written in September 2002, concluded that the system developed in 1996 was a failure (in practice, if not in concept). In their report, the committee specifically noted that the widely accepted conditions for shared use trail systems simply did not exist in the Wissahickon and questioned whether the FOW should promote these conditions or ban mountain bikes. Feeling unqualified to make the appropriate decisions, the primary recommendation of the committee was for the FOW to hire qualified, outside experts to resolve the problems.

Hiring expert consultants was the primary recommendation of the mountain bike committee report. By voting to accept the report, the board was committed to follow its recommendations. After a six-month delay, they agreed to engage a well-recognized, outside expert. As with the deer committee, the FOW had demonstrated that hiring

David Dannenberg (1962–)

David Dannenberg grew up in Mt. Airy and teaches at the Crefeld School, a progressive school in Chestnut Hill. He was recruited by Stainton in 1998 to join the FOW board and became a member of the conservation committee.

From the beginning, he brought an holistic understanding of ecological ideas to the conservation committee. Both a strategist and a hands-on worker in the park, he seized the trail issue in all its complexities and pushed it to the forefront of the FOW agenda. Dannenberg and co-chair Susan Wilmerding followed Wallis as head of the conservation committee. As the deer issue was resolved, Dannenberg took up the cudgels for trails, recognizing that one of the keys to a healthy forest in a public park was a sustainable trail system.

In 1999, in response to complaints about mountain bikes, the FOW formed a mountain bike subcommittee with Dannenberg as its chair and David Pope and Louise Johnston as members. The unspoken subtext was that this committee would recommend banning mountain bikes from the park. Without bias, Dannenberg led this committee through a process of learning about trail design and usage, and in the end, the committee came to a radically different conclusion. This process led to the "Sustainable Trails Initiative," which Dannenberg started and has continued to nurture.

Dannenberg reads widely about park issuess and is committed to using professional consultants as the framework for volunteer activities. His tenacity and thoroughness in covering, in detail, all the areas of concern have led to the remarkable success of the trails plan and demonstration projects.

He has brought to all his work for the FOW an accurate sense of the fabric of the park and of its needs, whether asking the Philadelphia Water Department to use Wissahickon schist when working in the gorge, or when bringing FOW attention to the potential loss of gutters on Kitchen's Lane.

David Dannenberg looking out over Wissahickon gorge on a tour of the demonstration work of the Sustainable Trails Initiative along the Orange Trail on the east side of Wissahickon Creek.
Source: Photograph by CLF

acknowledged experts to make recommendations and develop a plan helped overcome public objections and led to a focused, effective program. By reaching out to nationally accepted experts, the mountain bike committee was reinforcing a tradition begun by the deer committee.

Gradually Dannenberg abandoned the idea of eliminating mountain bikes. There could be no positive influence on the park without including bikers, and banning bikes would be virtually impossible to implement. The committee members realized that if no action were taken to rehabilitate the trail system, the existing trails would still continue to contribute to the degradation of the ecosystem, even if no one—walker, jogger, biker or equestrian—were to enter the park.

Dannenberg realized that there could be a critical connection between mountain biking and a major initiative to rebuild Wissahickon trails. Redesigning and repairing deteriorating trails was crucial to the health of the forest and to the quality of the visitor experience. If the trails were rejuvenated and there were still problems with bikers, then mountain bikes could be banned at that time and Wissahickon Park would have a better trail system. On the other hand, if the FPC simply banned bikes, a major constituency would no longer enjoy the park and there would still be an unsustainable trail system actively contributing to park deterioration.

In trying to find appropriate trail experts, Dannenberg, who was reading widely about the subject, found references to a doctoral dissertation by Alan Bjorkman on the impacts of mountain bikes on park trails. He gave Bjorkman's name to Pope who then set out to locate him and explore the issues further. Bjorkman recommended that Pope visit Kettle Moraine Park in Wisconsin and meet Ray Hajwesky, the park manager. At his own expense, Pope traveled to Kettle Moraine and to the Cook County Forest Preserves that circle the City of Chicago. He returned with changed views about biking and the recommendation that the FOW hire Bjorkman and Hajewski.

In seeking the advice of experts, Pope and Dannenberg were careful to ensure a process that was open and fair—hoping, of course, that everyone would reach the same conclusions. They contacted Dlugach's new organization, the Wissahickon Restoration Volunteers (WRV), who were fiercely anti-mountain bikes, and Jay Jones of the Delaware Valley Mountain Biking Program (DVMBP), with information about Bjorkman and Hajewki. Both groups accepted these consultants as neutral parties qualified to evaluate biking in the park and understood that accepting these experts did not mean endorsing their conclusions.

The Bjorkman and Hajewki report recommended that the entire Wissahickon trail system be rebuilt to International Mountain Biking Association (IMBA) standards—pointing out that, ironically, the group that could best design trails were mountain bikers themselves. With a proposal from this group, the approval of two committees and a vote of the board, the FOW began the process of hiring IMBA, only to face further controversy from a few board members. The proposal was then put out for public bid and IMBA won hands down, but many months were lost and IMBA considered suing the FOW for shopping their bid to competitors.[41]

In June 2004, the FOW announced to its membership that it would sponsor and oversee a comprehensive analysis and redesign of the entire Wissahickon Park trail system. In the fall of that year, they hired Trail Solutions, the design, construction and management arm of IMBA, to create a system of sustainable trails.

IMBA Trail Solutions was established in 2002 out of a need to have multi-purpose trails that reconciled the needs of all users. Working with the topography and the ecosystems of each site, they brought an in-depth knowledge of what it takes to make durable and effective trails in high use urban and wilderness parks. In addition, their trails are designed to solve social conflicts. The design of the trail "informs" users how and where to go—by their vertical and horizontal alignments, widths and materials. Educational programs, workshops with park users and signage reinforce the design.[42]

The most important lesson learned from site visits, wide reading and consultation with experts was that the problem was not mountain bikes, but poorly designed trails. Everything that matters about trails—from user behavior to environmental impact—originates in the design and construction of the trail. Happily, designs that elicit good behavior are also those that ensure minimal user impact and maximum trail sustainability.

The process, from initial ideas to acceptable plan, was a long journey to the realization that the FOW had been trying to solve the wrong problem. The problem had been seen as an irreconcilable conflict—keep bikes out of the park and preserve the "wilderness" experience, or permit some active recreational uses and destroy its character and quality. This conflict was the latest iteration of a long debate begun with the founding of the park. By the 21st century, the answer was no longer an either-or proposition. A new solution would come from unexpected places and from a fusion of the needs of all constituencies. It would be inclusive and offer benefits to all park visitors. No constituency would be excluded, and instead, the group previously considered "the problem" would be the key to creating a more complex and long-lasting solution.

FOW Initiatives | Sustainable Trails Initative

The general purpose of the Sustainable Trails Initiative's demonstration projects is to help assess the resources, materials, manpower, machinery and money, required for future trail improvements. The projects also help to field test various techniques for constructing, reconstructing and closing trails. Perhaps most importantly, these demonstrations raise public awarenedss and support.

Two trail plans were the product of Phase II of a three-phase Sustainable Trails Initiative. The project is a joint undertaking of the Fairmount Park Commission and the Friends of the Wissahickon, funded by the Pennsylvania Department of Conservation and Natural Resources and private donors. Working with FOW staff members and volunteers from the International Mountain Biking Association (IMBA), Trail Solutions Program mapped and evaluated the existing trails, created a sustainable trails plan and identified demonstration sites.

In explaining the Sustainable Trails Initiative, Dannenberg has written,"From a user standpoint the purpose of the project was to provide a better experience for all users. Meeting this goal requires occasional compromises. Were those trails created and rebuilt only to enhance the mountain biking experience, they would have been designed and constructed differently."[1]

For the trail design, the FOW welcomed input from running groups, cyclist clubs, equestrians, fishermen, birders, rock climbers and dog walkers. As the Sustainable Trails Initiative evolves, continued input has been solicited from stakeholder groups to evaluate completed projects and to select and design future projects.

Trails that are currently open to biking will remain open; those currently closed to mountain biking will remain closed. With better signage, enhanced educational outreach and enforcement, it is expected that cyclists will use only the trails open to them. It will be possible for walkers and joggers to complete a path loop without encountering bicycles. It is critical that all users, including dogs, remain on the existing trails at all times, so that new "rogue" trails are not created. The existence and maintenance of high quality trails should reduce the incentive for people to create their own.[2]

1.　　　2.　　　3.

Legend: Trail Assessment
1. Trails that can be restored,
2. Trails that must be relocated
3. Trails that cannot be made sustainable and should be closed.

1.

Legend: Sustainable Trails
1. Redesigned trails

This trail plan combines the IMBA Trail Assessment and the Sustainable Trails Plan. It shows both the existing trails and their evaluation, as well as proposed routes for the core trails that parallel Wissahickon Creek. Access paths and paths in Carpenter Woods and the Andorra Natural Area are not shown. Source: IMBA Trail Solutions

Orange Trail Demonstration #1

The first demonstration site was on the Orange Trail, located on the Chestnut Hill side of the creek, from the Indian statue, and Towanda Street to the north. This path was the upper footpath on the east side and runs parallel to Wissahickon Creek. The project was undertaken in late summer 2007 by the FOW, the FPC, IMBA Trails Solutions and volunteers.

Despite running generally along the contours, two sections of this trail had grades over 20 percent. These gullies were filled and terraces built to reduce all steep grades. A variety of "armoring" techniques—steps, ledges and ramps—helped to hold the fill and stabilize the trail. Wherever possible, local soil and stone found on the site were used. Additional schist was trucked in to complete the job.

Excavation of the outside edges reduced the width of the trail and provided soil and stone for recon-struction. This excavation disturbed over 1,000 square feet of hillside, which was then planted with bottle-brush grass (*Elymus hystrix*), chestnut oak (*Quercus dentata*) and acorns and ferns harvested from other areas of the park. Whenever possible, the topsoil was preserved and spread over the excavated areas and covered with leaves and duff gathered nearby.

All reconstructions were designed to be compatible with a variety of trail users—walkers, runners, cyclists and equestrians. The team worked a total of 660 hours (300 from volunteers) on this 555-foot section of the Orange Trail. Volunteers received valuable on-the-job training that could be used in future trail work.

Wigard Avenue Trail Demonstration #2

In early autumn 2007, the same partnership tackled a second demon-stration project. This project began at the foot of Wigard Avenue where it dead-ends in the park. Wigard Avenue is the access road to a small colonial farmhouse located off Henry Avenue on the Roxborough side of the creek. For many years, this house has been used by the Boy Scouts.

The Wigard Avenue Trail is a steep trail down to the creek that joins the Yellow Trail. The Yellow Trail is the hillside trail parallel to Forbidden Drive that runs from Ridge Avenue, at the beginning of the park, to Bell's Mill Road. Some parts of this path were eroded into deep gullies.

IMBA's design for repair of this path section included a variety of techniques. The path was regraded to form more than 20 gentle "rolling dips." Rolling dips are "grade reversals" and form tiny valleys on the trail—an average of one every 24 feet. They create small catchment areas that capture stormwater before it can rush down the path, gathering velocity and erosive force. These dips are practical solutions to the problems of erosion and improve the path experience for all users. The mini-valleys are not steep enough to be readily noticeable, but they slow bicycles and make a more exciting and varied trail.

Due to the steepness of the path, this project focused on trail closure and new trail construction. The team, employing over 300 volunteer hours, succeeded in constructing nearly two-thirds of a mile of new sustainable trail, reclaimed over 2,000 feet of existing trail and did maintenance work on another 1,000 feet of trail.[1]

Some sections of trail were deemed unusable and had to be closed permanently, with large Wissahickon schist rocks and fallen logs. Compacted soil was scarified, local fill brought in, organic material spread over the bare ground and local ferns, shrubs and native trees were transplanted to stop erosion and help the land recover. The cost for this demonstration was $37,000, not including the value of time, equipment and materials contributed by Fairmount Park staff.

1. David Dannenberg, chair, FOW trails committee, to Steve Jones, president Wissahickon Restoration Volunteers, November 23, 2007.

2. Richard Edwards, IMBA Trail Solutions, Report of Trail Reconstruction Demonstration: A Project of Friends of Wissahickon, Sustainable Trails Initiative, August 14, 2007.

Stages in Trail Repair

"Fall-line" trails—trails that go straight down the hillside—are an example of poorly designed and heavily degraded trails in the Wissahickon gorge. Stormwater erodes these trails into deep gullies, often creating a surface of loose rock and debris. Tree roots are exposed and sediment is carried down into the creek. As walkers and bikers move around obstacles, they widen these trails or create unofficial new ones— "rogue trails." Here, volunteers are closing one of these "fall-line" trails. The old trail is blocked off with fallen branches and tree trunks. The new trail is realigned and will follow the contours.

Volunteers gather to receive instructions from Richard Edwards and Jill Van Winkle, trail specialists from IMBA, Trail Solutions.
Source: Photograph by CLF

New signs alerted park users that a trail would be closed and redesigned.

Trail Closed

This area is resting.
Please follow the new trail.

This trail section has been causing significant erosion. It has been rerouted as a part of the Sustainable Trails Initiative.

For more information, visit the warming shed kiosk at Valley Green Inn, or go to: www.FOW.org

Friends of the Wissahickon

Respect the land, Respect the trail.

Before: "Fall-line" trail eroded into a deep gully.
Source: Photographs by Jon Pearce,
Philadelphia Mountain Biking Association.

During: "Fall-line" being blocked with tree trunks. Ultimately, this gully will need to be filled.

Student volunteers carry a tarpaulin full of leaves to cover the newly filled gullies on the closed portion of the trail. The leaves will be used to cover the bare earth and form a natural mulch to prevent erosion and allow native ferns and wildflowers to grow.
Source: Photograph by CLF

Stages in Trail Repair *(Continued)*

Volunteers build a rock drain to carry water from the hillside across the trail without eroding a gully In the path.
Source: Photographs by Jon Pearce, Philadelphia Mountain Biking Association

The new trail section is flagged and then raked to show the new alignment.

Barely finished, this new trail section is already being tested and enjoyed.
Photographs by CLF

A finished trail. Large logs have been placed at the edge of the trail to provide technical challenges for bikers and a place for walkers to sit. Source: Photograph by CLF

Volunteers cut branches overhanging the new trail section. Source: Photograph by Jon Pearce, Philadelphia Mountain Biking Association

Finished trail with new stone steps. Where it is not possible to reroute the trail, shallow terraces are made and retained with shallow, stone steps. These terraces are sloped to shed water evenly off the trail. Source: Photograph by CLF

Community Workshops

In 2007 and again in 2008, the Philadelphia Mountain Biking Association (PMBA), working closely within the framework suggested by IMBA, began a series of workshops with horseback riders at the Courtesy Stables (a non-profit equestrian facility within Wissahickon Park). The workshops brought bikers and horseback riders together to overcome trail conflicts. During the day-long training session, the needs of each group were discussed and a win-win solution was created for each typical trail situation.

Both days were strenuous, fun and a great success. These efforts will not only diminish conflict between different users on the trails, but also will open new possibilities for learning and for fun in the park. These workshops have reinforced the park's role as common ground —an integrator of social groups.

Illustrating the character and temperament of a horse to mountain bikers.
Source: Photographs by Jon Pearce. Philadelphia Mountain Biking Association (PMBA)

Riding in the park, bikers and horseback riders practice going in opposite directions on a trail.

The workshop took place at the Courtesy Stables in Upper Roxborough, where a variety of exercises gradually sensitized each group to the other's needs.

Source: Photographs by Jon Pearce,
Philadelphia Mountain Biking Association

Other FOW Initiatives

15:23-26

There have been several other significant FOW initiatives since reorganization. Under Stainton. The structures committee has repaired all the WPA buildings in the park and has also tackled many other park features—from small pedestrian bridges to kiosks for park notices. With the addition of professional staff, the easement committee is aggressively pursuing buffers between Wissahickon Park and adjacent private properties. They are also hoping to acquire land or conservation easements to better preserve the presently unprotected tributaries. Under Debra Wolfe Goldstein, the easement program is being extended into the middle and upper Wissahickon Valley. Improvements to the Valley Green Inn and

15:23

Edward Stainton (1933–)

In 1998, "Ed" Stainton, an enormously popular teacher, retired from Chestnut Hill Academy (a local, boys' private school) after many years of teaching woodworking. Following his retirement, he became the second president of the FOW, since reorganization.

Over the years, Stainton would go into the park and simply fix what needed to be repaired. Like Dlugach,

he was impatient to achieve results and often ignored both bureaucratic niceties
and the complexities of an issue in order to get projects moving. Unlike Dlugach, Stainton was politically saavy, working successfully with park directors and a variety of politicans. As president of the FOW, he supported the deer management campaign and worked closely with

Ernesta Ballard to win over the leadership of the Pennsylvania state legislature.

In 1996, he spearheaded the formation of a structures committee—a subcommittee of the conservation committee. He began work on the WPA structures, obtaining permission from then FPC director William Mifflin to restore all of them in Wissahickon Park. Over the next decade, Stainton and volunteers have repaired the 13 remaining WPA structures—guardhouses, picnic shelters and toilet buildings.

Without Stainton's tireless work much of the cultural richness of the park would now have disappeared. Countless small pedestrian bridges, bulletin boards, gates, railings, the warming sheds at Valley Green and even the well at the Andorra Natural area have been reconstructed by the structures committee. Stainton has brought consummate skills to the job and inspired others to join him. He has found imaginative ways to leverage park staff using his own shop and equipment at home to tackle large projects like the warming sheds.

Stainton with Larry Moy building new guard rails at Valley Green. Moy, a board member of the FOW and retired employee of the Philadelphia Streets Department, oversaw the Valley Green landscape improvement project.

Source: Denise Larabee, *FOW Newsletter*

its surrounding landscape was the first large construction project undertaken by the FOW. This project has greatly improved a tattered and abused landscape, stabilized the inn financially, and reinforced Valley Green as the heart of Wissahickon Park.

Galvanizing the Fairmount Park Commission

Changes in the FOW, starting in the early 1990s, led the way for a major reorganization of Fairmount Park administration. With 65 parks and 9,100 acres within its jurisdiction, the Fairmount Park Commission faced a multitude of challenges. The frayed physical fabric of the park system reflected an ignorance of the environmental crisis, a lack of funding, blindness by the city government to the importance of the park and lack of political will. The time was past due for intervention and change.

By the late-1980s, a radical change had occurred in the lower Wissahickon Valley. In contrast to the "sleepy park" of earlier decades, about three-quarters of a million people were now using Wissahickon Park every year, with 55 percent of them living outside Philadelphia. Some 1,200 visitors came to the park daily—and on a typical weekend, over 4,000 people. Heightened interest in the park—by visitors and by an increasingly mobilized and active friends group—led Philadelphia foundations and high level Fairmount Park staff to confront the deteriorating conditions in the Wissahickon Valley—and by analogy—to acknowledge problems in the other city stream corridor parks.

Earlier, in 1983, Fairmount Park had undertaken the first master plan in its 128-year history. Prepared by architects and planners, Wallace, Roberts and Todd (later WRT), this plan established goals, policies and guidelines for park preservation along with strategies for land acquisition and management, financial support and park administration. To clarify overlapping jurisdictions and to streamline park operations, the plan identified three types of areas: the designed landscape with gardens and historic structures; recreational facilities; and "natural lands." Designating the natural lands as a separate category would later lead to a new focus on Fairmount Park's "wildlands" as a special resource—in need of a different management approach and dedicated funding.[43]

Lacking a strong director and without the institutional framework to raise money independently, little of the 1983 plan was implemented. Nearly twenty years later, a 2001 article in the *Philadelphia Daily News* entitled "Acres of Neglect" found "a park system that looks lush from the outside, but is slowly decaying from the inside after years of ineffectual city leadership."[44] Vandalism and abandonment had made many of the stream corridor parks isolated and dangerous.

At about the same time as the FOW reorganization, Peter O'Dell, then assistant director of Fairmount Park—using the lessons of the Gorgas Lane project and the experiences of the Central Park Conservancy in the North Woods—drafted a proposal to fund a study of the park's neglected natural lands. Working closely with Claire Billet, Leslie Sauer and others, O'Dell wrote a grant to the William Penn Foundation. In 1996, to celebrate its 50th anniversary, this foundation gave Fairmount Park the largest single grant ever given to a municipal park system—a proposed total of $26.6 million.

FOW Initiatives | Structures

In 1996, "Ed" Stainton, then an FOW board member, spearheaded a structures committee (a subcommittee of the conservation committee). This committee was a successor to the earlier Wissahickon Rebuilding Project (WRP). The structures committee was charged with formulating policy for the repair of all the historic houses, stables, guard houses, WPA buildings, public toilets, bridges, benches, ruins, fountains, fireplaces, picnic tables and statues in Wissahickon Park.

This committee represented the voice of those who felt that the structures were an important part of the park's heritage and that the park was richer for its fusion of natural and cultural features. Dlugach was the main voice of opposition on the FOW board, and the committee was created only when he was absent. Ironically, it was the FOW itself, in the 1930s, which had vehemently opposed the construction of these WPA shelters.

In the beginning, the structures committee had to face many of the problems with the FPC staff that had troubled the WRP. These issues included claims that volunteers would be unskilled, concerns about insurance for non-city workers and union opposition to volunteers. In the end, the most difficult obstacle was opposition from union shop stewards (from the local carpenters, masons, electrians and plumbers unions). The structures committee reached out to the unions to reassure them, and in 1997, the committee received permission from the FPC to repair all the WPA structures in Wissahickon Park.

One of the structural members of locally harvested black locust (*Robinia pseudoacacia*) is lowered into position to rebuild the former WPA guardhouse at Forbidden Drive and Mt. Airy Avenue.
Source: Photograph by Richard Berman

Tom Bryan (1996-98) headed this committee initially and was followed by "Buzz" Wemple (1999-02) and then by Stainton (2003-). For the first project in 1996, they installed a new roof on the building near the Rex Avenue Bridge, which was then reused as a tool shed for FOW projects. Architect Gerald Linso drew plans pro bono for this project, as well as for several others. The following year, the committee

renovated the picnic pavilion and the toilet building at the entrance to the Orange Trail near Bell's Mill Road, with assistance of the FPC, the Fairmount Park Ranger Corps, Fairmount Park District #3 staff and students from the Crefeld School.

In 1998-99 the structures committee tackled its most ambitious project, the restoration of the six-stall warming shed at the Valley Green Inn that had once provided shelter for horses, carriages, riders and drivers. For models of how these sheds were constructed, members of the structures committee visited several Quaker meeting houses where old warming sheds still survived.

The main project for 2000 was the restoration of the "Ten-Box" shelter, where Forbidden Drive ends at Lincoln Drive. In 2004, they tackled the shelter at Thomas Mill Road near the covered bridge. When arson destroyed the already repaired guard-house at the foot of Mt. Airy Avenue in 2006, the team rebuilt it with the assistance of Weavers Way Co-op, which contributed $1,200 toward this project.[1]

1. *FOW Newsletter*, Winter 2006. Ed Stainton, Interviews by authors, March 20 and June 28, 2008.

The finished guard shelter. To be less attractive to vandals, this once closed guardhouse was redone as an open sided pavilion. Probably originally constructed of American chestnut (*Castanea dentata*), the repairs were made with "standing dead" or fallen red oak (*Quercus borealis*) and Black Locust (*Robinia pseudoacacia*), harvested from the park. This decision was in keeping with the original agreement between the FOW and the WPA to use only indigenous materials.
Source: Photograph by CLF

FOW Initiatives | Conservation Easements

Since World War II, many privately owned open spaces and forested properties bordering the park had been subdivided and developed. New building increased the density, the impervious cover and the non-native vegetation adjacent to a vulnerable natural area, contributing to the deterioration of the forest.

In the early 1990s, the Chestnut Hill Historical Society (CHHS) began accepting facade easements on building fronts and occasional easements on entire buildings in Chestnut Hill. This architectural easement program became the springboard for the FOW and the CHHS to offer a joint "landscape conservation" easement program that began in 1994. The goal of this program was to establish long-term open space easements on private property directly adjacent to Wissahickon Park.

"Facade" easements protect structures from any significant alteration of the architectural features and are usually limited to the outside of a building. "Conservation" easements protect land from future development or preserve cultural features in the landscape, such as gardens or terraces that are an integral part of the house and its grounds. Facade and conservation easements compliment each other by preserving both the integrity of the architecture and its historic setting.

In a 1996 brochure, the FOW/CHHS defined a conservation easement as "a legal agreement between a property owner and a qualified third party that conveys specific development rights from the property owner to the third party in perpetuity."[1] Under such an agreement, owners voluntarily restrict the type and amount of development that may take place on their land. These restrictions include giving up the right to subdivide the property, the right to erect more structures, remove trees, block views, grade, dump, quarry or dispose of waste.

Such limitations would "run with the deed," and bind any future owners.

Property owners retain full ownership and the right to sell, lease or bequeath their land. Easements must be assumed by an organization recognized by the Internal Revenue Service (IRS), and a significant public benefit must result. Public benefits can include scenic enjoyment (but not access), protection of public open space, preservation of important wildlife habitat and preservation of a historically important area.

Landowners granting easements are entitled to multiple financial benefits. Under section 170(h) of the IRS Code, they may deduct the amount of decreased property value from their taxes as a charitable donation to an IRS recognized non-profit. The gift and commensurate deductions can be spread out over 16 years. A case can also be made for a lower assessment of value for city property taxes.

One of a number of FOW presentations on conservation easements. This presentation, "Conservation of Your Wissahickon Valley Property," was given by Debra Wolf Goldstein, Project Manager, FOW Protect Our Watershed Program. It was held at the Valley Green Inn on June 23, 2008.
Source: Photograph by CLF

Other financial benefits allow a property to be appraised at a lower value at the time of the owner's death, reducing estate taxes. Just as important as the tax benefits is the owner's satisfaction in knowing that the property is preserved.[2]

To initiate the easement process, the property to be donated must be mapped, an appraisal made and an agreement drawn up. This process incurs costs for the land stewardship trust, the surveyor, appraiser and lawyer. All these fees must be paid by the donor but are tax deductible.

The FOW/CHHS has received 32 landscape easements, totaling 64 acres and 12 historic facade easements over a 10-year period. These landscape easements form a critical buffer for the Wissahickon corridor.[3]

1. *FOW Newsletter*, Spring 1994; "Preserving Chestnut Hill: Easements in Perspective," *Chestnut Hill Local*, April 11, 2002. See also Brenda Lind, *The Conservation Easement Stewardship Guide* (Washington, D.C., 1991).

2. "Managing Development and Promoting Preservation: The Conservation Easement Program of the Chestnut Hill Historical Society and the Friends of the Wissahickon,"1996.

3. *FOW Newsletter*, Spring 1994; "Preserving Chestnut Hill: Easements in Perspective," *Local*, April 11, 2002; Chestnut Hill Historical Society Homepage, Easement Program Website: chhist.org/easements. See also Brenda Lind, *The Conservation Easement Stewardship Guide* (Washington, D.C., 1991). Debra Wolf Goldstein, Project Manager, FOW Protect Our Watershed Program, "Conservation of Your Wissahickon Valley Property," June 23, 2008.

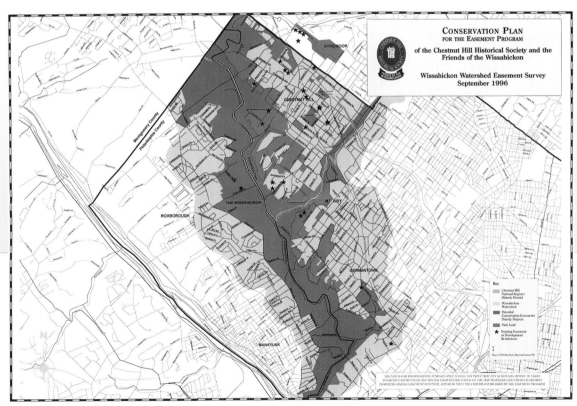

In 1996, Martha E. Moffat, the easement planner at CHHS, produced a handsome brochure with a map showing the landscape easements already acquired and those properties targeted for future action. Source: FOW/CHHS

FOW Initiatives | Conservation Easements *(Continued)*

The FOW has recently hired Debra Wolf Goldstein, from Conservation Matters, LLC, to head up a new program—Protect Our Watershed. Through a series of meetings with potential donors, the FOW is trying to acquire additional conservation easements in the entire Wissahickon Valley. They have produced a brochure, "Protecting Your Land with a Conservation Easement," and sent it to more than 200 owners of properties designated as "high priority."

A map compiled by the Natural Lands Trust shows the existing FOW/CHHS easements and priority land parcels, along the creek and its tributaries—both within the City of Philadelphia and in Montgomery County, in the middle and upper valley. It also identifies priority projects.
Source: Natural Lands Trust

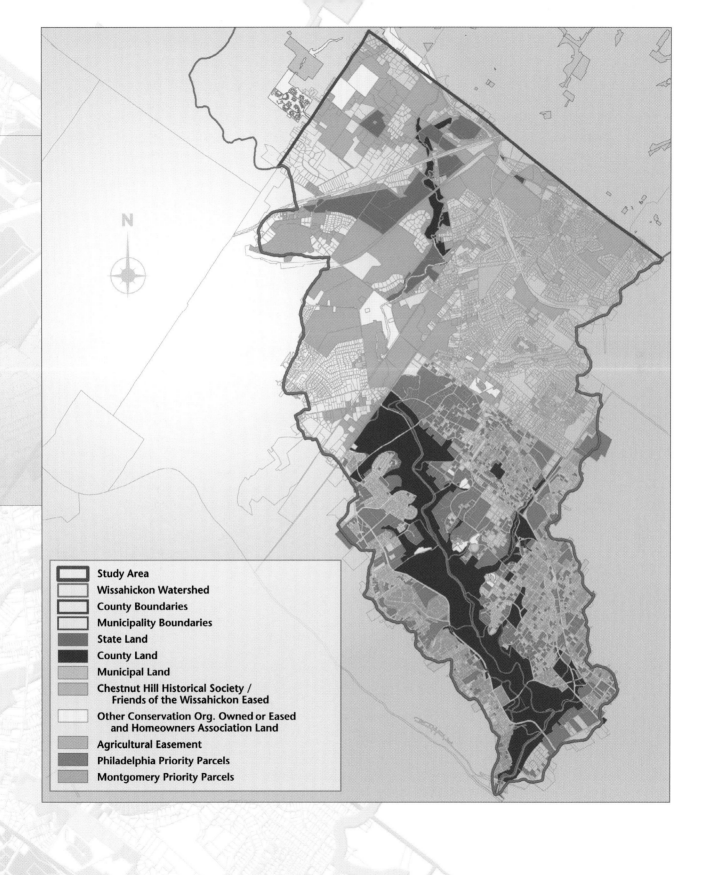

Study Area
Wissahickon Watershed
County Boundaries
Municipality Boundaries
State Land
County Land
Municipal Land
**Chestnut Hill Historical Society /
Friends of the Wissahickon Eased**
**Other Conservation Org. Owned or Eased
and Homeowners Association Land**
Agricultural Easement
Philadelphia Priority Parcels
Montgomery Priority Parcels

FOW Initiatives | Valley Green Inn

The FOW understood that the Valley Green Inn and its surrounding landscape was the lynchpin of park experience. However, for the inn to survive in the park, it needed to be economically viable. The inn was too small and its kitchen and bathrooms were old-fashioned and cramped. There was also a need for additional parking, but the increasing numbers of cars crowded into a poorly defined parking area were beginning to unravel the quality of this important site.

In the mid-1990s, Koey Rivinus, president emeritus of the FOW, spear-headed the restoration of Valley Green Inn, working closely with Ella Torrey. They worked tirelessly to raise the needed funds to update the inn, enlisting support from the FPC, the city and private foundations. In 2002, an enlarged snack bar and a new banquet room were added to the old building. The bathrooms and the kitchen were modernized.

The ambitious renovation of the inn, along with more parking, allowed Valley Green to host weddings and other events. The FOW realized that a more attractive and coherent landscape was the only way to reconcile the proposed expansion with a better park experience.

Water pours off the parking lot, carrying sediment into the creek. Source: Photograph by Colin Franklin

Before:
Panorama of the Valley Green landscape in 2004. An abundance of
undefined paving, poorly organized parking and a general deterioration
of the landscape gave the inn a shoddy look, despite recent renovation
of the inn building and the warming sheds.

After:
Valley Green in 2008 showing the reorganization of the landscape.

Below:
New "rain garden" captures some runoff
and sediment during heavystorms.
Source: Photographs by Colin Franklin

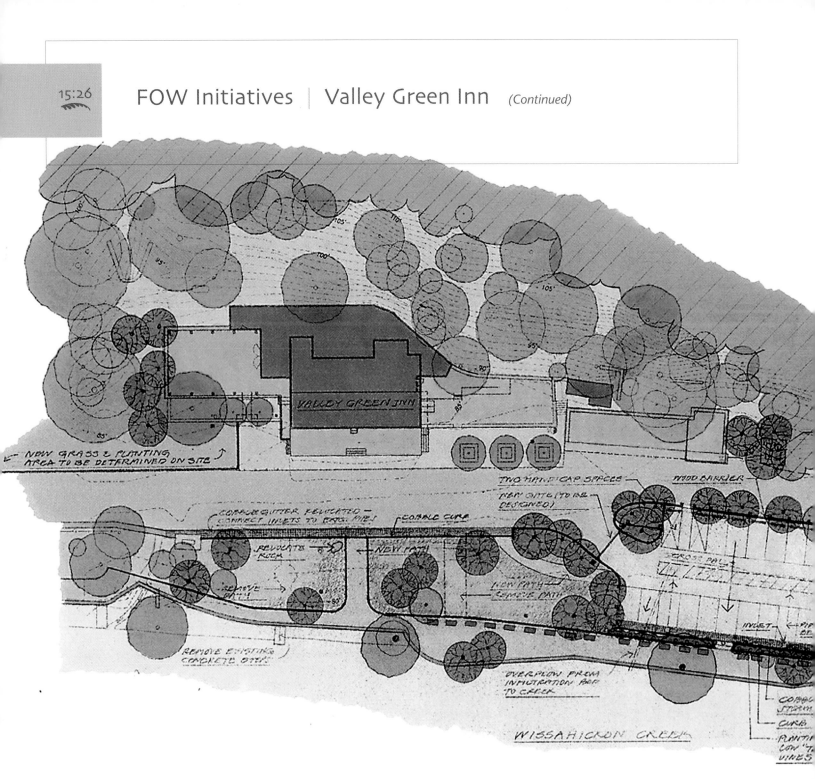

Plan for the Valley Green landscape.
Improvements included reorganized parking, with an additional 25 spaces.
Reorganized drainage included a new "rain garden" to help capture some of the
water that poured off the roadway and parking lot in severe storms, directly into
the creek. The plan also showed a reorganized waterfront now protected from
cars by a "recharge channel" planted densely with shrubs.

Source: Andropogon, 2004

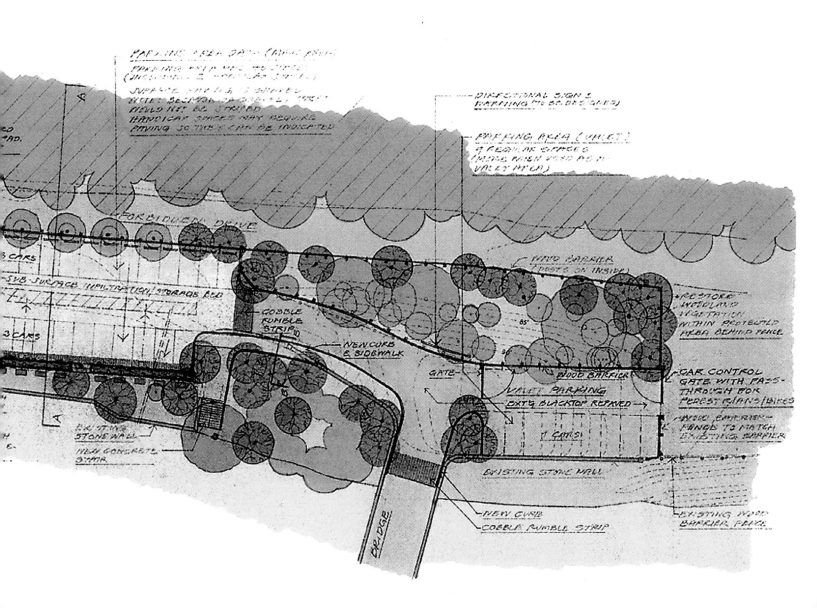

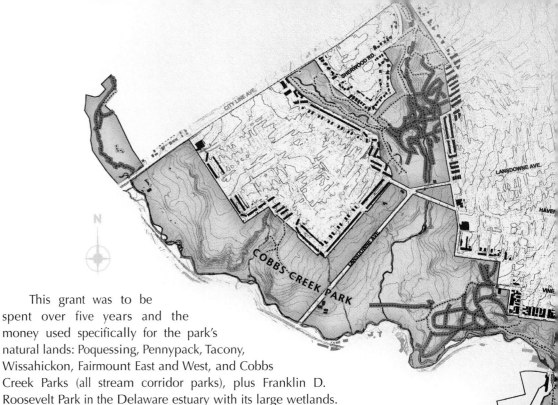

Plan showing the existing trails at Cobbs Creek Park. Poor trail design leads to bad behavior, frustrating experiences for park users and severe environmental damage.
Source: Trail Master Plan for Cobbs Creek Park, Fairmount Park Commission, Natural Lands Restoration and Environmental Education Program
Andropogon, 2001

This grant was to be spent over five years and the money used specifically for the park's natural lands: Poquessing, Pennypack, Tacony, Wissahickon, Fairmount East and West, and Cobbs Creek Parks (all stream corridor parks), plus Franklin D. Roosevelt Park in the Delaware estuary with its large wetlands.

A new administrative structure within the park system, called the Natural Lands Restoration and Environmental Education Program (NLREEP), would oversee and implement this grant. Nancy Goldenberg was the first program administrator, succeeded by her assistant Mark Focht. For the first time in many years, the park's management focus went beyond lawns, buildings and playing fields.[45]

NLREEP began with master plans for the seven parks—the Natural Lands Restoration Master Plan. They hired the Academy of Natural Sciences, which put together a team of botanists, zoologists, stream bioengineers, landscape architects, and planners. Led by the (Ruth) Patrick Center for Environmental Research and Biodiversity at the Academy, this team included the academy's Environmental, Systematic Biology and Public Programs Groups, as well as experts from a wide variety of regional institutions and private consultants—the Morris Arboretum, the University of Delaware, the Natural Lands Trust and Munro Ecological Services. The master plan included a long overdue assessment of the resources of the parks' natural lands. It compiled historical records of park plants and animals, inventoried existing plants and animals, documented invasive plants, identified ecologically important sites, assessed vegetation and stream health—all mapped in geographical information systems format (GIS).

Reports prepared for each of the stream valleys, and for the Delaware estuary, established priorities and proposed critical areas for restoration. The master plan also developed site-specific recommendations for invasive plant control and revegetation with native plants, reintroduction of selected animal species, repair of stream banks, rebuilding infrastructure, the creation of new environmental centers and the development of educational and volunteer programs.[46]

NLREEP then hired consultants to create a trail plan for each of the stream valley parks—except for the Wissahickon, which had already completed its trail plan. Prepared by Andropogon, with Campbell Thomas and Hunt Engineering, these plans rationalized redundant, confused and degraded circulation systems.[47]

Two major problems plagued the trails in the seven parks. The narrowness and fragmentation of a number of these parks made it difficult or impossible to have a continuous trail system with a coherent hierarchy of paths. Few existing paths led to desired destinations, some park areas were without path access and some paths were unnecessarily duplicated. Many paths stopped abruptly and spawned a spaghetti of rogue trails. This off-trail usage was a major source of damage to park natural systems.

The Wissahickon was spared the worst of the problems found in the other stream corridor parks. This park was relatively wide and continuous, allowing a major trail to follow the creek from the beginning of the park to the edge of the city. There was also room for continuous trails along the upper slopes (the Yellow Trail on the Roxborough side and the White and Orange Trails on the Mt. Airy/Chestnut Hill side).

The NLREEP program required ten new staff. These employees, largely untainted by patronage considerations, infused a new spirit of intelligent hard work—in contrast to a long tradition of doing little, taking no initiative and literally sleeping on the job.

One of the new staff positions under NLREEP was a woodland manager and volunteer coordinator whose task was to organize, train and supervise volunteers to repair damage to the natural lands, particularly to remove invasive exotics and replant forest vegetation. The part-time volunteer coordinator hired by the FOW set the precedent for this new staff position. The volunteer coordinators were under a director of stewardship

The lower portion of the Yellow Trail (also called the Ten Box Trail) parallels Wissahickon Creek at the bottom of Lincoln Drive. New stabilization measures included retaining walls—where the path was undermined by the widening creek channel. Other improvements were new drainage, railings, path surface and lighting. The trail was an important commitment to a pedestrian and bicycle link from Center City to Wissahickon Park. The work has greatly improved the usability of the trail. However, the massive retaining walls, with their expressway character, did not enhance the park experience.

Source: Photograph by CLF

and a stewardship coordinator, and they were responsible for four areas of the city—Northwest Philadelphia (which included Wissahickon Park), West and Southwest Philadelphia, Center City and South Philadelphia and Northeast Philadelphia.[49] The FOW persuaded the FPC to hire David Bower, their woodland manager, as a full-time coordinator with responsibility for Northwest Philadelphia.

In Wissahickon Park, NLREEP decided to work primarily on the main promenade—Forbidden Drive—as well as on the trail that connects Forbidden Drive to East and West Parks. This trail is sometimes called The Ten Box Trail after the WPA shelter at the southern end of Forbidden Drive. A second NLREEP project was the reconstruction of a small section of Forbidden Drive just above Valley Green. The roadway was resurfaced; the drains at the side of the drive cleaned out and repaired and a new, stronger barrier fence replaced the picturesque but easily rotted rustic rails. This project was designed by Simone and Jaffe (later Simone Collins landscape architects) and installed by professional contractors. The Forbidden Drive project included new interpretive and wayfinding signage by the environmental graphic design firm of Cloud Gehshan.[48]

By 2002, the NLREEP grant had run its allotted five-year course. Integration of NLREEP into park operations and the extensive use of scientists and consultants for studies and plans had taken up much of the budget for the first two years, leaving only three years for project implementation. The William Penn Foundation was especially concerned that a portion of the grant be used to build a constituency for the park through environmental education. This goal led to a requirement that the park commission build or renovate an environmental education center in each of the parks. This requirement proved difficult for many reasons. In the end, only two of the seven proposed environmental centers were actually built or renovated.

Estimating that three more years were needed to complete the various projects under the grant, the Fairmount Park Commission applied for an extension. They were turned down, possibly because the foundation had conceived of this grant as an extraordinary, one-time gift to celebrate its 50th anniversary. Fairmount Park was unable to use about $7 million of the promised grant monies. These remaining funds had not yet been dispersed, so actual money was not returned. Although the timeframe for the original grant was not extended, the foundation has continued to fund specific restoration projects in the park.[49]

As the NLREEP grant was expiring, the mayor's office, with mixed motives, commissioned a strategic plan for Philadelphia's park system. Despite the impetus of NLREEP, the Fairmount Park Commission had fallen woefully short in creating imaginative policies

Fairmount Park Executive Directors from 1980

Executive Director:

Alexander L. "Pete" Hoskins	1980-1988
Joe Guignan	1988-1989
William Mifflin	1989-2002

Acting Executive Director of Fairmount Park:

Phillip R. Goldsmith	2002-2004
Karen Lloyd Borski	2004-2005

Executive Director:

Marc A. Focht	2005-

and strategic initiatives for the reorganization of management, staff, physical resources and fundraising. Leon Younger and PROS, a nationally known parks and recreation consulting firm, were hired. Their task was to identify the means to establish and maintain Fairmount Park as one of the nation's premier park systems, to conduct a comprehensive study and formulate a strategic plan. The report solicited community and stakeholder input and reviewed park operations, finances, facilities, programs, financial resources, partnerships and governance.

Called "Bridge to the Future," the plan was published in 2004. Its recommendations called for: greater synergy and efficiency between Fairmount Park and the Department of Recreation; a policy-shaping role for the Fairmount Park Commissioners; enhanced leadership and management capacity at Fairmount Park; improved management policies practices for every area of operations; and positioning the park system as a key economic driver for the City of Philadelphia. This plan was to be realized through 29 specific objectives and over 70 detailed strategies for action.[50]

Some of the most important of these strategies were: hiring a strong executive director for Fairmount Park who could serve as an agent of change; defining the role of the commissioners as policy-makers and focusing them on the larger park issues such as watershed management, preservation and acquisition of new lands, land use and land management; formulating specific criteria and implementing a transparent evaluation process for the selection of commissioners; establishing a separate Fairmount Park Conservancy to raise money and to ensure that these funds are used specifically for park projects and do not end up in the city's general budget; introducing higher park-user fees and using the increased revenue to hire a marketing director and a chief financial officer; forging a better alignment between Fairmount Park and the Philadelphia Department of Recreation, with Fairmount Park concentrating only on self-directed recreation, environmental education, historic preservation; and the Recreation Department emphasizing programmed facilities and activities.[51]

Following these recommendations for reorganization, Fairmount Park integrated the NLREEP staff and structure into a newly established department called the Environmental, Stewardship, and Education Division, with Nancy Goldenberger and then Mark Focht as director. This new department moved its headquarters to share a common space with the recreation department. These two entities, one quasi-independent and one a city department, were to rationalize the land under their jurisdiction. Ballfields, tennis and basketball courts were to go to the recreation department in exchange for pieces of natural land that had previously been under their jurisdiction.[52]

The importance of the William Penn Foundation grant cannot be overstated. This intervention by a private non-profit lifted the park out of the paralysis of city politics and the commission's well meaning, but very limited vision. Even though all the projects envisioned by the grant were not carried out, the reorganization of the Fairmount Park administration and the recognition of natural lands set a new and hopeful agenda. This change in administrative structure set the stage for a clear differentiation between the Philadelphia Recreation Department and Fairmount Park. The department had overseen some natural areas, while Fairmount Park was in charge of a number of ballfields and other recreational facilities. The NALREEP grant began the process of separating functions under a joint jurisdiction.

NLREEP | A New Environmental Center

Building a constituency to protect Fairmount Park through environmental education and public stewardship was a major goal of the 1996 William Penn Foundation grant to Fairmount Park for the Natural Lands Restoration and Environmental Education Program (NLREEP). This goal led to the foundation's requiring the park commission to build or renovate an environmental education center in each of the designated parks.

For Wissahickon Park, this requirement was problematic, since there were already several reasonable, preexisting facilities—the Saul School of Agricultural Sciences, the Schuylkill Center for Environmental Education (not within the watershed but very close), the Boy Scout House at Wigard Avenue and the Tree House at the Andorra Natural Area. Each of these facilities offered environmental education programs and were themselves in desperate need of funds to maintain and upgrade their existing buildings and curricula. Sioux Baldwin, then director of the Andorra Natural Area, made a plea to the FOW and to NLREEP staff asking that the money intended for a new nature center be given instead to the Tree House.

An alternative solution, well-suited to the realities of Wissahickon Park, was the option to use the money to buy and incorporate inholdings (the small, privately owned properties within park boundaries). Stainton, president of the FOW at the time, had discovered an in-holding for sale on Wise's Mill Road. This in-holding included a beautiful Wissahickon-style stone house and considerable land along Wise's Mill Run. Acquisition of

The inholding along Wise's Mill Road would have made an appropriate new environmental center. The site is directly above Forbidden Drive.

This property has several abandoned water features created when Wise's Mill Run was diverted into a series of fountains and pools. Here, in a parallel to the Wissahickon style, nature and culture blend together to make "half-rooms"—outdoor spaces for people that provide an intimate contact with the character of the valley. Source: Photographs by CLF

this picturesque house and environmentally fragile property had the potential to provide a handsome educational facility. It would also resolve a number of problems. For example, acquisition of this property would allow park users to avoid walking on Wise's Mill Road, which is a heavily trafficked road.

Despite FOW concerns and better alternative uses for the money, NLREEP moved ahead and hired consultants to review potential sites and propose a location for a new environmental center. The consultants chose a site adjacent to the Boy Scout House. In its favor, this site was centrally located on the Roxborough side, with potentially synergistic relationships to Saul School and the Schuylkill Environmental Education Center. Working against this choice was its proximity to a mature and relatively healthy forest (considered one of the best bird-watching areas in the park) and the wastefulness of creating and then maintaining yet another facility in the area. Regardless of these issues, architects were selected and designs presented to the community in a public forum.

The NLREEP grant would provide start-up funding for environmental education, with each center staffed by two environmental educators and one administrative assistant. There was an expectation that the city would continue to fund these positions.[1] In the end, this facility was never built, as the NLREEP staff came to realize that its operating budget could not provide funds for either ongoing staffing or building maintenance. Instead of building a new center in Wissahickon Park, the Fairmount Park administration ultimately decided to support and enlarge the older facility at Andorra, under the new name of the Wissahickon Environmental Center at the Andorra Natural Area.

The "Tree House" at Andorra Natural Area.

The tree house had been the home of the Andorra Nursery propagator, Adolph Steinle. Steinle built the porch of his house around a large sycamore tree (*Platanus occidentalis*) and the family named their home the "Tree House." In 1981, the sycamore had to be cut down, but a slice of the huge trunk remains inside.[2]

This existing facility was ultimately chosen to receive the money for the environmental center in Wissahickon Park. The interior has been renovated and has a large new mural of the Wissahickon, painted by Paul Barker.

Until 2002, NLREEP money paid for an environmental educator at this center. When the grant ceased, this money was cut off. After protest from five community organizations, the city agreed to refund this position.[3]

The Tree House at Andorra Natural Area. Source: Photograph by CLF

Despite internal repairs, and a tree that once pierced the porch, NLREEP money did little to integrate this facility with its surrounding site.

1. *FOW Newsletter*, Spring 2002, Sarah West, "Green Alert, Continued Funding in Doubt for Wissahickon Environmental Center," 2.

2. Website: fow.org/wec.php

3. *FOW Newsletter*, Spring 2002, Sarah West, "Funding Restored for Park's Environmental Centers," 6.

Examples of new signage
along Forbidden Drive
Source: Courtesy Cloud Gehshan

NLREEP Projects in Wissahickon Park | New Signage

As part of the NLREEP improvement projects in Wissahickon Park, Forbidden Drive was refurbished with new guardrails, granite mile markers, new path surface and new interpretive and way-finding signs. Continuing debate about the character of Wissahickon Park (natural preserve or cultural landscape) spilled over into controversy about signage. Advocates of a "natural preserve" feared that the experience of the wild and scenic landscape would be spoiled by visible signs.

After much public debate, elegant and informative new signs, designed by Cloud Gehshan, a local graphics firm with a national reputation, were placed in strategic locations along Forbidden Drive. Theresa Stuhlman, the historic preservation officer for the FPC, provided the images and text. These new signs, located only along Forbidden Drive, enriched the experience of the main park route.

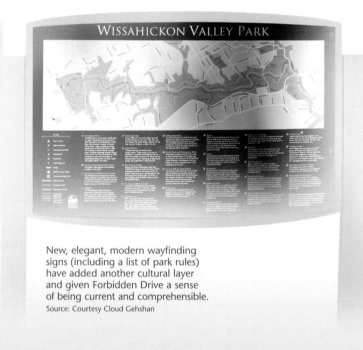

New, elegant, modern wayfinding signs (including a list of park rules) have added another cultural layer and given Forbidden Drive a sense of being current and comprehensible.
Source: Courtesy Cloud Gehshan

The William Penn Foundation

Private foundations across the country represent an extraordinarily important American tradition of partnerships between public institutions (including municipalities) and private charities. These partnerships are especially crucial in an age when cities have neither the political will nor the resources to fund their departments at sufficient levels.

The William Penn Foundation was established in 1945 by Otto and Phoebe Haas. The money came from Rohm and Haas, a large research and chemical manufacturing company based in Philadelphia. The foundation is named for William Penn, "the 17th century Quaker, whose pursuit of an exemplary society and understanding of human possibilities, led him to found Philadelphia."[1] From the beginning, the foundation has focused exclusively on needs in the Greater Philadelphia region so that their funds can have the most concentrated impact in a highly urbanized setting.

The foundation gives grants in three areas: arts and culture; children, youth, and families; and environment and communities. On the environment, its goal is to "conserve and improve the natural resources of our region; to further access to, and stewardship of, these resources; and to assist local, neighborhood, and regional organizations in creating desirable and enduring communities."[2]

The foundation has funded major initiatives for both the Fairmount Park Commission and the FOW. In 1996, to mark its 50th anniversary, the foundation made two, one-time grants to Philadelphia institutions: $26.4 million to Fairmount Park and $18 million to the Free Library of Philadelphia. The park grant created NLREEP—the Natural Lands Restoration and Environmental Education Program—within the Fairmount Park Commission's organizational structure. The foundation also funded a strategic plan for Fairmount Park—"A Bridge to the Future"—in concert with the City of Philadelphia and the Fairmount Park Conservancy.

In 2004, the foundation gave a three-year grant of $275,000 to the FOW. NLREEP had identified more than 180 priority projects for Wissahickon Park, but it was clear that the city had no budget to address these needs and that the FOW, with only a part-time staff, did not have the resources to oversee additional restoration work.[3] The grant to the Fairmount Park Commission and the money to the FOW allowed both these organizations to move to a greater level of organizational effectiveness and relevance.

---

1. Website: williampennfoundation.org/info-url_nocat3558/info-url_nocat.htm

2. The William Penn Foundation,"Guidelines for Applicants."

3. FPC, Natural Lands Restoration Master Plan, Volume I, General Observations, 1-3.

Otto Haas
Source: Morris Arboretum of the
University of Pennsylvania

A Push for Change

The National Geographic Traveler has named Philadelphia the "Next Great American City."[53] With the revitalization of Center City and a new influx of people, Philadelphia's overall population is relatively stable. However, the neighborhoods have continued to decline since the 1950s. According to the Pennsylvania Environmental Council, for Philadelphia to compete with other American cities, it "must find ways to have more of what makes cities great—parks and open spaces, redeveloped riverfronts, efficient transportation, better air and water quality, recycling and waste programs that work, and leadership in green building implementation, among others."[54]

Despite this increasing consensus on the importance of parks to great cities, Fairmount Park has suffered from decades of neglect, blinkered leadership, lack of adequate funding and gradual loss of its political independence. This loss of independence was officially sanctioned by a municipal charter change approved by Philadelphia voters in November 2008. The Fairmount Park Commission was abolished and the park system placed under a new city department of parks and recreation.

The most recent push for change began in June 2001 when the Philadelphia Daily News ran a special investigative article called "Acres of Neglect" on the park's many problems. The Daily News reporters found a park, which "looks good from the outside but is slowly decaying from the inside after years of ineffectual city leadership.... Underfunding and understaffing is so severe that, ultimately, people, animals, trees and plants are all at risk."[55]

The article reminded readers that Philadelphia was one of the few cities in the United States where two different entities—the Fairmount Park Commission and the Department of Recreation—managed multifaceted park resources. The article concluded that this split management structure had led to numerous inefficiencies because of overlapping responsibilities and staff positions.[56]

After much pressure, the Fairmount Park Commission undertook a strategic plan, published in 2004. Called "A Bridge to the Future," this plan suggested that the separation of the park commission and the recreation department had led to a "confusion of roles and responsibilities citywide, dilution of resources, and inefficiencies in the delivery of services . . . ." To address this problem, the plan recommended a "more efficient and effective operation" and realignment of responsibilities between the two agencies, with the idea that the park commission would preside over the more "passive" activities in the park, while the recreation department would be in charge of the more "active" uses. However, the strategic plan did not call for an immediate merger of the two entities, stating that three to five years of exploration and discussion would be needed before such a move should be seriously considered.[57]

In 1993, then Philadelphia Mayor Edward "Ed" Rendell had called for a merger of the park commission and the recreation department, but voters turned down this proposal in a citywide referendum. Protest was organized around the belief that Philadelphia city government had been notoriously corrupt in the past and that the independently chartered Fairmount Park Commission was the only buffer—no matter how weak—against greedy and self-seeking officials, whether city council or the mayor.

In June 2005, Philadelphia City Council members Darrel L. Clarke, from the 5th council district, and council woman at-large, Blondell Reynolds Brown, introduced legislation that would consolidate the park commission and the recreation department. One of their most potent arguments was the alleged administrative efficiency that a merger would bring, and, with it, cost savings to the city. This bill would have required a ballot question in the general election to amend the Philadelphia Home Rule Charter and allow transfer of all the powers and duties of the Fairmount Park Commission to the Philadelphia Department of Recreation.[58] A number of park supporters objected, and the vote was postponed to allow further discussion. These discussions took place at a Town Meeting at the Free Library on December 13 and at City Council hearings on December 14, 2005. The overwhelming opinion of those who testified at these two venues was that the proposed legislation was premature.[59]

Then FOW president Robert "Bob" Lukens reminded city council that the city's 2004 Strategic Plan for Fairmount Park had recommended taking three to five years to explore the issues involved in a merger. Former FOW president David Pope concurred: "If the merger is, indeed, such a good idea, it will be an even better idea after proper review and public input." He and other members of the FOW also expressed fears that the park commission was the only protection against plans by city authorities to sell off or lease parkland for development or other non-park uses.[60]

Testimony against the legislation from the FOW, the Parks Alliance, the Pennsylvania Horticultural Society and several other interest groups nevertheless underscored the need for reforms and for a properly funded park system. Lauren Bornfriend, executive director of the Philadelphia Parks Alliance (a non-profit, advocacy group founded in 1983, which builds coalitions and educates the public), opposed the merger legislation at this time, but insisted that "the status quo for Fairmount Park and the park system was unacceptable." Bornfriend added that the alliance's constituents were willing to support major changes in park admin-istration, but only if they promised significant improvements. She also criticized the method of having the Board of Judges select park commissioners "as outdated and opaque, distancing park leadership from the elected officials who should be held accountable for the state of the park system."[61]

Three years later, the same council members introduced a somewhat modified bill, and on June 9, 2008, this legislation passed. By then, the Philadelphia Parks Alliance had changed its position against the merger and became one of the major voices calling for charter change. The reasons given were that all the other major cities in the United States had a combined park and recreation department, that the city would appropriate more money for the Fairmount Park system and that a new park commission would be appointed in an open and transparent process and would concentrate on policy.[62] The great fear is that since this new commission is only advisory it would likely be toothless.

In January 2008, Michael Nutter became Philadelphia's new mayor. Nutter was the strongest mayoral supporter of Fairmount Park in many decades. During his campaign in 2007, he had developed "The Nutter Plan for a Sustainable Philadelphia Environment," where he stated, "Building on this valuable but neglected asset [will be] the foundation for a commitment to environmental goals throughout city government."[63] This plan proposed the reform of the governance of Fairmount Park and a significant increase in park funding.

To following up on this commitment and to lay the groundwork for acceptance of the merger of Fairmount Park with the recreation department under the city administration, Nutter approved a $2.3 million in increased park funding for 2008 and promised a 46 percent increase in the park budget over the next five years. This initial appropriation, and the promise of more money to come, blunted demands for a delay in park reorganization until the system was effectively funded.[64] Ironically, in 2009, the city and the nation experienced one of the worst economic downturns in the last 75 years. The resulting budgetary crisis forced the mayor to withdraw even this modest increase and to cut the park budget from a proposed $15.6 million to $12.5 million—more than a half million dollars less than the previous year's budget of $13.1 million.[65]

In 2008, Mayor Nutter threw his support behind the revised merger legislation. The resultant charter change, approved by the voters, abolished the 140-year-old Fairmount Park Commission. Parks and recreation was divided into two equal portfolios—a deputy commissioner, Mark Foulk, former director of Fairmount Park, was put in charge of natural lands and a second deputy commissioner, Susan Slawson, a lieutenant from the police department, was put in charge of recreation. These deputies would now report to a new overarching commissioner of parks and recreation. Mayor Nutter has said publically that the new organizational structure would be more akin to a marriage than a merger, respecting the missions, history and staff of both entities.[66]

The mayor appointed Michael DiBerardinis commissioner of the newly merged entity— now called the Philadelphia Department of Parks and Recreation. DiBerardinis had been director of the Philadelphia Recreation Department under Mayor Rendell, and later Governor Rendell's director of the Pennsylvania Department of Conservation and Natural Resources. All the appointees are well qualified for their new posts, but they will be severely handicapped by the ever-decreasing park budgets (in both real and relative terms).

Despite good people in charge, the merger has raised strong fears that the Fairmount Park system will be at the mercy of developers, greedy council members and a future corrupt mayor who might sell or lease parkland, gutting this remarkable system. The new 15-member commission on parks and recreation has been created to allay these fears, but this commission has no official decision-making authority. It must rely on the quality, prestige and expertise of committee members, and the willingness of the mayor and city council to follow through on their recommendations.

The city conducted a broad talent search to find nine citizen commissioners. The other six members are ex-officio: the heads of the two departments of parks and of recreation, the director of the department of streets, the heads of the water department and of the department of streets and public property, the president of city council, and the executive director of the city planning commission. Their roles and responsibilities are to "(1) adopt standards and guidelines for lands use, preservation of green space, watershed management, sustainability and the conveyance and acquisition of park and recreation land or facilities…; (2) assist and advise the parks and recreation commissioner to promote, support and enhance the image of the Fairmount Park System and other city parks and Recreation facilities… (3) convene quarterly public meetings…."[67] Probably the most pressing need is for this new commission to establish strong, effective policies on the sale, lease, development and acquisition of parklands that can be translated into strong and effective legislation.

The ongoing campaign of the Fox Chase Cancer Center to obtain an 80-year lease to expand onto 19 acres of the 69 acre Burholme Park is an alarming example of what can happen. Burholme Park is partially wooded and partially "park" with old stately trees in sweeping lawn. It is an oasis in densely built-up Northeast Philadelphia. Robert Waln Ryerss willed the property with its mansion to the city in 1895, "for the use and enjoyment of the people forever."[68] Today the park has a museum, a stream and woodlands, a golf-driving range and ballfields. The 800-million-dollar plan for the expansion of Fox Chase Hospital into Burholme Park would eliminate the picnic grove, the driving range and much of the woodlands.

Mayor Nutter brokered the deal with Fox Chase. Members of the Fairmount Park Commission appointed by the mayor overruled the independent commissioners and approved the Fox Chase takeover. Councilman Brian O'Neill persuaded Philadelphia City Council to change the zoning in the area to accommodate the hospital. To make the deal palatable, Fox Chase promised to contribute $4 million to the city's capital program, preferably (but not required) for the acquisition of open space.[59] There will always be pressure to peel away pieces of the Fairmount Park system, allowing these pieces to be sold or leased to private interests. After the mayor had made repeated promises to protect and enhance parkland, he nonetheless became a major player in furthering the transformation of this park into large buildings and parking lots.

A citizens group, Save Burholme Park, filed suit in Philadelphia Orphans Court, which has jurisdiction over wills, to stop the Fox Chase expansion. In December 2008, the court ruled against Fox Chase and the city. Judge John W. Herron wrote, "So long as a community or neighborhood actively uses dedicated park land, the city is required to hold such land in trust for their use, …and is required to maintain these open spaces as public parks."[70] This issue is still unsettled because Fox Chase Cancer Center continues to appeal the decision and continues to purchase property in the area for its 20-year development plan.

Even more frightening than the piecemeal surrender of parkland for private uses was the sweeping legislation proposed in spring 2009 by councilwoman Joan Krajewski. Her bill submitted to city council would rezone all recreation land to allow construction of museums, conference centers, single family dwellings, public and private parking lots and commercial recreation. Fortunately, there was a huge outcry by the Philadelphia Parks Alliance, the *Philadelphia Inquirer* and the Fairmount Park Commission in one of its last meetings. The outcry forced Krajewski to withdraw the bill but such legislative proposals are like many-headed hydras. Although they are apparently stopped, multiple new efforts reappear.[71]

Among American cities, Philadelphia has one of the worst reputations for corruption and "pay-for-play," with a long-standing and unholy association between local law firms, developers and politicians.[72] The strong mayor system, established in the early 1950s, was intended to end the worst corruption in city government. Instead, after the initial impetus of the Philadelphia Renaissance, voters have not always sent the most honest and capable people to City Hall. Even with the civil service, there is still ample opportunity in Philadelphia government for corrupt politicians to appoint incompetent cronies and relatives to municipal positions. These employees have had a poor reputation for their commitment to the job and for the quality of their work.

All these issues cast a dark shadow over the future of Fairmount Park. For this reason, the Commission on Parks and Recreation, newly established in 2009, must provide strong policy guidelines and ensure that they are enacted into law by municipal legislation. The citizens of Philadelphia have given the mayor the final responsibility to protect Fairmount Park and to ensure that those in charge of the city's natural lands will continue to be of the highest quality.

Rebuilding Natural and Social Capital

In the last decade of the 20th century and the first years of the 21st, a number of institutions and groups, both public and private, woke up to the deterioration of the Wissahickon's ecosystems and cultural landscapes. A renewed and energized FOW embarked on an ambitious program of park preservation and rehabilitation. Two programs—deer management and a sustainable trails initiative—propelled this organization into regional leadership as a very effective, professional non-profit. Under the prodding of a number of foundation and state grants that provided money for studies and action programs, Fairmount Park recognized its natural lands as a separate entity requiring special expertise and management skills. Restructuring to create an Environmental Stewardship and Education Division at Fairmount Park provided a more stable administration for the park's natural lands, orchestrating all repair and capital improvement projects and institutionalizing a massive volunteer effort. The merger of the Fairmount Park Commission with the Philadelphia Recreation Department opens the way for new opportunities. However, the loss of the independent commission poses new dangers in a city notorious for mediocre and self-serving politicians.

Middle Valley Renaissance

1975-2010

16

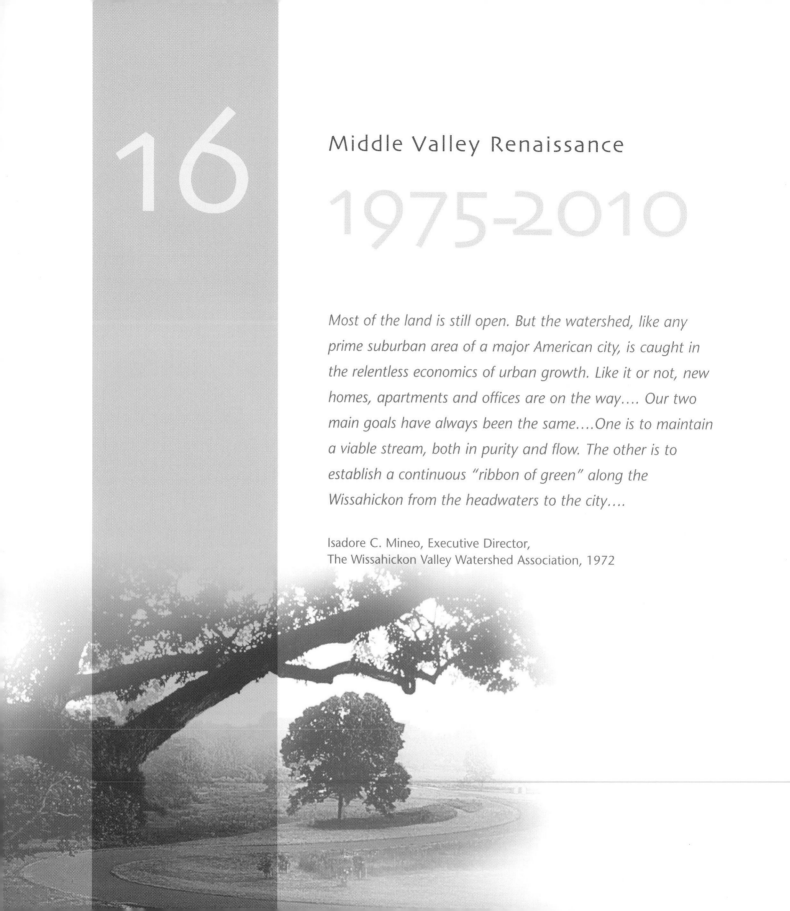

16

Middle Valley Renaissance

1975-2010

Most of the land is still open. But the watershed, like any prime suburban area of a major American city, is caught in the relentless economics of urban growth. Like it or not, new homes, apartments and offices are on the way…. Our two main goals have always been the same….One is to maintain a viable stream, both in purity and flow. The other is to establish a continuous "ribbon of green" along the Wissahickon from the headwaters to the city….

Isadore C. Mineo, Executive Director,
The Wissahickon Valley Watershed Association, 1972

Renewal in the middle valley was in some ways parallel to the three renaissances discussed earlier—Philadelphia, Chestnut Hill and later the FOW. In all three instances, administrative change, coupled with strong leadership, laid the foundation for meaningful physical change. The Philadelphia charter reform, led by individuals and civic groups, provided the foundation for major urban renewal projects. In Chestnut Hill, the reinvention of community government, spearheaded by area business people, paved the way for a revitalization of the commercial district. The resurgence of the FOW was necessary for the reorganization and professionalization of this conservation non-profit, which in turn generated multiple programs for park repair. In each instance, new structure, creative direction and a redefinition of purpose were central to the survival and effectiveness of a city, a community and an organization.

In some ways, there was a parallel awakening in the middle valley between the mid-1970s and the present. The middle valley suffered from a lack of overarching identity. In contrast, Philadelphia was one political unit, Chestnut Hill was a coherent community and the lower Wissahickon Valley was a beloved and recognized entity. A renaissance in the middle valley was more attenuated and came later.[3]

While the open space corridor along Wissahickon Creek in the city is entirely public parkland, open space along the creek in the middle valley is a patchwork of ownership: state and county parks; institutions and large private properties. During this period, middle valley institutions woke up to the fact that the landscape was their major asset, and surrounding communities also realized the value of the landscape to their quality of life.

Postwar Prologue

The landscape of the middle valley, still mostly rural just after World War II, was subject to an avalanche of development in the 1950s and 1960s. Organizations working to protect the lower valley had flourished for over a century, but similar groups took hold in the middle valley only with increasing development pressures. The most potent of these pressures was the completion of the Pennsylvania Turnpike above Philadelphia, along with the 309 Fort Washington Expressway.[1] Malls and tract housing followed almost immediately.

Increased flooding was one consequence of this intense and largely unplanned development. A new civic organization, the Wissahickon Valley Watershed Association (WVWA), was founded in 1957 to address this issue. Initially, the organization focused on opposing development. Then, in the 1970s, they launched a bold program to buy land, designate a portion for parkland and resell the remainder with deed restrictions. Later, the WVWA would focus almost exclusively on acquiring conservation easements.

In the 1970s, the large institutional properties in the middle valley faced a number of crises. The Morris Arboretum, Chestnut Hill College and Carson Valley School lacked a clear sense of purpose, reflected in insufficient endowments and operating funds. These institutions, as well as large private properties—Erdenheim Farm (formerly Erdenheim Farms), the several golf courses and Highway Materials (formerly Corson Quarries)—were in danger of being sold and developed.

WVWA

Two back-to-back hurricanes—Connie on August 13, 1955, and Dianne five days later on August 18—caused over $5 million in flood damages in Montgomery County.[2] The magnitude of the problems forced county and state officials to acknowledge that this flooding was not simply a natural phenomenon, but the result of environmentally destructive land use practices in the Wissahickon watershed.[3] These floods triggered the formation of the WVWA in 1957. This organization was founded by nine local conservation activists: Edward Altemus, Phillip Dechert, Antelo Devereaux, John Hamilton, Alston Jenkins, Frederick Lewis, Ross Pilling, Sr., Charles Uhle and Polly Miller.[4]

After the hurricanes of the mid-1950s, local residents asked the Army Corps of Engineers to create a flood control plan for the entire Wissahickon watershed—the first of its kind in Pennsylvania. The 1954 Watershed Protection and Flood Prevention Act (PL 83-566) provided the authority for the U.S. Soil Conservation Service, later the U.S. National Resource Conservation Service (NRCS), to cooperate with other federal, state and local agencies to survey river basins and develop coordinated water resource programs, floodplain management studies and flood insurance programs. In late 1961, the corps began a year-long study of flooding in the whole 15-mile length of Wissahickon Creek in Montgomery County. The study called for nine "low-head" dams, two on the main stem in the upper valley and seven on the various tributaries (including three dams on Sandy Run). The WVWA vigorously opposed this plan, finally defeating it in court.[5]

By the early 1970s, the WVWA recognized that simply saying "no" to bad development was not an effective tool to manage a watershed. Confronted by skyrocketing land values and taxes, they changed tactics. Receiving a grant from the C. Mahlon Kline Foundation in 1971, they hired the Philadelphia land planning firm of Rahenkamp, Sachs and Wells (later Rahenkamp Sachs Wells, Associates) to evaluate the landscape of the Wissahickon Valley above the gorge and determine what parts of the valley should be protected or developed.

The plan suggested three strategies: acquire land by outright purchase; permit some development with strict environmental guidelines; and preserve a significant portion of the area for limited outdoor recreation, wildlife habitat and flood protection.[6] A corridor park of 4,000 acres along both sides of the main stem of Wissahickon Creek and its tributaries would extend eight miles and would include six townships and four boroughs, in both the middle and upper valley. There would be an additional 4,000 acres of open space, secured by conservation easements, to act as a buffer between the park and adjacent development.[7] The idea for a "green ribbon" along Wissahickon Creek had its origins in this plan.

A second grant from the Kline foundation gave the WVWA "seed money" to buy land and work with qualified developers to design and build approved plans. The WVWA would act as advisor and consulting developer, encouraging creative designs that protected ecological and aesthetic values. This strategy paralleled the actions of the Chestnut Hill Reality Trust—to buy property, select developers and direct the design, with community values foremost. Unfortunately, the WVWA plan, begun with such promise, never materialized. Escalating land costs, and a move away from the commitment to a regional framework, defeated these farsighted ideas.[8]

By the late 1970s and early 1980s, corresponding to the withdrawal of the FOW from the broader public arena in the lower valley, the WVWA retreated from regional proposals and abandoned organized protests against poor development. This withdrawal was a reflection of a larger national apathy towards environmental concerns and a backing off from regional solutions. Instead, the WVWA redirected their activities to acquiring control over land along the Wissahickon Creek and its tributaries. By 2008, this organization had protected a total land area of 1,100 acres, through a combination of outright purchase, donation and conservation easements.[9] They have continued to pursue this goal, hampered only by lack of funds. However, for the middle valley, the impetus for audacious, area-wide plans had withered.

Morris Arboretum: Fulcrum and Catalyst

The first of the middle valley institutions to reorganize and reinvent itself was the Morris Arboretum. In the early 1970s, 40 years after its bequest to the University of Pennsylvania, the arboretum had not fulfilled its potential. Administered by the botany department, with a succession of academic directors, the institution had focused narrowly on horticultural issues. The leadership did not value the rich cultural and natural fabric of the former Morris Estate. Above all, the arboretum failed to forge relationships with the larger community, looking inward instead.

Without a plan or a focus, the Morris heritage—plants, gardens and garden features— had deteriorated. In 1968, the university demolished "Compton," the old Morris mansion, a rambling Victorian house, viewed as an expensive nuisance. Without the house, a landmark visible from everywhere on the grounds, visitors lost a pivotal point of spatial orientation.

Like good Victorians, Lydia and John Morris had set out to acquire and display the world's diversity. They collected garden styles as well as individual plants. On their property, they brought together a number of European and Asian gardens to display their acquisitions. In contrast, the university focused exclusively on the collection and classification of individual plant specimens, grouping them together by families for study and display. Gradually the garden spaces were filled in and the original landscape organization was lost.

The University, as new owners, made few efforts to create the necessary facilities to transform a private estate into a public institution. A single carriage loop, left over from the old estate, was the only path system through the grounds. Over time, a "rats nest" of discontinuous and confusing paths grew up. A new entrance was built at the bottom of the valley, which failed to orient visitors in this complex landscape. The first year it opened to the public (in 1933-34) the arboretum received over 30,000 visitors. By the 1970s, only a few thousand people came annually. There was little to see, little to do, no clear route and no visible destinations.

After years of decline, the university no longer saw a compelling reason to own an arboretum. The diminished role of traditional botany, and the rise of the new discipline of microbiology, had made a "garden of collected plants" irrelevant. The university considered selling the property for condominiums. In 1972, Otto Haas, retired president of Rohm and Haas Industries, a member of the University of Pennsylvania's Board of Trustees and an ardent advocate of the arboretum, became chair of the Morris's advisory board of managers. Deeply concerned about the deteriorating condition, Haas initiated several important structural changes by moving the arboretum out of the botany department and into the University's Interdisciplinary Resource Center, under the provost. There it was aligned with other university cultural resources—the University Museum, the Institute of Contemporary Art (ICA), the Annenberg Theater and the university radio station (WXPN). These changes put the arboretum on a new administrative footing, and allowed it to link to other university departments.[10]

16:1

Haas also recognized the need for a full-time director. Earlier directors had been academics—and only part-time. In 1977, the university hired William M. Klein, the assistant director of the Missouri Botanical Garden (MBS) in St. Louis. Klein was a visionary. He excited others with his ideas. He was also extremely imaginative in devising strategies to achieve his goals. His drive, energy and vision transformed this rundown and neglected garden.

MBS had just completed its master plan, and Klein had come to appreciate the power of a plan to give a sense of direction and act as a vehicle for fund-raising. When he arrived, the arboretum was broke and the university unwilling to support it financially. Klein could not afford a full-scale plan. A "can-do guy" and a strategic thinker, he cleverly began the process by documenting the arboretum's physical decline, with estimated costs of repair. In 1978, he commissioned Andropogon Associates (later Andropogon) to create a "Program of Renewal" for potential donors. With this document in hand, he enlisted supporters and raised the funds for a comprehensive master plan to reinvent the arboretum as a contemporary institution.

16:2-6

The master plan called for facilities to welcome and serve the public (a visitor's center, entrance road, parking, an extensive path system, exhibits and maintenance facilities). Every intervention was to demonstrate the arboretum's commitment to the larger social and natural communities. For the first time since the Morrises, the Wissahickon Creek, which formed the western boundary, became an important part of the garden.

Recognition of the Wissahickon context—the creek itself, the forest and the two tributaries (Paper Mill Run and the Swan Pond Stream)—helped to shape the new plan. Beyond the historical gardens, the natural areas—once the unexploited framework for the garden—were now themselves considered exhibits. Treated as "curated natural habitats," they enlarged the diversity of plants on display and the variety of experiences for arboretum visitors.[11]

William McKinley Klein, Jr. (1934–1997)

Along with Otto Haas, it was William "Bill" Klein, hired as executive director in 1977, who made a moribund institution into an arboretum of substance and purpose. Klein came to the Morris from the Missouri Botanical Garden in St. Louis, where he was the assistant to its renowned director Peter Raven. During Klein's tenure at the Morris Arboretum (1977-91), its annual budget increased from $300,000 to over $2 million. He also raised $14 million to restore the grounds and the key historical features. He launched a number of research projects and reinvigorated the arboretum's plant-collecting expeditions to Asia.

Klein took both a scientific and humanistic view of the arboretum, seeing it, according to Judy McKeon, rosearian at the Morris, "as part of an art form, as well as an ecosystem."[1] He was a tireless promoter, building both the institution and the staff. He was fond of saying that the arboretum was dedicated to "growing people" as well as plants. Paul Meyer, the next director, characterized Klein's achievements: "He laid the foundations for the whole master planning effort, which transformed a rundown estate garden into what has become the world class public institution it is today."[2]

In 1988, the state legislature designated the Morris as the "Arboretum of the Commonwealth of Pennsylvania." This designation came about partly as the result of Klein's brilliant handling of the controversy over the new entrance road. Steve Wodjak, an arboretum neighbor and the City of Philadelphia's chief lobbyist in Harrisburg, raised vehement objections to the initial design. Klein then appointed Wodjak head of the committee to redesign the proposed road—making him an enthusiastic supporter. With the road now curving away from his house, Wodjak lobbied for funds for the arboretum in the state legislature. He also played a major role in designating the Morris as the official state arboretum.

Klein left the arboretum in 1991 to become director of the Fairchild Tropical Botanic Garden in Miami, Florida. He was the author of several books, including *Gardens of Philadelphia and the Delaware Valley* (1995) and *The Vascular Flora of Pennsylvania* (1989), in collaboration with Ann Rhoads of the arboretum.[3]

---

1. Quoted in *New York Times*, February 14, 1997.

2. Ibid.

3. For obituaries on Klein see *Philadelphia Inquirer*, February 14, 1997; *New York Times*, February 14, 1997; *Honolulu Advertiser*, February 13, 1997.

Klein perched in a huge tree at the former arboretum director's residence on Bethlehem Pike in Chestnut Hill, c. 1988. Source: Photograph by Nick Kelsh

New emphasis on the natural areas as exhibits persuaded the arboretum to repair Paper Mill Run and to reestablish the large wetland in the farm fields that John Morris had drained in the early 1900s. In an exhibit called "Penn's Woods" the arboretum also restored the Wissahickon forest on the steep slopes above the creek. These displays have been a great success and have opened up previously unused parts of the property. The wetland has encouraged a noticeable increase in the number and variety of bird species, bringing in bird-watchers as a new constituency.

16:7-11

16:2
Morris Arboretum |
From Private Victorian Estate to Public Garden

These diagrams illustrate the devolution of the arboretum, showing the effect of the university's research program in botany on the Morris estate.

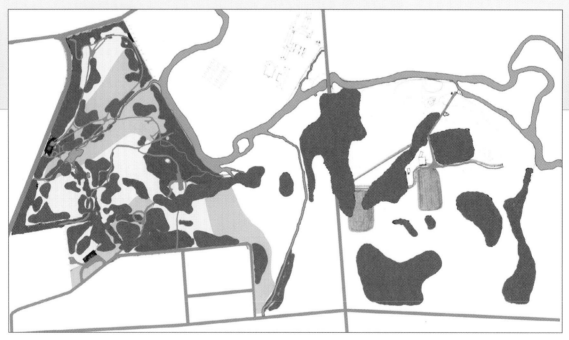

Disregarding the original layout and the spaces of the individual gardens at the Morris Estate, the structure of the landscape was obscured by new plant collections. Source: Andropogon, Morris Arboretum Master Plan, 1978

Enlarging the context to include Wissahickon Creek led to partnerships and interventions beyond the arboretum boundaries. Working with the FOW and private donors, the Morris later extended the restoration of Penn's Woods into Wissahickon Park. With state, county and local agencies, it sponsored a plan for the Green Ribbon Trail (from Wissahickon Park to Fort Washington State Park) and donated a portion of their land for this trail. The arboretum also collaborated with Chestnut Hill College, forging ties between these two institutions on opposite sides of the creek.

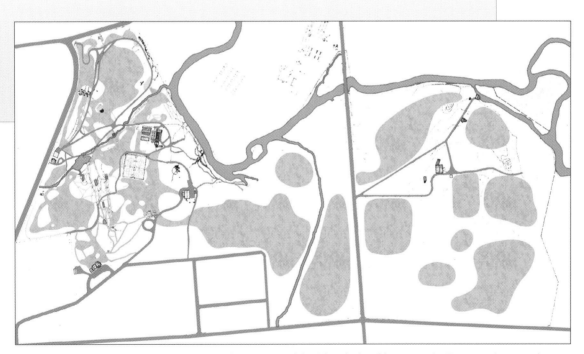

The university had not provided any facilities and visitors were left with only the old estate paths. To access the grounds, visitors and staff had created a "spaghetti" of unauthorized "rogue" trails. Source: Andropogon, Morris Arboretum Master Plan, 1978

Exploration of what the Morris Arboretum had been and what it could become began by "holding up a mirror to the institution"—recognizing its unique resources: its Victorian design; its context along the Wissahickon Creek; its local community; its position between city and suburbs; and its important collections of Northeast Asian trees.[12] Out of these assets, the arboretum built its central themes. The Victorian vocabulary was retained and reemphasized. The plant collections were refocused on the temperate forests of the world, particularly those of Northeast Asia. In recognition of its historical significance, the Morris was placed on the National Register of Historic Places in 1978.

Thirty years later, the arboretum has traveled a great distance—from a neglected and underused plant collection run by the botany department of the University of Pennsylvania,

16:2

Morris Arboretum
From Private Victorian Estate to Public Garden *(Continued)*

The first diagram shows the organization of the original Morris Estate. There are several types of landscapes on this historic property— farm, park, gardens and natural areas. The second diagram shows how these original relationships could be adapted as the basis for the modern plan. It reveals where new facilities should (or should not) be sited. For example, the maintenance facility was located in the former carriage house at the heart of the garden. This area was inappropriate and inefficient. Arboretum operations needed to be moved to the "working landscape" at Bloomfield Farm, where they could be consolidated and expanded. Once vacated, the carriage house could be adapted as a new education center.

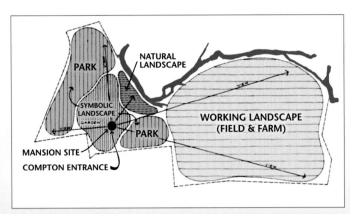

This diagram shows the landscape types of the historic property (Compton and Bloomfield)—the estate park, the gardens, the natural woodlands and the working farm.

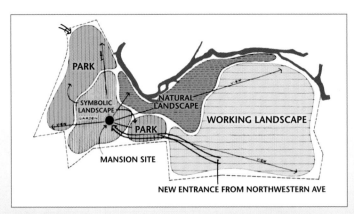

This diagram shows that in the new plan, the former landscape types were retained, but given different sizes, shapes and relationships. The public arboretum includes the estate park and gardens, and the natural woodlands. The old farm at Bloomfield, the "working landscape," is now the center of maintenance and operations, and the site of the new Horticultural Center.

Source: Andropogon, diagrams by Colin Franklin

The Morris Arboretum, looking north
from the top of the Chickies quartzite ridge
down into the limestone valley. In the distance is the
second Chickies quartzite ridge—Militia Hill—
that marks the northern edge of the Whitemarsh Valley.
Source: Photograph by Paul Meyer

Morris Arboretum |
From Private Victorian Estate to Public Garden   *(Continued)*

The maintenance facility, originally housed in a former carriage house at the center of the garden. This location was inappropriate and inefficient.

Maintenance operations were moved from the heart of the "symbolic landscape" to the "working landscape" at Bloomfield Farm where they could be consolidated and expanded. Once vacated, the carriage house could be adapted as a new education center.

Source: Photographs by Colin Franklin

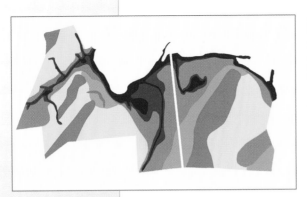

Diagram showing the landforms of the Morris Arboretum. The Wissahickon Ceek and its tributaries, the Swan Pond Stream, Paper Mill Run and a tiny stream along Northwestern Avenue, are shown in dark blue. Their floodplains are in light blue. The arboretum buildings are strung along the ridges. These ridges are marked in red and are the Chickies quartize ridge at Compton and the dolomite ridge at Bloomfield.
Source: Andropogon, drawing by Colin Franklin

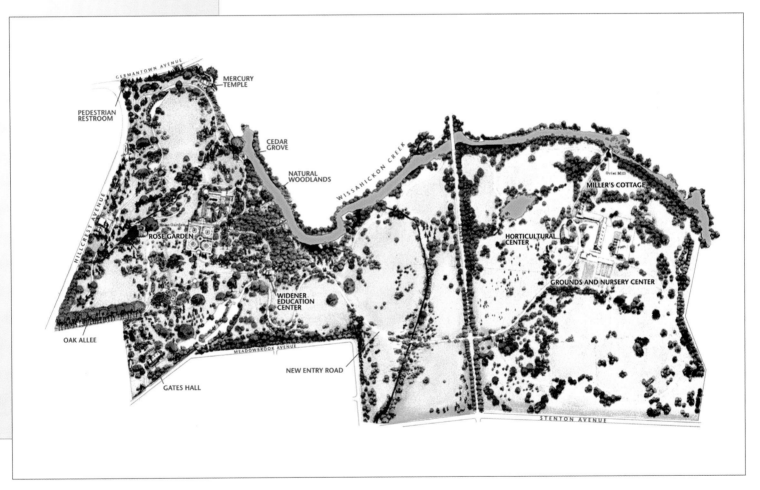

The master plan grew out of a combination of the historic organization of the Morris Estate, the natural structure of the landscape and visitor needs.
Source: Andropogon, Morris Arboretum Master Plan, 1978

Morris Arboretum | Entrance Road

Road, parking and paths immerse the visitor in the experience of the site. The wet meadow is crossed on a ford of cobblestones. Over Paper Mill Run, the bridge is an open grating. In heavy storms, the stream can flood through the grating and the open railings. From the bridge, the road winds up the hill and arrives at a new parking lot where visitors enter the garden. The Morris mansion once stood at this location overlooking the estate grounds.

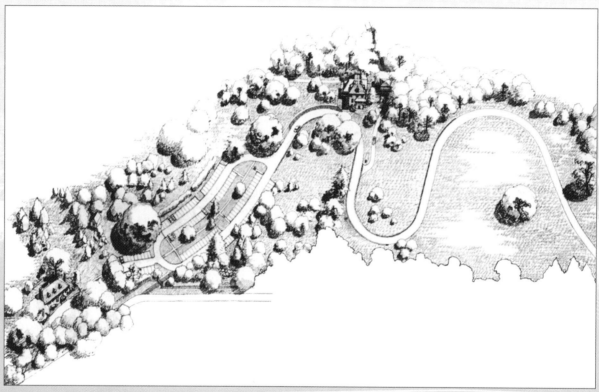

Configuration of the new entrance road with parking curved into the contours of the hill.
Source: Andropogon, drawing by Colin Franklin

New entrance gates to the Morris Arboretum welcome visitors to an elegant Victorian garden. The gates form a big elliptical forecourt that dissolves the boundary between public and private space, allowing Northwestern Avenue to seem like a part of the arboretum.

The bridge over Paper Mill Run, near the beginning of the entrance road, is designed to "go with the flow" and offer the least resistance to the inevitable floods. To raise the bridge above the frequent flood levels would have been prohibitively expensive and would have created a large, ugly structure that was out of scale with the landscape. The grated decking and open railing allows Paper Mill Run to rise up through the bridge during high water.
Source: Photographs by CLF

At each turn, the road reveals a previously hidden landscape—the little stream of Paper Mill Run, the floodplain meadows, the slope up from the broad limestone valley and the Chickies quartize ridge at the top of the hill. This is a journey of anticipation and surprise, designed to make visitors feel that they have left the ordinary world.
Source: Photograph by Nick Kelsh

Morris Arboretum | Permeable Parking

The parking lot at the Morris Arboretum is carefully set into the "military crest" on both sides of the ridge top, hidden from visitors in the gardens below and curved to follow the contours. Between the parking bays, a pedestrian walkway collects visitors and connects the arboretum's two main buildings—the Widener Education Center and the administrative offices at Gates Hall.

The lot recognizes the invisible interconnection between the land and the creek. It was designed as a series of level terraces to catch rainwater and snow melt. Paved with permeable asphalt, a gravel basin underneath holds and slowly releases water into the ground. From the top of the hill, this water gradually moves underground into Paper Mill Run—and then into Wisshickon Creek.

Water runs off the conventional asphalt of the road and is absorbed into the permeable asphalt of the parking bays.

Source: Photographs by CLF

This parking lot is a multifunctioning landscape—holding cars, collecting stormwater runoff and recharging ground water. A large basin (sized to hold stormwater runoff from a 50-year storm), engineered by T. H. Cahill & Associates, was constructed under the entire lot. The parking bays were paved with permeable asphalt. In this system, the parking lot, basin, site and soil type work together. Stormwater infiltrates into the soil in the uplands where it falls, instead of being collected in an inlet and piped to an already rain-swollen waterway. The parking lot was installed in 1986, and has never been repaved.

Source: Andropogon

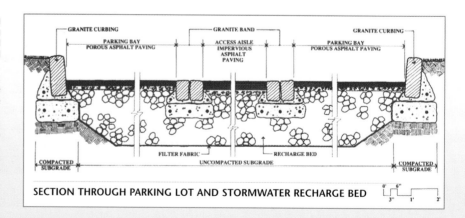

SECTION THROUGH PARKING LOT AND STORMWATER RECHARGE BED

Morris Arboretum | Lighting

The light standards were originally produced for the Smithsonian Institution in Washington, D.C. and were designed by Luke Tigue, of Tigue Lighting, Inc. These tall, substantial fixtures reinforce the Victorian theme. The light poles follow the central pedestrian pathway down the ridge to the visitors center.

In these light fixtures, the bulbs are recessed. There is no glare and the light shines only on the area to be illuminated–not into neighbors' windows. The spectrum of light is calibrated to moonlight and the illuminated globes appear like floating moons in the landscape.
Source: Photograph by CLF

to a multi-faceted and internationally significant institution. It has a wealth of programs and immaculately cared for grounds, with the historical features lovingly restored and integrated. Membership and visitation are at an all time high. Every year there are new gardens and exhibits. In 2009, the new horticultural center and a new canopy walk over Penn's Woods were built. The walk will give visitors another sense of connection to Wissahickon Creek.

16:12–13

Following Klein, Paul Meyer, who had been director of horticulture, became the new arboretum director. His quiet friendliness belies his extraordinary competence and genius at fund-raising. Meyer focused on the arboretum's growth and conserved its resources. He slowly but inexorably fulfilled the master plan's intent. He also unflinchingly took the arboretum into experimental areas, going beyond the master plan but maintaining its spirit. Two strong directors—one reinforcing what the other had begun—built the board, staff, programs, facilities, partnerships and a solid financial base. Their leadership is at the heart of the arboretum's success.

Morris Arboretum | A Hierarchy of Paths

The main path loop around Compton uses portions of the old carriage drive.

Secondary paths take the visitors to special events that are not along the main loop.

Smaller paths lead to individual exhibits. A view to a grassy path that takes the visitor to the Wisteria walk.
Source: Photographs by CLF

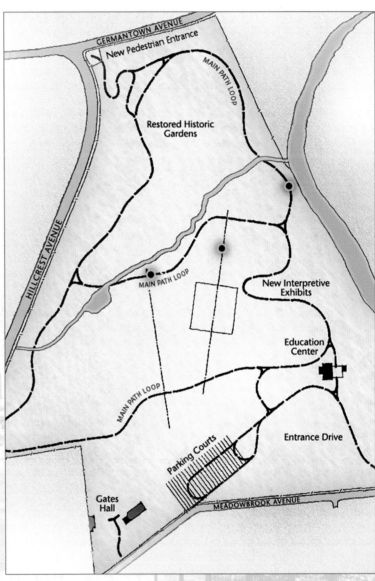

Plan of the circulation at Compton.
Source: Andropogon, Morris Arboretum Master Plan, 1978

Morris Arboretum | New Wetlands, Stream Repair and Penn's Woods Restoration

Klein understood that an arboretum served several different but related purposes—education, research and display. Changing attitudes toward the environment have led arboreta and botanic gardens to include an additional purpose—conservation. These institutions have chosen to conserve the biological diversity represented by their own collections on their own properties (in-situ), and in the collections of sister institutions around the world (ex-situ). Later, by extension, "conservation" also included the preservation and restoration of historic and cultural resources.

As conservation became an important mission for the arboretum, the areas of concern expanded to the repair of Paper Mill Run (a tributary of Wissahickon Creek), reestablishment of the historic wetlands in the abandoned farm fields adjacent to Paper Mill Run and to the rehabilitation of "Penn's Woods" along steep slopes above Wissahickon Creek.

Conservation concerns also resulted in the restoration of areas of the arboretum where historic features and environmental interventions fused together. When the storms of August 2004 blew out the Swan Pond stream and the Swan Pond itself, the arboretum used the insurance money to restore these highly crafted, historic garden features, which received the heavy load of stormwater from the surrounding neighborhood.

Aerial view of Paper Mill Run (called out by the diagonal tree line). A new wet meadow can be seen in the upper right hand corner, and a new wetland in the lower left hand corner.
Source: Morris Arboretum of the University of Pennsylvania

Morris Arboretum | Wetlands

New wetlands were created at the Morris Arboretum in
the limestone valley. The drain tiles left over from John
Morris's agricultural experiments were broken up and a
hole dug. Some of the water supply for the wetland comes
from subsurface flow from the remaining drainage tiles still
in place across the entrance road.
Source: Photograph by Paul Meyer

Morris Arboretum | Swan Pond Stream

The Swan Pond Stream after the August 2004 storm had poured raging flood waters out of a pipe at the edge of the property, ripping away the Victorian rockwork that lined the stream channel.

The Swan Pond Stream further down, where the channelized banks have been entirely ripped away.

The Swan Pond Stream after repairs. An extraordinary contractor, Paul Steinbeiser, was responsible for this sensitive and elegant restoration work. These repairs were paid for, in part, by the University of Pennsylvania's insurance policy, which covered the Morris Arboretum.   Source: Photographs by Colin Franklin

Morris Arboretum | New Projects: Horticultural Center

Aerial rendering and perspective of the Horticultural Center at Bloomfield. Following the initial master plan, horticultural operations were moved to the "working landscape." Taking their cue from the farm character of the existing site, these "Leed Platinium" facilities, designed by Overland Partners, Architects, blend into the texture and fabric of the pastoral landscape of the middle valley.
Source: Watercolors by Overland Partners, Architects

Morris Arboretum | New Projects: Out on a Limb

Visitor surveys and community focus groups indicated that the arboretum's audience is evolving from adults only to multigenerational families. The arboretum initiated a new interpretive master plan. A 275-foot canopy walk, designed by Metcalfe Architecture & Design (who specialize in interpretive exhibits), with Andropogon, is one of the new exhibits in this plan. Called "Out on a Limb," this new exhibit brings visitors right out over the steep rocky slopes to the edge of Wissahickon Creek. Source: Andropogon, drawings by John Collins, from drawings by Metcalfe Architecture & Design

Chestnut Hill College: Reconnecting Campus and Creek

The two decades after World War II were a time of expansion for Chestnut Hill College. The administration hoped to reclaim land in the floodplain for a student center, parking lots and athletic facilities by cutting off a major bend in the creek. In the process, they filled in the old Dewees millrace and millpond, and created a new, connecting channel several hundred yards to the southeast. Whereas in the earlier period, the sisters had made the meandering creek, along with the millpond and wetlands, an integral part of Catholic life and student activities, this "floodplain reclamation" increased the separation between the buildings and the lower campus.

These changes caused serious ecological problems. After flowing through the limestone valley, Wissahickon Creek cuts a channel through the Chickies quartzite ridge between the college and the arboretum. When floodwaters rush downstream, they hit the hard rock ridge and are deflected into the open meadow of the lower campus. Historically, millpond, wetlands and the multiple channels of the creek absorbed these floodwaters. With the water now constricted to a single, straight channel—and with the increased runoff from developing Springfield Township—the entire lower campus flooded in every major storm. Topsoil that had covered the fill material was washed away, exposing bricks, old bathroom tiles and asphalt slabs.

As late as the 1960s, an insular, interior and monastic mentality continued to keep Chestnut Hill College from forging closer ties with other institutions and local groups. The college had remained largely a school for white, Catholic women at a time when American society was grappling with issues of integration and inclusion. By the mid-1970s, enrollment had begun to fall alarmingly because other private colleges were going co-educational. With declining enrollment, the diminishing revenues made it difficult for the college to add new programs or to maintain its aging physical plant. Like the Morris Arboretum during this same period, the college was at a crossroads and had to adapt to new social and cultural realities or face closing.

The situation continued to deteriorate into the early 1990s when the board appointed a strong, new president, Sister Carol Jean Vale, S.S.J. Vale is a take-charge person, willing to face the reality of the situation and to take risks to bring about change. Like Klein and Meyer, she slowly built a board that understood the problems, that was inspired by her initiatives and that would raise the necessary money.

To show prospective donors that the institution had a future, Vale commissioned a master plan. Designed by Mark B. Thompson, Associates, Architects, in collaboration with Andropogon, this plan reinforced the college's original organization along the ridge and its powerful relationship to Wissahickon Creek. The plan reflected the four long bands that followed the landforms of the campus: the narrow ridge; the steep escarpment; the gentle transitional valley slope; and the broad, flat floodplain. These bands recognized a progression from the world of buildings on the hill, to the natural landscape along the creek.

16:12–14

Flooding at Chestnut Hill College

Below the college buildings on the ridge in the lower campus of Chestnut Hill College is the designated 100-year floodplain of Wissahickon Creek. The campus experiences a significant flood two or three times a year. These floods have cut off the access road from Northwestern Avenue and flooded large parts of the lower parking area.

Increasing urbanization upstream has caused more runoff. The channel now has to carry a greater volume and velocity of water, exacerbating the natural tendency of this area to flood. In addition, there is more volatility in the precipitation patterns, due to the effects of global climate change. Increased flooding limits the uses of the lower campus.

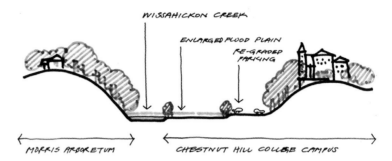

The college raised the playing fields adjacent to the creek to keep them from being inundated by floodwaters. However, raising the playing fields constricted the floodway, causing worse flooding.

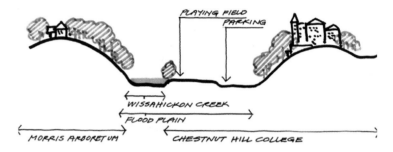

Instead, the playing fields should be lowered and used to store floodwaters and the parking lots adjacent to the ridge raised to protect the cars.

Aerial photograph of the Chestnut Hill College campus showing the college on the hilltop, bottom left, and the parking, tennis courts and soccer field below in the floodplain.
Source: Photograph by Colin Franklin

When it encounters the hard rock of the Chickies quartzite ridge, Wissahickon Creek makes an abrupt right turn. This bend encloses the northeastern part of the campus. When the creek floods, the narrowing gorge acts as a dam, backing up water and flooding large areas of the lower campus, the Morris Arboretum, the Wissahickon Valley Country Club golf course and Northwestern Avenue.
Source: Andropogon, diagrams by Colin Franklin

Flooding at Chestnut Hill College

Plan of Chestnut Hill College, showing the 100-year floodplain as well as the original creek channel, oxbow and millrace. This drawing also shows the realignment of the stream by the college in the early 1960s.

The old stream channel, oxbow and millrace were filled with construction debris and covered with a thin layer of topsoil. During heavy storms, this topsoil erodes badly. Circles show the locations of the historic photographs of the 1967 flood.

Source: SaylorGregg Architects (formerly Dagit Saylor Architects), Chestnut Hill Master Plan: 2007, drawing by Andropogon

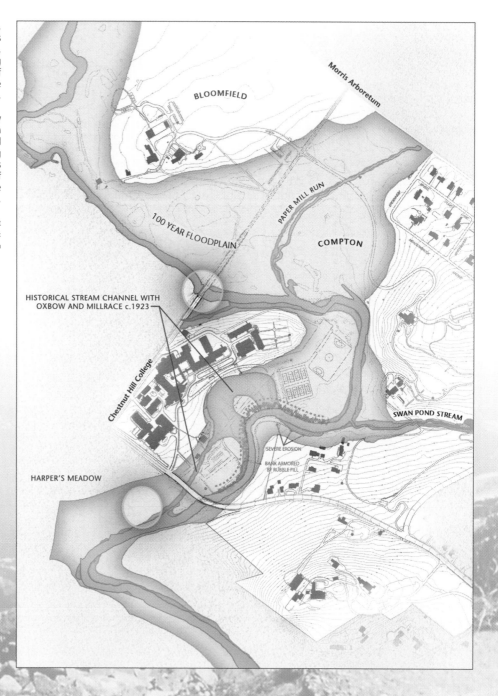

BLOOMFIELD

Morris Arboretum

PAPER MILL RUN

100 YEAR FLOODPLAIN

COMPTON

HISTORICAL STREAM CHANNEL WITH OXBOW AND MILLRACE c.1923

Chestnut Hill College

SWAN POND STREAM

SEVERE EROSION

BANK ARMORED BY RUBBLE FILL

HARPER'S MEADOW

As a result of the August 2004 flood, the banks of Wissahickon Creek at Chestnut Hill College were washed away, exposing the fill from the 1960s.

Floodwaters topped this small wall making a waterfall that gouged a parking lot.
Source: Photographs by CLF

Flooding along Wissahickon Creek

Flooding along Northwestern Avenue, late winter, looking southwest towards Germantown Avenue. The Morris Arboretum is in the foreground, with Bloomfield on the right and Compton on the left. Chestnut Hill College can be seen in the distance on the upper left–hand side. Photograph, 1967. Source: CHHS

To avoid putting buildings into the floodplain and to break down the physical and psychological wall between upper and lower campuses, the plan proposed new facilities built into the steep, southern hillside. These buildings would step down the slope with broad staircases to join hill and valley. The new "green roofs" would become plazas, giving the campus much needed outdoor gathering spaces. A new pond and wetlands would reestablish the school's presence on the creek, at the same time creating flood storage and outside study areas for the college's environmental science program.[13]

As a part of the master planning process, Vale hired Schultz & Williams, strategic planning consultants for non-profits, to do an enrollment study. Despite strong evidence to the contrary, this firm recommended that the college remain for women only, and despite the renovations of existing buildings, enrollment continued to decline. Vale then put together an ad hoc committee to review the question of coeducation. In 2001,

Flooding in Harpers Meadow, across Germantown Avenue from Chestnut Hill College. Photograph, 1967.
Source: CHHS

the college commissioned Miller/Cook Associates to undertake a second enrollment study, which now recommended that the college admit men. In the fall of 2003, the college became coeducational in all its programs for the first time. This change resulted in an immediate and dramatic rise in enrollment and in fiscal health.

The student body, which had fallen to about 350 in 2002, nearly doubled to 700 by 2005 and has continued to rise. With a projected goal of 1,500 students, there was an urgent need for new dormitories, classrooms and a center for student life. The college then commissioned Dagit Saylor Architects (later SaylorGregg Architects), with Andropogon, to begin a facilities master plan update. Almost serendipitously, within a few months, the large, adjacent property known as "Sugarloaf" was suddenly on the market and potentially available to the college. The facilities master plan was then expanded to include this new property.[14]

16:15

Chestnut Hill College | Master Plan

The organization of a campus is deeply tied to its intellectual and financial success. The interplay of two dense centers on opposite hillsides, with the scenic Wisssahickon Valley becoming the common recreational spine that joins the two campus, could transform Chestnut Hill College into a dynamic and memorable collegial experience. This new vision for the college is also a catalyst to transform the village of Chestnut Hill.

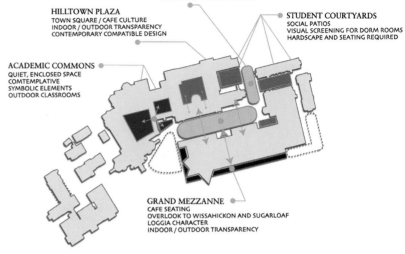

STUDENT FORUM
ACTIVE HUB FOR STUDENT INTERACTION
EMERGENCY VEHICULAR ACCESS

HILLTOWN PLAZA
TOWN SQUARE / CAFE CULTURE
INDOOR / OUTDOOR TRANSPARENCY
CONTEMPORARY COMPATIBLE DESIGN

STUDENT COURTYARDS
SOCIAL PATIOS
VISUAL SCREENING FOR DORM ROOMS
HARDSCAPE AND SEATING REQUIRED

ACADEMIC COMMONS
QUIET, ENCLOSED SPACE
COMTEMPLATIVE
SYMBOLIC ELEMENTS
OUTDOOR CLASSROOMS

GRAND MEZZANNE
CAFE SEATING
OVERLOOK TO WISSAHICKON AND SUGARLOAF
LOGGIA CHARACTER
INDOOR / OUTDOOR TRANSPARENCY

Diagram showing the proposed organization of the main campus—large buildings along a main spine, alternating with courtyards.
Source: SaylorGregg Architects (formerly Dagit Saylor Architects), Chestnut Hill Master Plan: 2009

View of the main campus on the Chickies quartzite ridge, from Sugarloaf.
Source: Perspective by Art and Design Studios. Courtesy, SaylorGregg Architects
(formerly Dagit Saylor Architects) Chestnut Hill Master Plan: 2009

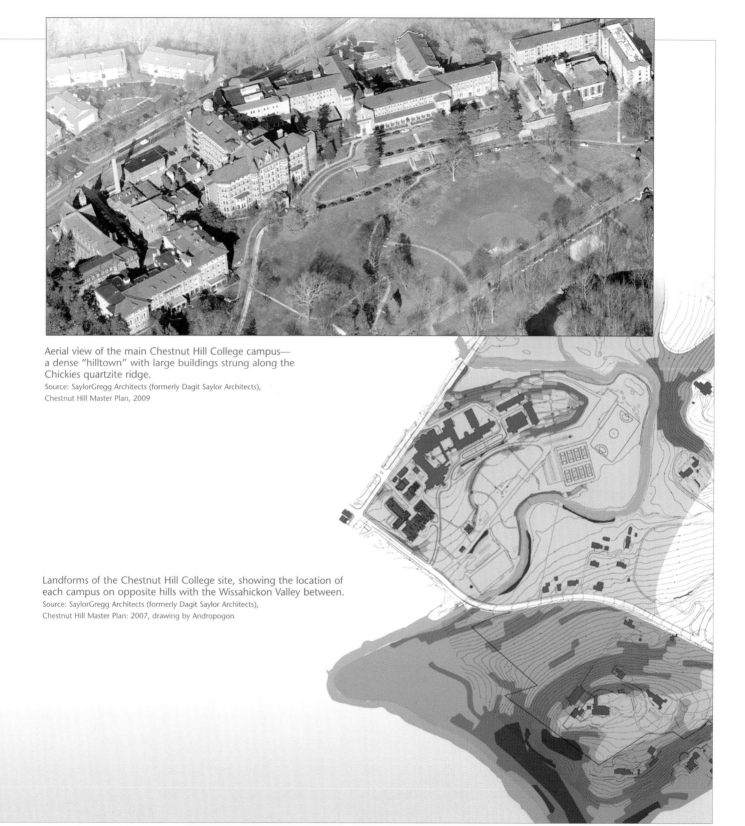

Aerial view of the main Chestnut Hill College campus—
a dense "hilltown" with large buildings strung along the
Chickies quartzite ridge.
Source: SaylorGregg Architects (formerly Dagit Saylor Architects),
Chestnut Hill Master Plan, 2009

Landforms of the Chestnut Hill College site, showing the location of
each campus on opposite hills with the Wissahickon Valley between.
Source: SaylorGregg Architects (formerly Dagit Saylor Architects),
Chestnut Hill Master Plan: 2007, drawing by Andropogon

Chestnut Hill College | Master Plan   (Continued)

The analysis of campus spatial requirements, by SaylorGregg Architects, concluded that at least 1.2 million square feet of new facilities were needed.

On the main campus, new dormitories would extend out in fingers towards Wissahickon Creek with spectacular views of the water and the valley. Taking advantage of the grade change, these buildings would be multi-layered and open underneath to accommodate hidden parking and service bays. Additional surface parking is pulled close to the edge of the ridge and out of the floodplain. The new student center steps down the south-facing hillside in tiers, and a new "green" replaces the old traffic circle. Campus buildings would be serviced from underneath. Elevators and stairs would bring people to and from the lower campus.

Strong pedestrian and vehicular connections between the two sites would maintain close relationships, keeping Sugarloaf from being seen as a "satellite" campus. Long, elevated walkways over Wissahickon Creek and Germantown Avenue would link a proposed student center to the large projecting residence hall on the Sugarloaf side.

Built into the hillside, new facilities at Sugarloaf have the potential to provide access to the upper levels of both parts of the campus without having to climb stairs. New dormitories would be built on the top of a 500-car parking garage set into the steep hillside. These buildings would also reach out in long fingers towards the main campus, mirroring the plan for residence halls across the creek. The roof of the garage is designed as a green plaza.

The large college buildings had been sited on the ridge top. In the 1960s, the lower campus was preempted when the millpond, with its picturesque islands, rustic bridges and tree-lined creek walk, were replaced by roads, parking lots and athletic facilities. As a result, there was little place on campus for student life.

Source: Photograph by Peter Saylor

CHESTNUT HILL
COLLEGE

MORRIS
ARBORETUM

FAIRMOUNT PARK

SUGAR LOAF
PROPERTY

WOODMERE
MUSEUM

EXISTING
CONDITIONS

PROPOSED
NEW FACILITIES

Source: SaylorGregg Architects (formerly Dagit Saylor Architects), Chestnut Hill Master Plan, 2005

A perspective rendering of the proposed student center built out over the wall. Traffic would be rerouted and the upper area turned into a pedestrian green. The new building encloses and shelters this central space. The upper campus would then have an academic quadrangle, with the qualities of both a college green and a Mediterranean plaza. Most importantly, the new student center, entered from both above and below, reconnects the college with the lower campus and Wissahickon Creek.

Source: Perspective by Art and Design Studios. Courtesy, SaylorGregg Architects (formerly Dagit Saylor Architects) Chestnut Hill Master Plan, 2005

A New Campus at Sugarloaf

Facing page
Plan showing ownership, easements and deed restrictions, both on the main campus and at Sugarloaf. Almost half the site was acquired through a "Growing Greener" grant from the Commonwealth of Pennsylvania. In accepting Growing Greener money, the college agreed to place a 10-acre easement around the Sugarloaf property.
Source: SaylorGregg Architects (formerly Dagit Saylor Architects), Chestnut Hill Master Plan, 2007.
Drawing by Andropogon

16:16

Sugarloaf, the old Albert M. Greenfield Estate, was a nearly 30-acre tract adjacent to Wissahickon Park. Located diagonally across Germantown Avenue from the college, this property was willed to Temple University as a conference center at Greenfield's death. It reverted to the Greenfield Foundation when Temple relinquished the property.

The college purchased Sugarloaf in August 2006. Many developers had bid for this prime, undeveloped tract in upper Chestnut Hill. Greenfield Foundation President Pricilla Luce, explaining why the college was chosen, emphasized the foundation's commitment to Philadelphia's civic and community life: "We felt the college had a wonderful plan to use the property for the campus expansion…and we wanted to support their educational mission and purpose…. Their promise to maintain the green space factored positively into the decision."[15]

Given the specter of 35 new houses on the site, both the college and the Chestnut Hill community recognized that the acquisition of this property offered mutual advantages. Concerned with providing stimulating and safe venues for student life, the college saw that its campus would now be within easy walking distance of the "top of the hill."

The initial facilities master plan was enlarged to include a feasibility study for Sugarloaf that evolved into a master plan for the entire campus. The plan for Sugarloaf kept the "estate" landscape visible from both Germantown Avenue and Bell's Mill Road. New buildings would be placed in the middle of the site buffered from Germantown Avenue to leave a forested buffer. This buffer would protect both park and neighbors from a direct view of the new college buildings.

The college is seeking to change the current zoning from R-2 Residential to an Institutional Development District. Such a district is common practice for Philadelphia institutions (Temple University, the University of Pennsylvania and Saint Joseph's University). It would formalize the master plan and allow the college to complete all the projects shown within the plan without returning to the Philadelphia Board of Zoning Adjustment for a variance.

Located between Wissahickon Park and the Morris Arboretum, the college is a crucial link in a band of contiguous open space along Wissahickon Creek. With the Morris Arboretum, Woodmere Art Museum, Norwood/Fontbonne Academy and Fairmount Park, there is a nexus of institutions at this boundary between city and suburbs. The Chestnut Hill Renaissance revitalized the village of Chestnut Hill and the surrounding neighborhood. A half a century later this energy has run its course and the rest of the country has caught up with and in some cases moved beyond these ideas. Imaginative master plans that recognize and incorporate the Wissahickon Valley, formalized in a Multi-institutional Development District, could create a framework for environmentally sensitive development at this critical juncture of geologies, landforms and political boundaries. Bold, integrated development could provide the energy and the inspiration for a second Chestnut Hill Renaissance and a strong initial springboard for the future Wissahickon corridor.

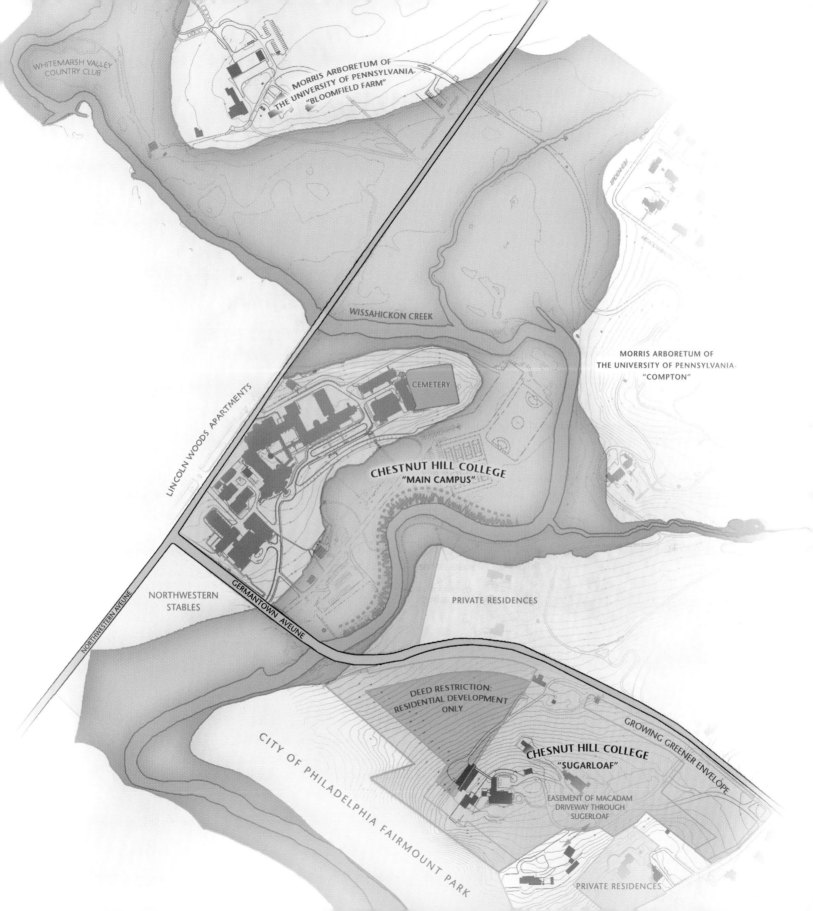

WHITEMARSH VALLEY
COUNTRY CLUB

MORRIS ARBORETUM OF
THE UNIVERSITY OF PENNSYLVANIA-
"BLOOMFIELD FARM"

WISSAHICKON CREEK

MORRIS ARBORETUM OF
THE UNIVERSITY OF PENNSYLVANIA-
"COMPTON"

LINCOLN WOODS APARTMENTS

CEMETERY

CHESTNUT HILL COLLEGE
"MAIN CAMPUS"

NORTHWESTERN
STABLES

NORTHWESTERN AVEUNE

GERMANTOWN AVEUNE

PRIVATE RESIDENCES

DEED RESTRICTION:
RESIDENTIAL DEVELOPMENT
ONLY

GROWING GREENER ENVELOPE

CHESTNUT HILL COLLEGE
"SUGARLOAF"

CITY OF PHILADELPHIA FAIRMOUNT PARK

EASEMENT OF MACADAM
DRIVEWAY THROUGH
SUGERLOAF

PRIVATE RESIDENCES

Chestnut Hill College | Sugarloaf Campus

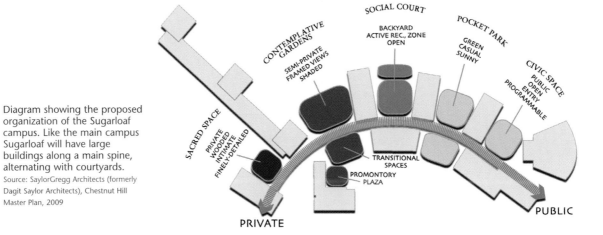

SACRED SPACE
PRIVATE
WOODED
INTIMATE
FINELY-DETAILED

CONTEMPLATIVE GARDENS
SEMI-PRIVATE
FRAMED VIEWS
SHADED

SOCIAL COURT
BACKYARD
ACTIVE REC., ZONE
OPEN

POCKET PARK
GREEN
CASUAL
SUNNY

CIVIC SPACE
PUBLIC
OPEN
ENTRY
PROGRAMMABLE

TRANSITIONAL SPACES

PROMONTORY PLAZA

PRIVATE

PUBLIC

Diagram showing the proposed organization of the Sugarloaf campus. Like the main campus Sugarloaf will have large buildings along a main spine, alternating with courtyards.
Source: SaylorGregg Architects (formerly Dagit Saylor Architects), Chestnut Hill Master Plan, 2009

Like the main campus, Sugarloaf will be developed as a dense "hilltown" built on top of a multi-story parking garage. This design preserves the maximum amount of open space, which allows the forest of the Wissahickon Valley to surround and filter into the new campus.
Source: SaylorGregg Architects (formerly Dagit Saylor Architects), Chestnut Hill Master Plan, 2009

Aerial photograph showing the main campus in the far right with the Sugarloaf campus in the bottom left.
Source: SaylorGregg Architects (formerly Dagit Saylor Architects), Chestnut Hill Master Plan, 2009

Section showing the parking garage terraced into the hill. The top of the garage is the foundation for the college buildings—dormitories and classrooms separated by "green roofs" that provide outdoor spaces for student life.
Source: SaylorGregg Architects (formerly Dagit Saylor Architects), Chestnut Hill Master Plan, 2009

Saving Erdenheim Farm

The 444-acre Erdenheim Farm is the largest undeveloped parcel in the middle valley. On his death in 1971, George Widener bequeathed this property to his nephew, Fitz Eugene Dixon, Jr.—with the exception of 113 acres along the Wissahickon given to the Natural Lands Trust (NLT). Dixon had a life interest in the NLT parcel, which allowed him to use the land.[16] With his wife, he maintained the property as a "gentleman's farm," where they raised prize-winning Black Angus cattle, Cheviot sheep and thoroughbred horses, occasionally adding pieces of adjacent property. Under the Dixons' stewardship, this iconic pastoral landscape of rolling fields and wooded hills, with picturesque barns and outbuildings and the Wissahickon Creek meandering through it, has survived and thrived. Steven L. Nelson, Deputy Chief Operating Officer of Montgomery County, has described this land as, "A unique treasure and landmark in our region, showcasing a consummate example of land stewardship and a historic agricultural landscape to thousands of motorists every day. Its preservation is important to maintain open space in the Wissahickon Valley, to provide a riparian buffer for the creek and to aid in stormwater recharge. The County recognizes its critical importance and is ready to work to save it."[17]

Erdenheim Farm is located between large and contiguous lands along the main stem of Wissahickon Creek, still mainly in open space. To the south, these properties include the Morris Arboretum, Chestnut Hill College and Whitemarsh Valley Country Club; to the west, Carson Valley School; and to the north, the Philadelphia Cricket Club. Other important large properties are: Highway materials (the old Corson Quarries), St. Thomas Church, and Fort Washington State Park.[18] If developed, Erdenheim Farms would cut a gaping hole out of this open space. Preserved in its entirety, it could become the focus and showpiece of an open space corridor that stretches from Fort Washington State Park at the mouth of Sandy Run, to the edge of Philadelphia at Chestnut Hill.

Erdenheim Farm is located mainly in Whitemarsh Township, with a small portion in adjoining Springfield Township. It is near a network of super highways: the Pennsylvania Turnpike, I-476 (known locally as the Blue Route) and the Route 309 Expressway. With this access, land prices have risen to record levels and every possible open space has been proposed for a wide variety of intensive development—from high-rise apartments to "McMansions." Private properties in the middle valley are the most vulnerable. The purchase of property from Dixon for a retirement complex, was an "alarm bell in the night."

Up until this time, local residents had assumed that Erdenheim Farm would remain unchanged forever. Concerned residents formed the Whitemarsh Township Residents Association (WTRA), initially, to stop any development at Erdenheim Farm, and later, to broker a deal that would minimize the damage. With the exception of the NTL piece, the remaining 331 acres of Erdenheim Farm were unprotected from development, a danger that suddenly became very real in 2000-2001, when retirement village developers acquired 54 acres, to be joined to the adjacent 42-acre Eugenia Hospital site. Called the Hill at Whitemarsh, the houses and apartments of this $220 million continuing care and retirement community were to be built on the gentle hillside sweeping down towards the Wissahickon Creek and known as the "Angus Tract" (from the angus cows grazing on it).

16:17-19

16:20

Erdenheim Farm

View of the 113-acre Natural Lands Trust parcel. Wissahickon Creek is in the center. The former Dixon house and its immediate grounds are to the left, out of the photograph, and are not part of the NLT tract. Source: Photograph by CLF

The Natural Lands Trust

In 1953, Alston Jenkins, one of the founders of the Wissahickon Valley Watershed Association (WVWA), spearheaded the Philadelphia Conservationists, which was later renamed the Natural Lands Trust (NLT). This organization continues to be an important player in the middle and upper Wissahickon Valley. The trust is the largest land conservation organization in Southeastern Pennsylvania. It specializes in land protection (through easements or acquisitions), conservation planning for large landowners and land management.

NLT has two major divisions. One is the recently established Center for Conservation Landowners (CCL). The other is the Conservation Action Center (CAC). The CCL offers training in land stewardship and provides a range of consulting services to private landowners, municipalities, institutions and non-profit organizations interested in preserving and restoring native habitats. These services include stewardship assessments, plans and project consultations. Project consultation includes contractor referrals, project oversight, monitoring, guidance on site management and advice on funding sources. The role

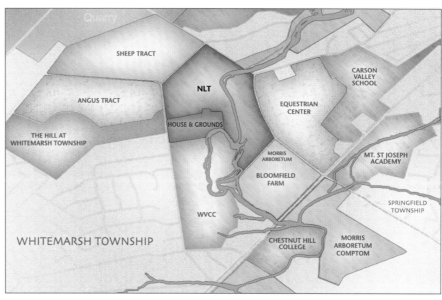

of the CAC is to educate the public about conservation issues and how citizens can become involved.

NLT participates in a number of partnerships that have had a significant impact in the Wissahickon Valley. One of these partners is Growing Greener: Conservation By Design, a state-wide program that helps municipalities and developers to build new homes and businesses and at the same time protect important local open space. This program is a collaboration between the Pennsylvania Department of Conservation and Natural Resources (DCNR), the Governor's Center for

Local Government Services and NLT. Chestnut Hill College used Growing Greener monies to help purchase the Sugarloaf campus.

NLT has been very active in Montgomery County, supporting the county's conservation efforts. In addition to direct efforts, NLT has a partnership with the Montgomery County Lands Trust (MCLT), which greatly increases their impact. NLT owns 113 acres of Erdenheim Farm, donated to them by George Widener in 1972. This parcel, a gift to the NLT as part of Widener's original conservation agreement, has been recently renamed "the Wissahickon Tract."

Map showing the Erdenheim Farm parcels and their relationship to the Wissahickon Creek corridor: the 109-acre "Sheep Tract," the 98-acre "Angus Tract" and the 101–acre Equestrian Center. Shown in yellow, and southwest of the NLT parcel, is the 23-acre piece with the Dixon house and estate offices. The NLT's portion of Erdenheim Farm is shown in green, in the center of the map.
Source: NLT

Transition between the Lower and Middle Wissahickon Valley

Composite map showing the transition between the lower valley in the City of Philadelphia and the middle valley in Montgomery County. The map illustrates the pivotal role of the Morris Arboretum and Chestnut Hill College at the boundary between city and suburbs and the critical importance of private open space to a coherent Wissahickon corridor. Public open space is shown in dark green and private open space in light green.

Source: Upper section adapted from a map by Gannet Flemming, Inc., Whitemarsh Township Open Space, for the Whitemarsh Township Parks and Recreation Commission. Lower section adapted from a map of the Wissahickon Park, courtesy FOW

The Hill at Whitemarsh

In 2000-2001, Whitemarsh Retirement Partners, LLC, headed by John J. Fleming (the son of a Chestnut Hill resident) purchased 54 acres of the Angus Tract from Fitz Eugene Dixon, to be joined with the adjacent 42-acre site of the abandoned Eugenia Hospital. Called the "Hill at Whitemarsh," it was to be a retirement community with apartments and single homes surrounding a central hospital and nursing facility. Most of the investors—known collectively as the "Founders"—were from the Whitemarsh Valley-Chestnut Hill area, and many now live at the retirement complex.

The initial design proposed to put an extensive facility on the hillside sweeping down to Flourtown Road. The residents of surrounding communities were appalled at the possible loss of this extraordinary landscape, which many had remembered since childhood and "believed" was theirs by right.

In the fall of 2000, a large group of concerned individuals formed the Whitemarsh Township Residents Association (WTRA) to oppose the Hill at Whitemarsh. The Eugenia Hospital part of the property was already zoned institutional, but the additional 54 acres from Erdenheim Farm required rezoning and township hearings. At these hearings the public was invited to review the plans. More than 1,000 residents, supported by WRTA, expressed their opposition to the initial design at meetings of the Whitemarsh Township Planning Commission. The crowds were so large that the township building could not hold them all.[1]

Whitemarsh Retirement Partners, LLC, presented a rigid and unimaginative scheme that sprawled down over the Angus Tract meadow. The township planning commission, citing the "density and intensity" of the proposed development and the additional run-off into Wissahickon Creek, turned down the rezoning application.[2]

After much behind the scenes negotiation, an agreement was worked out with the landowner, the developer and the WTRA. A revised plan for the Hill at Whitemarsh moved the buildings to the plateau on and around the old Eugenia Hospital grounds. Relocation preserved most of the familiar and much loved view shed—the long sloping meadow. Buildings would be clustered to provide 40 percent open space. A conservation easement preserved the 12-acre woodland at the top of the hill as a buffer to the neighbors.

The agreement included an option for the larger community to purchase the 97-acre "Angus Tract," exercisable at Dixon's death. The developers would contribute $1 million towards the purchase and preservation of this 97-acre parcel. An additional $107,000 a year would be given to the open-space acquisition fund.

Entrance drive with view to main hospital building. The site plan is formal in an informal landscape. The hospital and community facilities are massed at the top of a rise, making them seem extra large and oppressive. The "Swiss Chalet" style is unsympathetic to the quality and character of the rambling, agricultural vernacular of the middle valley.
Source: Photograph by CLF

The township agreed to earmark all property taxes from the Hill at Whitemarsh for the fund. Through use of an important new conservation tool called "Tax Increment Financing," a special fund was set up for 20 years to be used to purchase designated Erdenheim Farm parcels. Hugh Molton, chair of the Whitemarsh Foundation, explained: "We were... fortunate to have a landowner, a private developer and three separate public taxing authorities who were willing to work together... Once the Hill at Whitemarsh is complete... it will generate new tax revenues. These revenues would normally flow to three separate taxing authorities: Montgomery County, Whitemarsh Township, and the Colonial School District."[3]

Protection of this evocative, rural landscape as open space will benefit the whole community, especially the residents of the Hill at Whitemarsh, where the Angus Tract will become their "front lawn." Other benefits to the township include the stabilization or even increase of property values, which will translate into revenue from property taxes.

Finally, the agreement established the Whitemarsh Foundation to purchase and hold any Erdenheim Farm properties that the community would be able to acquire.[4] Making up the foundation board were representatives from the Hill at Whitemarsh, the WTRA, the Whitemarsh Valley Farms Community Association (a local neighborhood association), Whitemarsh Valley Country Club, and the Morris Arboretum. The Foundation will hire consultants to develop a compelling and achievable vision for the future of the "Angus Tract" to guide them in

Despite assurances that this complex would not compromise the viewshed, the developers cut down the little woodland at the crest of the hill where the new buildings are located, exposing the facility to public view from all nearby roads.

fundraising, and in the creation of preservation and land management strategies.[5]

As of early 2008, the Whitemarsh Foundation was in sight of raising the $14.5 million purchase price for the Angus Tract. Of that, $5 million came as part of a settlement (in December 2007) between the Commonwealth of Pennsylvania and the pharmaceutical firm, Merck and Company, which had spilled toxic chemicals into Wissahickon Creek from its Upper Gwynedd plant in June 2006. (Another $1.7 million from Merck will be used to create wetlands and a riparian buffer along the Wissahickon Creek. The company will contribute another $1.2 million for restoration).

Whitemarsh Township recently passed an earned income tax of 0.25 percent for open space protection and identified the preservation of Erdenheim Farm as a primary goal in its 2006 Open Space Plan. A portion of these new open space revenues will be directed towards helping secure the farm.[6]

1. WRTA to Dear WRTA Member, December 28, 2001; *Chestnut Hill Local*, February 21, 2002.

2. Kim Shepherd, telephone interview by Contosta, February 19, 2004.

3. *Philadelphia Inquirer*, December 15, 2007.

4. Hugh Molton, *Whitemarsh Vista*, July 2005.

5. *WTRA Newsletter*, July 2001.

6. Chris Van de Velde, Whitemarsh Township Manager Interview by authors, July 24, 2008.

Stormwater management was an opportunity to be innovative and protect Wissahickon Creek. Instead, the developers built a conventional and not very attractive retention basin.
Source: Photographs by CLF

The crisis over the Hill at Whitemarsh made many township residents aware that their board of supervisors was willing to go along with conventional suburban development and had initiated little positive action to promote the preservation of this exceptional open space. To change the political climate before elections, the WTRA held candidate forums. As a non-profit, the WTRA could not endorse any particular person seeking office, but responses to questions at these forums made members and other residents of the community aware of which candidates were in sympathy with open space preservation goals. Within four years, new supervisors, coming from both political parties, would replace the old board. These new supervisors would take a pro-active and environmentally aware approach to increasing development pressures in the township.[19]

With new supervisors and new public awareness, an agreement was drafted between Dixon and a consortium of public and private entities: The Hill at Whitemarsh, the Whitemarsh Foundation, the Whitemarsh Township Residents Association (WTRA), the Whitemarsh Valley Country Club, and the Whitemarsh Valley Farms Association. The agreement established the Whitemarsh Foundation to purchase and hold designated portions of Erdenheim Farm. On the foundation board there were representatives from the parties to the agreement with Dixon, with the addition of the Morris Arboretum.

The agreement included an option to purchase the 98-acre "Angus Tract," exercisable at Dixon's death. Whitemarsh Retirement Partners, LLC, would contribute $1 million toward the purchase, plus an additional $107,000 a year for the open-space acquisition fund. Montgomery County officials pledged $4 million for Erdenheim Farm open space protection—$2 million for the Angus Tract and $2 million for the Sheep Tract. Whitemarsh Township pledged $1.9 million from the state open space funding it had received.[20] The township also agreed to earmark property taxes from the Hill at Whitemarsh for the fund through the use of an important new conservation tool called "Tax Increment Financing" (TIF).

TIF, a pubic financing method, is a tool that uses future gains in taxes to finance current improvements.[21] Since there will be no school-age children living at the retirement complex, the Colonial School District would not face the additional expenses of new pupils and could forgo the estimated S15 million in tax revenues that the school district and the township would otherwise receive over a 30 year period. These "increased" revenues from the taxes on the new construction are the "tax increment." TIF dedicates the increased revenue to finance, in this case, a public land acquisition for conservation. This significant pot of money is collected yearly and is held by the foundation.

The TIF agreement with Whitemarsh Township is the first time in Pennsylvania, and perhaps in the nation, that this strategy was used to preserve a large swath of open space rather than to fund a construction project, and the first time this technique has been used to prevent, rather than to encourage development.

Other funds have come from the state, foundations and private sources. In July 2006, the Whitemarsh Foundation received a grant of $1 million from the Keystone 93 Fund administered by the Pennsylvania Department of Conservation and Natural Resources. Keystone 93 receives its support from 15% of the state's realty-transfer tax and provides grants mainly to acquire open space and fund the maintenance of park infrastructure. Dixon's death in July 2006, and the impending settlement of his estate, added urgency to plans to preserve as much of Erdenheim Farm as possible.

The Whitemarsh Foundation purchased the Angus Tract in 2008 for $13.5 million. Then, in 2009, the foundation bought the 91-acre sheep tract with $12.5 million in county and local funding. Agreements with the foundation will enable the Montgomery County Green Ribbon Trail to be completed between Fort Washington State Park and the Morris Arboretum, and the establishment of an environmental education center for Colonial School District.

While these purchases were being arranged, the foundation worked with all the interested parties to find a suitable buyer for the remaining 243 acres. A deal was eventually struck with Peter McCausland, chief executive officer of Airgas, to buy the land with extensive conservation easements. These easements will be held by the Natural Lands Trust. The McClausland family will live in the Dixon family home, overlooking Wissahickon Creek and continue to raise Angus cattle and Cheviot sheep. A member of the Dixon family will retain ownership of approximately 14 acres of the "Equestrian Tract" on the northeastern side of Stenton Avenue, also protected by conservation easements.[22] Agreements with the foundation will enable the Montgomery County Green Ribbon Trail to be completed between the Morris Arboretum and Fort Washington State Park. The agreement also provides for an environmental center for the Colonial School District and a small township dog park at Flourtown and Stenton Avenues, the western corner of the property.

Carson Valley School

The ups and downs of the Carson Valley School closely paralleled those of the Morris Arboretum and of Chestnut Hill College. In the decades after World War II, the school, in need of funds, drew up plans to develop parts of the property as an investment. The board considered abandoning the site altogether, as a number of other area institutions were threatening to do at the time and move to less expensive land further away from the city. Several obstacles kept Carson from relocating. The school was initially unable to secure the necessary bank loans to rebuild elsewhere. Later, Springfield Township refused to grant the necessary zoning changes.

For years, the child welfare community had been moving away from institutional care, insisting that foster care in real homes gave children a much better sense of family life. Fewer and fewer children were being placed in establishments like Carson. This attitude was part of a larger paradigm shift in 1960s and 1970s. The public began to believe that institutions mistreated their clients and that separating children from the larger community was detrimental.

At the same time, Carson could not reach out to Philadelphia's growing African American communities because its founder had limited enrollment to "whites only." In contrast to Philadelphia's all-white Girard College (which despite the name was actually an orphanage and a school), Carson's board voluntarily and successfully petitioned the courts to allow racial integration.[23] Under the leadership of chairman Anderson Page, the board took this position because it would help to increase their enrollment and because it was morally right. Like Chestnut Hill College and the Morris Arboretum, Carson had to open its doors to new and different constituencies to survive.

Again, like these other institutions, bringing on a strong, imaginative director was the key to leading the institution out of a constricted past. Like the arboretum, Carson hired a number of unsuccessful directors before bringing John Taaffe to the school in 1974.[23] Taaffe was pragmatic, innovative and energetic. He created a number of new programs, which emphasized short-term placement and diagnostic evaluation at Carson, so that children could be returned to their own families or sent to foster care. Carson Community Programs provided outreach facilities in Mt. Airy and North Philadelphia, which trained and supported foster care parents for children with special social and psychological needs. They also began programs to counsel families to prevent children from being taken from their homes.

Like the school's first director, Elsa Ueland, Taaffe was constantly on the lookout to forge ties with the larger community. The nursery school, established back in 1924, continued to serve parents in surrounding communities, some of them becoming donors to the institution or members of the board. These local residents sent their children to Carson because the picturesque cottages and the pastoral landscape charmed them.

One of Carson's greatest assets was land—altogether 100 acres. Their clustered buildings occupy only three to four acres. The rest of the land was given over to playing fields and farm fields. A 19th–century farmhouse and several attractive small barns front onto Bethlehem Pike, the main street of Flourtown, one of the old strip villages along historic roads out of Philadelphia. Taaffe recognized that Carson Valley School—this magical, fantasy village in the Wissahickon Valley—supported the children's emotional well-being. In 1986, after years of discussion, the board resolved that Carson would continue to require "a generous acreage for the fulfillment of [its] unique mission."[24]

These farm buildings and the land behind them suggest the possibility of using part of the Carson grounds for a Community Supported Agriculture (CSA) program. The house and barns along Bethlehem Pike make an inviting cluster that could be used for welcoming the public and selling farm products. The CSA could offer hands-on learning for adolescents at the school in a wide variety of disciplines—from horticultural to business organization. It could provide a real forum for the students to interact with the community and greater visibility for the institution. Locally grown fruits and vegetables would cut food costs, improve health and save money and energy. Most significantly, for the Wissahickon corridor, a CSA is a device to preserve farmland. It would give Carson a practical and self-sustaining use for its extensive open space.

By the early 2000s, the main institutions of the middle valley—Carson Valley School, Chestnut Hill College and the Morris Arboretum—had all renewed and reinvented themselves. By reconnecting to the local landscape and enhancing their original site plans and historic buildings, these institutions gained several benefits. They added to their legitimacy and stature by anchoring themselves in their rich pasts. By reaching out to new constituencies and creating partnerships with community groups, they found contemporary purpose. Without bold plans for a more relevant future, they would have decayed and eventually been sold for development. By preserving and incorporating the landscape of the Wissahickon Valley, they have enriched the fabric of the place.

Community Supported Agriculture

Community Supported Agriculture (CSA) could provide opportunities to preserve the working farmland in the middle valley. Carson Valley School is a prime location for such an experiment.

In describing CSAs, Suzanne DeMuth writes, "Community Supported Agriculture is a new idea in farming, one that has been gaining momentum since its introduction to the United States from Europe in the mid-1980s. The CSA concept originated in the 1960s in Switzerland and Japan, where consumers interested in safe food, and farmers seeking stable markets for their crops, joined together in economic partnerships. Today, farms in the U.S., known as CSAs, currently number more than 400. Most are located near urban centers in New England, the Middle Atlantic states, and the Great Lakes region, with growing numbers in other areas,

including the West Coast.

A CSA consists of a community of individuals who pledge support to a farm operation so that the farmland becomes, either legally or spiritually, the community's farm, with the growers and consumers providing mutual support and sharing the risks and benefits of food production. Typically, members or 'share-holders' of the farm or garden pledge in advance to cover the anticipated costs of the farm operation and the farmer's salary. In return, they receive shares in the farm's bounty throughout the growing season, as well as satisfaction gained from reconnecting to the land and participating directly in food production. Members also share in the risks of farming, including poor harvests due to unfavorable weather or pests. By direct sales to community members,

Behind the Carson farm buildings, fields that could support a CSA.   Source: Photograph by CLF

who have provided the farmer with working capital in advance, growers receive better prices for their crops, gain some financial security, and are relieved of much of the burden of marketing."[1]

---

1. Suzanne DeMuth, *Community Supported Agriculture (CSA): An Annotated Bibliography and Resource Guide*, September 1993.

Entrance into Carson Valley School from Bethlehem Pike, the main street of Flourtown. This view shows the complex of farm buildings available for a potential CSA. There are several large barns and ample parking.   Source: Photograph by CLF

The Golf Courses

The most fragile, and potentially least permanent open spaces in the middle valley are the three golf clubs with their extensive courses that add 631 private, undeveloped acres along the Wissahickon corridor. All private and semi-private lands (not under easement) are vulnerable, but golf courses are particularly so. They are at the mercy of their own popularity and of the popularity of the sport. If they lose members and are not financially viable, they must sell. Golf clubs in the area have a long history of selling their property and relocating on cheaper land farther from the city.

From north to south, the golf clubs of the middle valley are Sunnybrook Golf Club, the Philadelphia Cricket Club and Whitemarsh Valley Country Club. Well-known early 20th-century designers planned all three courses. Donald Ross, creator of North Carolina's Pinehurst Golf Course (in 1907), and the most celebrated of these designers, laid out the original Sunnybrook course. A. W. Tillinghast designed the course at the Philadelphia Cricket Club's Flourtown site.[25] The course at the Whitemarsh Valley Country Club was the work of George C. Thomas, Jr., who had sold the land to the club from his estate, Bloomfield Farm, with the rest being purchased by John Morris for the Morris Estate (later the Morris Arboretum).[26]

The fate of Sunnybrook Golf Club, founded in 1913 and originally located on East Mill Road along Sunny Brook in Flourtown, is a cautionary tale. In 1954, partly because the projected Route 309 Expressway would take some of its property, the club sold the easternmost end of the course to Springfield Township. This land was then leased as a nine-hole course to the Flourtown Country Club. Sunnybrook sold the rest of the property for tract housing. New impervious surfaces—roofs, driveways, streets and large open lawns—combined with the destruction of the natural drainage system to pour massive amounts of stormwater directly into Sunny Brook. Local authorities coped with these problems by putting the stream into a straight, open concrete channel, with little bordering vegetation. These "improvements" to this Wissahickon tributary leaves it engorged with water during storms and bone dry in intervening periods. Water gushes from the brook into Wissahickon Creek during a storm, but in periods of drought, Sunny Brook cannot contribute to the flow.

Sunnybrook Golf Club then built a new course further out in the middle valley, at the intersection of Stenton Avenue and Joshua Road. (The Gordon Brothers, creators of the famous Saucon Valley course in Bethlehem, Pennsylvania, designed the new course). This 135-acre site skirts Lorraine Run, an important tributary of the Wissahickon. In 2001, the club bought an additional 33 acres, which it placed under an open space easement with the Montgomery County Lands Trust and the Preservation Alliance of Philadelphia.[27]

The Philadelphia Cricket Club, with 321 acres and two eighteen-hole golf courses, is the largest of the three. In 2002, it opened its new Militia Hill course. This land had been left undeveloped since the early 1920s and allowed to return to successional forest. The designers of the new course, Micheal Hurzdan and Dana Frye, are also well-known designers of a number of American golf courses, including the Desert Willow/Firecliff Course in Palm Springs, California.

The design of the Milita Hill course builds on the successional landscape and preserves the regional character. Instead of a traditional manicured golf course, these links keep the "roughs" in meadow with groves of trees. Milita Hill offers an unusual and

16:22

Golf Courses

Although the Whitemarsh Valley Country Club protects an important section of Wissahickon Creek with its broad floodplain and oxbow, the lack of a riparian corridor, along with the runoff from greens and fairways, has taken a toll on the creek.

In contrast, the Philadelphia Cricket Club's new Militia Hill course represents a more aesthetic and ecological approach.
Source: Photographs by CLF

strikingly beautiful landscape, which together with the club's adjoining older course, protect the lower portion of Lorraine Run. These courses are the open space link between Erdenheim Farm and Fort Washington State Park.

Militia Hill, the larger and more challenging course, was intended to expand the club's membership and attract younger golfers. It has successfully reinvigorated this recreational resource. This major investment suggests that the Philadelphia Cricket Club will remain in the area.

The 122-acre Whitemarsh Valley Country Club is also a critical piece of the open space along the main stem of Wissahickon Creek. It is the connection between the Morris Arboretum to the south and the Natural Lands Trust portion of Erdenheim Farm to the north. This property protects the large oxbow along Wissahickon Creek. The backwater channel and the small island of this oxbow provide an important reservoir for floodwaters.

The better manicured the lawn, the greater the runoff. The Whitemarsh Valley Country Club grounds are almost entirely lawn. The creek floods frequently from the volumes of water upstream and from the runoff from the course itself. Low-lying areas are inundated even during small storms. The creek is not buffered by a riparian corridor because golfers believe that trees and shrubs would interfere with their game. As a result, the banks and the channel of the Wissahickon Creek, which passes through the Whitemarsh Valley Country Club, are badly eroded, with no deeply rooted vegetation to hold the banks, shade the water or provide nutrients for aquatic life.

To maintain the quality of the fairways and greens, all three clubs use large amounts of herbicides, pesticides and fertilizers. These chemicals add non-point source pollution to the runoff flowing into the creek and its tributaries. Nonetheless, if these properties were to be sold and developed, flooding, pollution and stream degradation would, almost certainly, become more severe.

The Quarries

The sale of the old Corson lime quarries to Highway Materials, Inc. opened the door for the new owners, the DePaul Group, to propose a huge office/apartment complex on the site. The land forms a triangle that separates the Philadelphia Cricket Club's golf course and Erdenheim Farm.

The quarries once included three holes of varying sizes. The oldest and smallest hole (54.36 acres) has been filled, the second hole (67.29 acres) is partially filled and the third (190.7 acres) is still operated to mine highway construction materials, chiefly aggregate.

In 2001, the DePaul Group submitted a sketch plan to the township for a mixed-use office park for the newly created land made by filling the first hole. This DePaul plan proposed a million-plus-square-foot development with four four-story office buildings, three seven-story apartment buildings and parking for 3,450 cars. The township's Traffic Impact Study estimated that this development would generate an additional 5,600 car trips per day on the area's narrow, two-lane roads. This additional traffic would ultimately force the widening of both Stenton Avenue and Joshua Road.[29]

Picturesque country roads are an endangered species in the middle valley. These roads roll up and down with the undulating landscape and give a sequence of shifting views. The outcry over the Angus Tract at Erdenheim Farm was over the loss of a viewshed

16:23

16:24

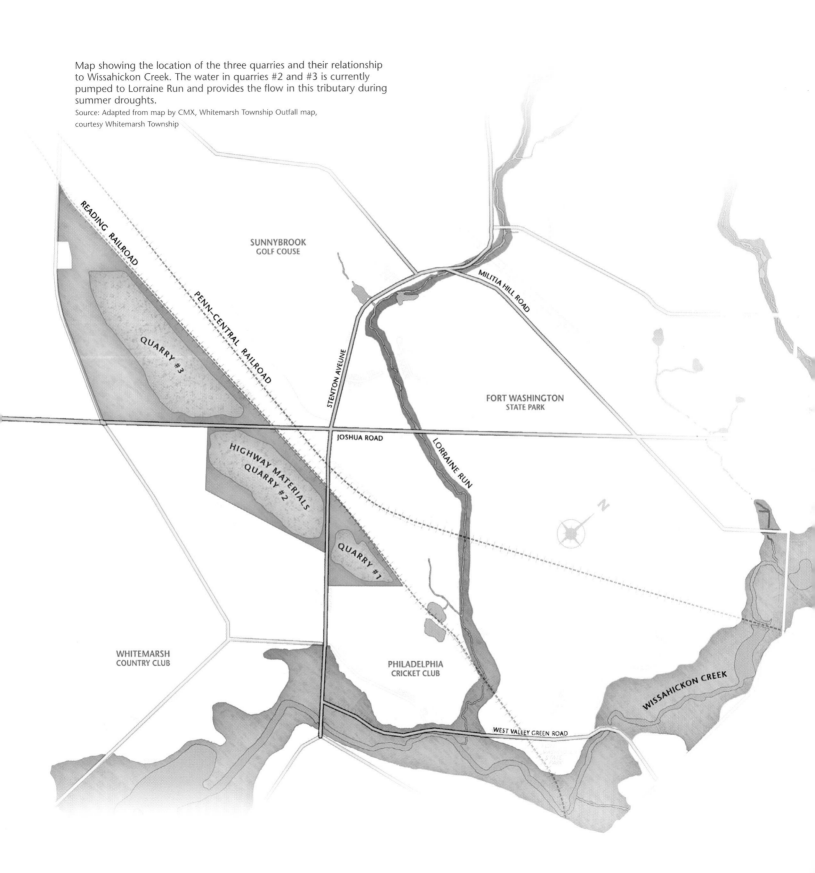

Map showing the location of the three quarries and their relationship to Wissahickon Creek. The water in quarries #2 and #3 is currently pumped to Lorraine Run and provides the flow in this tributary during summer droughts.

Source: Adapted from map by CMX, Whitemarsh Township Outfall map, courtesy Whitemarsh Township

READING RAILROAD

PENN–CENTRAL RAILROAD

SUNNYBROOK
GOLF COUSE

MILITIA HILL ROAD

STENTON AVEUNE

QUARRY #3

FORT WASHINGTON
STATE PARK

JOSHUA ROAD

HIGHWAY MATERIALS
QUARRY #2

LORRAINE RUN

N

QUARRY #1

WHITEMARSH
COUNTRY CLUB

PHILADELPHIA
CRICKET CLUB

WISSAHICKON CREEK

WEST VALLEY GREEN ROAD

The Quarries

The three quarries owned by the DePaul Group are in a critical location between Erdenheim Farm to the south and two golf courses to the east and north. Greedy and insensitive development of these quarries would negatively impact the entire middle valley. On the other hand, the quarries provide a very interesting opportunity to create a vibrant mixed used community, built into the quarry sides, largely invisible from the surrounding properties.

For Whitemarsh Township, Simone, Jaffee, Collins, Inc., Landscape Architects (later Simone Collins, Landscape Architects) identified three possible traffic scenarios: improvement of Flourtown Road as a connector from Stenton Avenue to the Blue Route and the Pennsylvania Turnpike at the existing Plymouth Meeting interchange; widening of upper Stenton Avenue as a connector to a new interchange at the turnpike; an improvement of Joshua Road

as a connector to a new interchange further east on the turnpike.

The key to a sucessful development here is providing site access, without destroying the fabric of the rural roads. Instead of making Stenton Avenue and Joshua Road into double lane divided highways, a network of new smaller roads should be created. These ideas are consistent with the latest and best thinking from traffic engineers such as Glatting Jackson.

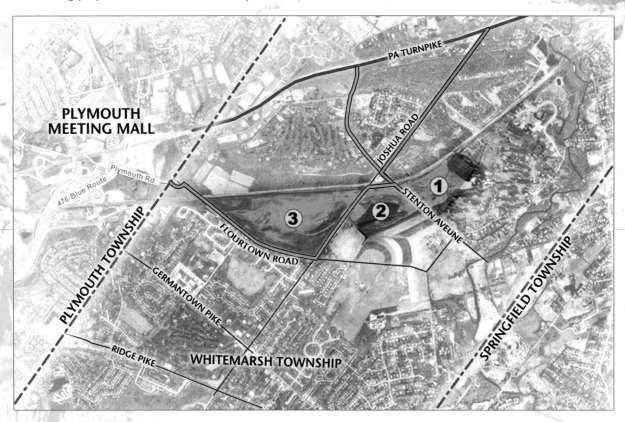

Plan showing the three potential traffic scenarios suggested by Simone, Jaffee, Collins, Inc., Landscape Architects (later Simone Collins, Landscape Architects).
Source: Simone, Jaffee, Collins, Inc., Whitemarsh Township Quarry Site, December 2001

The first quarry (filled).

The second quarry (partially filled).

The third quarry (operating).

Source: Photographs by CLF

Hedgerow of white ash (*Fraxinus americana*) and red maple (*Acer rubrum*) Source: Andropogon, drawing by Colin Franklin

Scattered groves of trees and dotted columnar red cedars (*Juniperus virginiana*) accent this gently rolling meadow. Wildflowers often grow along the fence where it is difficult to mow.

The Texture and Flavor of the Middle Valley

16:24

The texture and fabric of the middle valley grows out of the underlying geology, the gently rolling terrain and the remaining pastoral landscapes of hedgerows, meadows, woodlots, country lanes and rural vernacular architecture. Unlike the darker colors of the gorge, with its Wissahickon schist, the light limestone, ranging in color from almost pure white to ivory, sand and grey, is typical of the middle valley.

Most rural landscapes are characterized by simple, bold elements—with hedgerows, single specimen trees and geometric structures silhouetted against wide swathes of sky. Even with contemporary development, these evocative elements can be incorporated into new designs.

A typical older house in the middle valley covered with a white "limestone wash."
Source: Photographs by CLF

Tulip poplar (*Liriodendron tulipifera*) groves in this meadow create a savannah.

A country road rolls with the landscape.
Source: Andropogon, drawings by Colin Franklin

A country road in the middle valley, with overarching trees, views of fields beyond and no curb or gutter.

from a country road. When a country road becomes a highway, the experience is noisy and unsightly, and the attributes of the countryside are diminished. Narrow thoroughfares have many other benefits. They calm traffic, bring people through the landscape and, as part of a larger network of intersecting roads, provide alternative routes.

On October 18, 2001, the Whitemarsh Township Board of Supervisors voted to turn down plans for developing the first quarry, citing a range of adverse impacts, including traffic, building density, and environmental concerns. At the urging of the WTRA, the supervisors also unanimously voted to change the zoning of the quarries from "heavy industrial" to "extraction." This zoning would remain in place until quarrying operations were completed. The zoning would then change to AAA-residential, the same as the surrounding area, which only allows a single-family dwelling per acre.[29] The township had scrambled frantically to beat the DePaul submission by rezoning the land. However, they missed the submission by a few days. The plan conformed to the old zoning and was legal.

The developer filed two court suits against the township supervisors and leading township officials: a suit in state court challenging the legality of the township's zoning changes for the quarry site, and a suit in federal court charging discrimination. In 2008, Judge Kent Albright of the Montgomery County Common Pleas Court ruled against the township. The township appealed to the commonwealth court, but was denied. The township has no plans to appeal this decision.

In the midst of the recession of 2009, the developer expressed a desire to build intensive housing instead of the office park, particularly where the parcel abuts the Philadelphia Cricket Club golf course and Erdenheim Farm. The township had rezoned the site for one house per acre. Highway Materials, Inc. claimed they needed a denser development to realize their investment. According to the *Philadelphia Inquirer*, "Unless all parties find a way to compromise, Whitemarsh faces the prospect of a new office park that neither its would-be developer, nor the township seems to want."[30] Regardless of what happens at the smaller quarry, complete development of the entire 300-acre site will take decades. The length of time for filling the other two quarry holes is estimated at 15 years for the second hole and 40 years for the third.

At some point there will probably be a compromise. The developers' threat to go through with the office park is a way of gaining leverage with the township. The township is legally bound to allow an office park because its rejection of the DePaul plan was overruled by the courts. However, if the developers want to build intensive residential they will have to get the zoning changed, which would give the township substantial bargaining power.[31] The present glut of both housing and office space should delay any development for an indefinite period, but the threat of inappropriate development still poisons the gains of the preservation of Erdenheim Farm and the quality and character of the middle valley.

State and County Parkland

In the early 20th century, the dream of a number of civic leaders in both Chestnut Hill and in the middle valley had been to extend parkland along the Wissahickon from

Fort Washington State Park

In the early 20th century the state authorized the acquisition of a substantial riparian park along Wissahickon Creek in the middle valley. For a while, in the late 1940s and early 1950s, it looked as if this plan would become reality. The Fairmount Park Commission—a state chartered institution—continued to have charge of both Fort Washington State Park in the suburbs and Wissahickon Park in the city. This joint administration was theoretically in a position to manage the whole valley as an integrated system. After World War II, the commission began to take additional property for Fort Washington State Park. Legislators in Montgomery County saw these acquisitions as a "stalking horse" to annex the suburbs, causing the whole effort to grind to a halt. In 1953, Montgomery County legislators convinced the Pennsylvania General Assembly to strip control of Fort Washington Park from the Fairmount Park Commission and put it under the authority of the Pennsylvania Department of Forests and Waters (later known as the Pennsylvania Department of Conservation and Natural Resources, DCNR). The separation and segregation of these two parks along the Wissahickon revealed the hostility of the postwar suburbs to any cooperation with the City of Philadelphia.[1]

Over the next five decades, Fort Washington State Park added a few modest holdings, as they became available. Later acquisitions along Wissahickon Creek by Montgomery County, and still others by the WWA, would eventually tie these areas together (tenuously).

The Wissahickon Creek in Fort Washington State Park near Cricket Road.
Source: Photograph by CLF

the Philadelphia city limits to the village of Fort Washington. State lawmakers had passed enabling legislation, but largely failed to fund this project, mainly acquiring a few Revolutionary War sites in the 1920s. The state originally placed these properties under control of the Fairmount Park Commission because the Park Extension Committee had envisioned these two park properties as a single entity—both inside and outside municipal boundaries. Jurisdiction over both properties was possible because the Fairmount Park Commission held its charter from the state and was not a city agency. This extraordinary example of regional governance was an idea well before its time.

16:25-26

In the late 1940s, Fairmount Park Commissioners began to acquire more property for this park, in some cases taking land through eminent domain. In an increasingly suburban Montgomery County, these initiatives alarmed residents. State representatives convinced the Pennsylvania General Assembly to strip control of Fort Washington State Park from the Fairmount Park Commission and put it instead under the Pennsylvania Department of Forests and Waters (later known as the Pennsylvania Department of Conservation and Natural Resources, or PA DCNR).[32] Under state administration, Fort Washington State Park has added only a few small parcels. At the beginning of the 21st century, this park was only 393 acres, just 36 percent of the 1,100 acres authorized by the state legislature back in 1915, and only 143 acres more than the park had owned in 1935.[33]

This parkland was also fragmented into four separate pieces: one, just west of Flourtown; a second at Militia Hill; a third at Fort Hill; and a fourth along Sandy Run. Making up for the shortsightedness of the state, Montgomery County has gradually acquired an additional 143 acres to link these four pieces. Called Wissahickon Valley Park, this county property, together with Fort Washington State Park, forms the bulk of public parkland along Wissahickon Creek and its tributaries in the middle valley.

By 2008, there were over 3,000 acres of public, private and semi-private open space in the Wissahickon corridor, between the end of Fairmount Park in Philadelphia and Fort Washington in Montgomery County. Such a corridor offers remarkable opportunities for the whole region and the potential for the imaginative interfingering of natural and built areas that could transform this region into one of the most livable in the country.

16:27

However, while park acreage has increased in the middle valley, the protected pieces are often thin bands along the main stem—too narrow to safeguard the integrity of the creek. In several places, the creek is protected only on one side and almost all the tributaries—from Andorra Run to Sandy Run—directly abut houses, office buildings or commercial areas. These tributaries are in very poor ecological health and are vulnerable to further damage from insensitive development.

Linking the Middle Valley

A trail along the Wissahickon Creek corridor, now called the "Wissahickon Green Ribbon Trail," links the city's park system with the two public parks of the middle

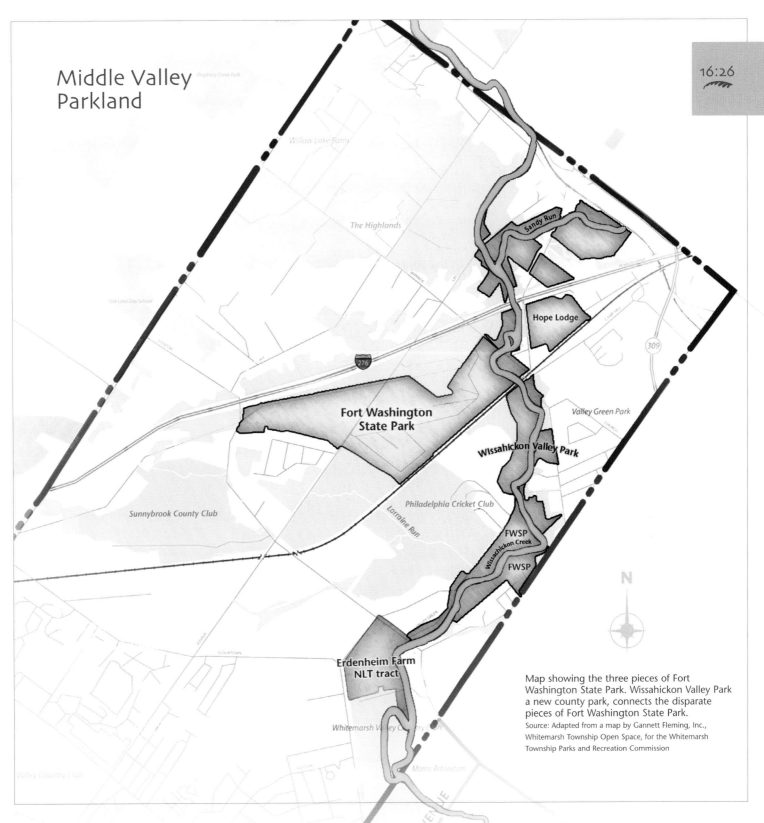

Middle Valley
Parkland

Willow Lake Farm

The Highlands

Sandy Run

Hope Lodge

309

Fort Washington
State Park

Valley Green Park

Wissahickon Valley Park

Sunnybrook County Club

Philadelphia Cricket Club

Lorraine Run

Wissahickon Creek

FWSP

FWSP

N

Erdenheim Farm
NLT tract

Map showing the three pieces of Fort
Washington State Park. Wissahickon Valley Park
a new county park, connects the disparate
pieces of Fort Washington State Park.

Source: Adapted from a map by Gannett Fleming, Inc.,
Whitemarsh Township Open Space, for the Whitemarsh
Township Parks and Recreation Commission

Whitemarsh Valley Country Club

Morris Arboretum

Open Space in the Middle Valley: 2005

Together the WWA, the Montgomery County Parks System and the State Park System have preserved 1,624 acres, giving this area almost as much public open space along the Wissahickon corridor as the Wissahickon portion of Fairmount Park in Philadelphia. With the holdings of semi-public institutions and large private properties in the middle valley, the land in open space totals 3078.5 acres.

(Listed in Alphabetical Order)

Property	Acres
Carson Valley School	98.0
Chestnut Hill College	47.0
Erdenheim Farm	398.0
Fort Washington State Park	493.0
Morris Arboretum	166.0
National Lands Trust (Erdenheim Farm)	117.0
Philadelphia Cricket Club	321.1
Sunnybrook Golf Club	188.0
Whitemarsh Valley Country Club	122.2
Wissahickon Valley Park (Montgomery County)	143.0
Wissahickon Valley Watershed Association	988.0
Total	**3,081.3**

View of fields at the Equestrian Center at Erdenheim Farm, typical of the pastoral landscape of the middle valley, still in farm fields, meadows and woodlands.

Source: Photograph by CLF

valley—Fort Washington State Park and Wissahickon Valley Park. Nearly 20 miles long, this trail begins at the confluence of Wissahickon Creek and the Schuylkill River in Philadelphia, and ends in Upper Gwynedd Township in Montgomery County.[23] Montgomery County has a long-standing history of trail development that began with the construction of the first phase of the Schuylkill River Trail in the late 1970s. This trail is a designated National Recreation Trail that connects Valley Forge National Historic Park to Center City, Philadelphia.

The Wissahickon Green Ribbon Trail is a joint effort of Montgomery County, DCNR and the WVWA.[34] It runs through the middle valley as a multi-use trail that will ultimately connect the Morris Arboretum to Fort Washington State Park. This trail will also join the Cross County Trail that loops back to the Schuykill River at Conshohocken. At present, there are significant gaps in this trail system with several sections incomplete and unresolved. With the new ownership of Erdenheim Farm, one section of this trail will border that property.

Several sections of the completed trail are uninspiring. They parallel roads and not the creek. Neither Chestnut Hill College nor the Morris Arboretum wanted a public trail to run through the center of their property, despite the fact that in both cases, the creek is well away from the main buildings, and the county would have fenced the trail along the creek to discourage off-trail wanderings. Where the trail is adjacent to a road, the experience is impoverished. The opportunity to make people aware of these institutions, and what they have to offer, has been lost.

16:28

A completed section of the Green Ribbon Trail curves around one corner of Bloomfield Farm at the Morris Arboretum of the University of Pennsylvania, on its way to connect with Forbidden Drive in Wissahickon Park. Although the trail is pulled back slightly from Northwestern Avenue, the main user experience is the asphalt road.
Source: Photograph by CLF

A critical connection is without an actual trail on a heavily trafficked road.
Source: Photograph by CLF

Possible trail route along Stenton Avenue at the Equestrian Tract of Erdenheim Farm. The horse path is defined by two parallel, split rail fences. Because it is raised above the road edge, the traffic all but disappears and the path seems to be a part of the field beyond. As an extension of the Green Ribbon Trail, this route would give a wonderful sense of travelling through the pastoral landscape of the middle valley.
Source: Photograph by CLF

At the edge of a piece of Fort Washington State Park, the trail is flush with the road and users experience neither the creek nor the thin band of parkland along it.
Source: Photograph by CLF

Wissahickon Green Ribbon Trail

In the middle valley, the Green Ribbon Trail runs through the lower section of Fort Washington State Park. In this broader, flatter floodplain the trail is located some distance from the creek to minimize flood damage. The surrounding forest often obscures views of the water. Without views of the creek and without the destinations and events along the journey typical of Wissahickon Park, this trail is relatively uninteresting.

Although very different in character from trails in Wissahickon Park, the Green Ribbon Trail can be beautiful in places. However, the forest here is very young. It is compromised by deer and by invasive exotics. At the Stenton Avenue entry and other places along the trail, the park is very narrow and is encroached on by housing.

Source: Photographs by CLF

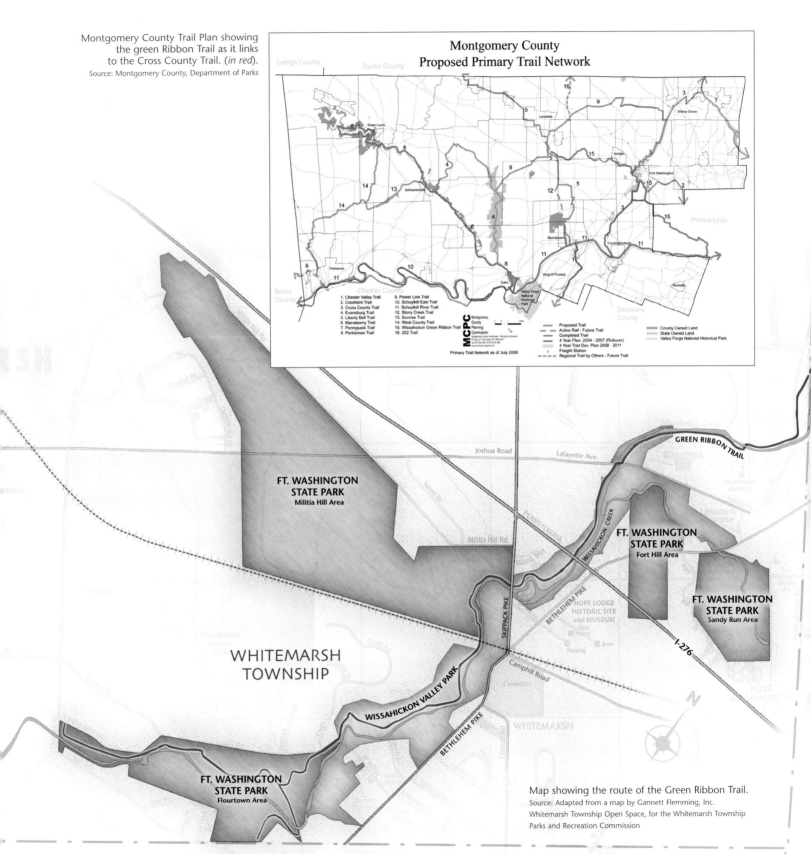

Montgomery County Trail Plan showing
the green Ribbon Trail as it links
to the Cross County Trail. (*in red*).
Source: Montgomery County, Department of Parks

Montgomery County
Proposed Primary Trail Network

1. Chester Valley Trail
2. Cresheim Trail
3. Cross County Trail
4. Evansburg Trail
5. Liberty Bell Trail
6. Manatawny Trail
7. Pennypack Trail
8. Perkiomen Trail
9. Power Line Trail
10. Schuylkill East Trail
11. Schuylkill River Trail
12. Stony Creek Trail
13. Sunrise Trail
14. West County Trail
15. Wissahickon Green Ribbon Trail
16. 202 Trail

MCPC
Montgomery
County
Planning
Commission

Primary Trail Network as of July 2008

Proposed Trail
Active Rail - Future Trail
Completed Trail
4 Year Plan 2004 - 2007 (Rollover)
4 Year Trail Dev. Plan 2008 - 2011
Freight Station
Regional Trail by Others - Future Trail

County Owned Land
State Owned Land
Valley Forge National Historical Park

GREEN RIBBON TRAIL

**FT. WASHINGTON
STATE PARK**
Militia Hill Area

**FT. WASHINGTON
STATE PARK**
Fort Hill Area

**FT. WASHINGTON
STATE PARK**
Sandy Run Area

HOPE LODGE
HISTORIC SITE
and MUSEUM

Joshua Road

Lafayette Ave.

Militia Hill Rd

PENNSYLVANIA

Wissahickon Creek

I-276

**WHITEMARSH
TOWNSHIP**

WISSAHICKON VALLEY PARK

Camphill Road

BETHLEHEM PIKE

Skippack Pike

WHITEMARSH

**FT. WASHINGTON
STATE PARK**
Flourtown Area

Map showing the route of the Green Ribbon Trail.
Source: Adapted from a map by Gannett Flemming, Inc.
Whitemarsh Township Open Space, for the Whitemarsh Township
Parks and Recreation Commission

SPRINGFIELD TOWNSHIP

Middle Valley Renaissance

Greed, lack of imagination and a disinterest in the idea of community characterized early post-World War II development in the middle valley. Multiple governing jurisdictions and weak political structures have made it difficult to create and administer a coherent open space system along the Wissahickon corridor. With vision and cooperative planning, the middle valley could become one of the most forward-looking and vital places to live in the Middle Atlantic States. Failure to take this opportunity will doom this once spectacularly beautiful area to the homogeniety of urban sprawl, and saddle it with increasing problems of flood and drought.

Notes

The notes and index for all four volumes of this work are found in Volume IV, pages 845-901. In addition, in a nod to reader friendliness, the notes for the first three volumes are repeated on un-numbered pages at the end of each of those volumes.

Chapter 12: Prosperity and Pressures (1945-1960s)

1. Website: Citizens Council on City Planning, library.temple.edu/collections/urbana/urb10-01.jsp?bhcp=1

2. John Andrew gallery, *The Planning of Center City Philadelphia: from William Penn to the Present* (Philadelphia, 2007), 32-34.

3. Joseph S. Clark, Jr., and Dennis J. Clark, "Rally and Relapse 1946-1968," in *Philadelphia: A 300 Year History,* 654-55.

4. Ibid.

5. *Philadelphia Daily News*, June 5, 2001.

6. Nathaniel Burt, *The Perennial Philadelphians* (Boston, 1963), 219.

7. Conversation with Mark A. Focht, Fairmount Park Director, May 8, 2008.

8. Fairmount Park Commission Fact Sheet, FPC; Mark A. Focht, (then) Program Administrator, FPC, interview by authors, May 6, 2003; Peter Harnik, *Inside City Parks* (Washington D.C.,. 2000), 42-44.

9. For a good contemporary account of Germantown's decay, see Mark Frazier Lloyd, "Germantown in Review, October 1978 through October 1979," *Germantown Crier* (1979), 89-91.

10. Wikiopedia, Redlining, Website: en.wikipedia.org/wiki/Redlining

11. Ibid.

12. See David R. Contosta, "Philadelphia's Miniature Williamsburg: The Colonial Revival and Germantown's Market Square," *Pennsylvania Magazine of History and Biography* (October 1996), 283-320.

13. Ironically, there was a remarkable stock of architecturally significant colonial-era buildings in the Germantown area, and the Germantown Historical Society had, over time, acquired a number of these, including several houses given by Lawrence and Eleanor Houston Smith. One of these was the Clarkson-Watson House, where John Fanning Watson, writer of the pioneering oral history, The *Annals of Philadelphia*, had once lived. The historical society, fixed on the idea of house museums, did not seek imaginative, adaptive reuses for these properties, and was eventually overwhelmed by the expense of maintaining them. In the end, many of these houses had to be sold.

14. The Chestnut Hill/Mt. Airy Businessmen's Association, established as early as 1913, had once been very active in community affairs, but had become moribund in the postwar period as its leaders aged or died. Lloyd P. Wells, interview by authors, March 2005. Lloyd P. Wells, interview by Contosta, September 8, 1985; Eli Schmidt, interview by Contosta, March 25, 1985; Russell L, Medinger, interview by Contosta April 22, 1985; Contosta, *Suburb in the City*, 216-30.

15. Helen Moak, "The Chestnut Hill Experiment: Renewal of an American Community," reprinted from *Chestnut Hill Local* in Lloyd P. Wells and Larry Lemmel, *Recreating Democracy* (Woolwich, Maine, 1998), xv-xvi.

16. Wells, note to authors, April 2006.

17. Wells founded the *Chestnut Hill Local* after the old paper, the *Herald*, came under new management, and was no longer willing to promote community projects. Wells, interview by authors, March 2005. For details on Wells's problems with the *Herald* and his decision to create a new newspaper, see Contosta, *Suburb in the City*, 236-38.

18. Contosta, *Suburb in the City*, 236-38.

19. Ibid., 216-230; Wells, interview by authors, March 2005.

20. Chestnut Hill Community Association, Land Use Planning Committee "Chestnut Hill Land Use Guidelines," (Philadelphia, 1982).

21. This unity of materials and treatment, which gives older villages in America and elsewhere in the world, their striking charm and coherence, is surprisingly absent in the outlying areas of most American cities, again, probably a result of the ruthless destruction of the old and the hasty, careless development in the post-World War II boom period.

22. Richard Wood Snowden, interview by authors, May 10, 2008.

23. Contosta, *Suburb in the City*, 245; Wells, note to authors, December 6, 2007.

24. Alexis de Tocqueville, *Democracy in America*, (reprint, New York, 2000), 630-32.

Chapter 13:
An Environmental Sensibility (1950-1976)

1. Kirkpatrick Sale, *The Green Revolution: The American Environmental Movement, 1962-1992* (New York, 1993), 5-9.

2. Ibid., 5.

3. Hal K. Rothman, *The Greening of a Nation: Environmentalism in the United States Since 1945* (New York, 1998), 121-25. Sale, Green Revolution, 11. One indication that Earth Day very quickly became a centrist event was the decision by the FOW to alert all its members to this celebration. See FOW Board Minutes, April 9, 1970.

4. Rothman, *Greening of a Nation*, 84-93.

5. FOW Board Minutes, October 10, 1950. FOW trail maps found at the CHHS archives were issued in 1940, 1950, 1954, 1972, 1974, 1978, 1990, 1995, 2001 and 2005.

6. National Park Service, Historic Landscape Initiative, Website: www.nps.gov/history/hps/hli/program

7. FOW Board Minutes, June 2, 1970.

8. Contosta, *A Philadelphia Family*, 119-20.

9. Eleanor Houston Smith, Interview by Contosta, December 11, 1984, and March 13, 1987. Eleanor Smith Morris, Interview by authors, May, 4, 2006, and letter to authors, May 9, 2006. The authors are also indebted to Morris for sharing her collection of articles relating to the development of Upper Roxborough.

10. Ibid.

11. FOW Board Minutes, March 5, May 6, and October 7, 1971, February 7, 1972.

12. *Chestnut Hill Local*, March 16, 1972.

13. *Philadelphia Inquirer*, March 22 and 24, June 21, 1972. See also *The Chestnut Hill Local*, January 6, March 16 and 23, August 31, and September 21, 1972.

14. *Chestnut Hill Local*, November 10, 1983.

15. Saul School Website: www.phila.k12.pa.us/schools/saul/

16. Robert Coughlin, interview by Contosta, April 7, 2003; *Chestnut Hill Local*, July 25 and August 12, 1976.

17. Robert Coughlin and Thomas Harmon, *Wissahickon Watershed Guidelines*, Philadelphia City Planning Commission, (Philadelphia 1976), 7. West Mt. Airy Neighbors (WMAN), *Mt. Airy Quality of Life Handbook*, Section V. Complete Guide to Zoning in West Mt. Airy. Website: wman.net/quality.htm#zoning. "The Philadelphia Zoning Code includes both a written description defining the zoning districts or classifications and a map that assigns a zoning classification to each parcel of land within the city. The text describes the uses permitted in each district as a matter of right and, in some districts, the uses that are permitted with a certificate from the Zoning Board of Adjustment. Each district also regulates the lot width and area; the occupied portion of the lot; the building setback line; front, side and rear yards; and the building height. Parking requirements may be included ...." Both the Zoning Code and zoning maps are available at the Philadelphia Planning Commission's Website, www.philaplanning.org.

18. *Wissahickon Watershed Guidelines*, 7

19. Ibid., 16.

Chapter 14:
The Wissahickon in Crisis (1975-1990)

1. United States Census Bureau, Census 2000.

2. Harnik, *Inside City Parks*, 41-45.

3. Ibid., 42-43.

4. William Hengst, "Park Guards in Danger of Abolishment, *FOW Newsletter* (Spring, 1998). See also ibid. (Spring, 1993) and *Chestnut Hill Local*, February 12, 1998.

5. *Philadelphia Evening Bulletin*, May 31, 1981.

6. John Naisbitt, *Mind Set!: Reset Your Thinking and See the Future* (New York, 2006), 15

7. Deborah J. Chavez, "Recreational Mountain Biking: A Management Perspective," *Journal of Park and Recreation Administration*, Fall 1993, 29-36; *FOW Newsletter* (Autumn, 1993): *Philadelphia Inquirer*, October 2, 1990. Bob D'Antonia, *Mountain Bike America: Greater Philadelphia* (Guilford, Conn., 2000), 38-51.

8. Nalbandian, interview by authors, April 15, 2008. See also EPA, Website: www.epa.gov/watertrain/protection/index2.html Stream Health

9. The authors are indebted to Thomas Cahill of Cahill Associates, Environmental Consultants, who, many years ago, brought to our attention the interconnection of water related issues—storm water, groundwater, wastewater, flood control and water supply—and who explained these ideas so clearly and convincingly.

10. Nalbandian, interview by authors, April 15, 2008.

11. City of Philadelphia, Combined Sewer Overflow Program, Philadelphia Water Department, Website: www.phillyriverinfo.org/CSOLTCPU/; *Philadelphia Inquirer*, May 26, 2003.

12. Ibid.

13. Pennsylvania Department of Environmental Protection, "Stream Redesignation Evaluation Report, Water Quality Standards Review, Wissahickon Creek," Segment: Source to Route 73 Bridge Drainage List: Stream Code: Water Quality Monitoring Section (APF), Division of Water Quality Standards, Bureau of Water Standards and Facility Regulation (October,2006), Website: www.depweb.state.pa.us/watersupply/cwp/view.aspa=1261&q=51770

14. For general soil information see David C. Coleman, D. A. Crossley and Paul F. Hendrix, *Fundamentals of Soil Ecology* (Burlington, Mass., 2004); Meet the Microbes, Fungi and Bacteria: The Fundamental Fertilizers. Website: www.microbeworld.org/microbes/mergers/fungi.aspx); Alexandra Contosta (doctoral student in soil ecology, University of New Hampshire), comments to authors, April 30, 2008.

15. Leslie Jones Sauer, *The Once and Future Forest, A Guide to Forest Restoration Strategies* (Washington D.C., 1998), 152. See also Ch. 17; E.A.Paul ed., *Soil Microbiology, Ecology, and Biochemistry* (Burlington, Mass., 2007).

16. Alexandra Contosta comments to authors, April 30, 2008; Wikipedia, Website: en.wikipedia.org/wiki/Mycorrhiza

17. Carleton S. White and Mark J. McDonnell, "Nitrogen Cycling Processes and Soil Characteristics in an Urban verses Rural Forest," *Biochemistry*, 1988, 243-262.

18. For a different view see Stephen J. Gould, "An Evolutionary Perspective on Strengths, Fallacies, and Confusions in the Concept of Native Plants," *Arnoldia, (*Spring, 1998), 3-10.

19. Chris Bright, *Life Out of Bounds: Bioinvasion in a Borderless World* (New York, 1998), 21.

20. Katalin Szlavecz, Sarah A. Placella, Richard V. Pouyat, Peter M. Groffman, Csaba Csuzdi and Ian Yesilonis, "Invasive Earthworm Species and Nitrogen Cycling in Remnant Forest Patches," *Applied Soil Ecology*, 2006, 32:54-62. See also Will Nixon, "As the Worm Turns," *American Forests* (Autumn, 1995), 36; Dennis Burton, "The Trouble With Worms," *FOW Newsletter* (Summer, 2003).

21. Bryon P. Shissler, Natural Resource Consultants, Inc., telephone interview by Contosta, March 2, 2004; *FOW Newsletter* (Summer, 1993, Fall, 1996); Stephen B. Jones et al., "Whitetails Are Changing Our Woodlands," *American Forests* (December, 1993), 20-25; *Philadelphia Inquirer*, November 9, 1995; *Chestnut Hill Local*, February 22, March 21, 1996, April 23, 1998; FOW Board Minutes, February 7, 1995; *FOW Newsletter* (Summer 1996, Spring, 1997).

22. Wikipedia, Website: Lyme Disease, http://en.wikipedia.org/wiki/Lyme_disease

23. G. R. Matlack and J.A. Litvaitis, "Forest Edges," in M.L Hunter, Jr. ed., *Maintaining Biodiversity in Forest Ecosystems*, (Cambridge, U.K., 1999), 210-233; C. Murcia, "Edge Effects in Fragmented Forests: Implications for Conservation," *Trends in Ecology and Evolution*, 1995, 10: 58-62. See Also Richard O. Bierregaard, Claude Gascon, Thomas E. Lovejoy, and Rita Mesquita, eds., *Lessons from Amazonia: The Ecology and Conservation of a Fragmented Forest* (New Haven, 2001); Larry D. Harris *The Fragmented Forest: Island Biogeograhy: Theory and the Preservation of Biotic Diversity* (Chicago, 1984).

24. P. Batáry and A. Báldi, "Evidence of an Edge Effect on Avian Nest Success", *Conservation Biology*, 2004, 18: 389-400; D. C. Lahti, "The 'Edge Effect on Nest Predation' Hypothesis after Twenty Years," *Biological Conservation*, 2001, 99: 365-74.

25. Lariviere, S. "Edge effects, Predator Movements, and the Travel-lane Paradox," *Wildlife Society Bulletin*, 2003, 31: 315-20.

26. Sarn Phamornsuwana, Effects and Solutions of Acid Rain, Website: www.geocities.com/capecanaveral/hall/ 9111/DOC.HTML "... pH is the measure used to determine whether a medium is acidic or alkaline, as measured by the ratio of the relative concentration of hydrogen ions. It is a logarithmic scale .... Most pH scales use a range from zero to fourteen. Any number below seven is considered to be acidic and above seven, alkaline. A pH from 6.5 to 8 is considered neutral."

27. Gene E. Likens, Charles T. Driscoll and Donald C. Boso, "Hubbard Brook Study," *Journal of Science*, 1996; Gene E. Likens, Charles T. Driscoll and Donald C. Boso, "Long-Term Effects of Acid Rain: Response and Recovery of a Forest Ecosystem," *Science*, April 12, 1996, 244-46; Jocelen Kaiser, "Acid Rain's Dirty Business: Stealing Minerals from the Soil," *Science*, April 12, 1996, 198; Douglas L. Godbold, Alloys Hüttermann eds., *Effects of Acid Rain on Forest Processes* (Hoboken, N.J., 1994). See also US EPA, Website: The Effects of Acid Rain on Forests epa.gov/acidrain/effects/forests.html

28. The United Nations Intergovernmental Panel on Climate Change (IPCC), *Climate Change 2007, the Fourth Assessment Report* (AR4), Working Group I, "Physical Science, The Basis of Climate Change, Summary for Policymakers (SPM)," revised February, 2007, Summary from Wikipedia, Website: http://en.wikipedia.org/wiki/Intergovernmental_Panel_on_Climate_Change.

This report concluded:
• "Warming of the climate system is unequivocal.
• Most of the observed increase in globally averaged temperatures since the mid-20th century is due to the observed increase in human greenhouse gas concentrations.

- Anthropogenic warming and sea level rise will continue for centuries due to the timescales associated with climate processes and feedbacks, even if greenhouse gas concentrations were to be stabilized, although the likely amount of temperature and sea level rise varies greatly depending on the fossil intensity of human activity during the next century.
- World temperatures could rise by between 1.1 and 6.4 °C (2.0 and 11.5 °F) during the 21st century causing sea levels to rise by 18 to 59 cm [7.08 to 23.22, shown in table 3]. There will be more frequent warm spells, heat waves and heavy rainfall. There will be an increase in droughts, tropical cyclones and extreme high tides.
- Both past and future anthropogenic carbon dioxide emissions will continue to contribute to warming and sea level rise for more than a millennium.
- Global atmospheric concentrations of carbon dioxide, methane, and nitrous oxide have increased markedly as a result of human activities since 1750 and now far exceed pre-industrial values over the past 650,000 years."

29. Tim Appenzelle and Dennis R. Dimick, "Signs from the Earth," *National Geographic Magazine* (September, 2004), 11.

30. John P. McCarthy, "Ecological Consequences of Recent Climate Change, *Conservation Biology* (April, 2002), 320. A. Menzel and P. Fabian, "Growing Season extended in Europe," *Nature,* 397: 659-60, (1999); C.D. Thomas and J.J. Lennon, "Birds Extend Their Ranges Northward," *Nature*, 399: 213, (1999).

31. *Nature*, 448: 1, 2007.

32. Leslie Jones Sauer, "Bring Back the Forests, Making a Habit of Reforestation, Saving the Eastern Deciduous Forest, *Wildflower*, (Summer, 1992), 31; John Dernbach, "What Global Warming Means for Pa.," *Sylvanian* (Newsletter of the Pennsylvania Chapter of the Sierra Club), (Summer, 2001,) 1,5. "There will be tremendous difficulties for plants to re-colonize over these distances, since following the last ice age, beeches dispersed themselves only about twelve miles per century. The movement of beeches and any other tree species will also be hampered by the fragmentation of the deciduous forest—increasingly separated by urban sprawl."

Chapter 15:
Rebuilding Natural and Social Capital (1985-2010)

1. Joseph Dlugach, telephone interview by Contosta, January 29, 2004. Interview by authors, April 17, 2004.

2. F. Markoe "Coey" Rivinus, then president of the FOW, was the liaison to the Wissahickon Rebuilding Project (WRP) and Bonnie Hay of the Wissahickon Valley Watershed Association (WVWA) was their representative.

3. Stephen Kurtz, interviews by authors, June 14 and 28, 2008. Kurtz, the owner of a major roofing company in the area, brought his extensive contracting skills to WRP for nearly a decade. The authors are indebted to Kurtz for his information and for providing the only extant records of the WRP.

4. Joseph Dlugach, Statement of Policy Regarding the Development of the Wissahickon, November, 1992: "All development [in Wissahickon Park should] be directed towards retaining the …natural features—the trees, plants, animal life, the stream, and the valley—in as close to a wilderness state as possible….It would mean no more paved roads, parking lots, ballfields, buildings, statues…[and] where indicated, existing ones [should] be removed or torn down."

5. Stephen Kurtz to David Pope, January 5, 1995, author's collection.

6. Rolf Sauer, notes on telephone conversation with Joseph Dlugach, December 17, 1986; Neil Korostoff, memorandum to Richard Nicoli, information director, Fairmount Park, November 12, 1986.

7. Joseph Dlugach, FOW Steering Committee, notice of formal formation of the conservation committee, January 14, 1991; meeting notice dated December 27, 1991; *FOW Newsletter*, Winter 1992-93.

8. David Pope, interview by authors, June 28, 2008, telephone interview July 12, 2008. The authors are indebted to Pope for his insightful summary of these years at the FOW and his detailed discussion of the administrative issues faced, as well as letters, pictures and other materials provided.

9. Edward Stainton, interviews by authors, February 12 and June 5, 2008.

10. David Pope, interview by authors, June 28, 2008, telephone interview July 12, 2008.

11. Ibid. Before sharing headquarters and one half of a director, the FOW had earlier partnered with the Chestnut Hill Historical Society (CHHS), collaborating with them on the sponsorship of conservation easements. These conservation easements expanded the program of the CHHS (preserving only house facades) into a complementary program to preserve the lands bordering the Wissahickon Creek and its tributaries.

12. Stainton interviews by authors, February 12 and June 5, 2008; Pope interview by authors, June 28, 2008, telephone interview July 12, 2008.

13. Ibid.

14. Peter Lapham, Executive Director, CHHS, interviews by David Contosta, December 9 and 17, 2003; Fairmount Ventures, Inc., "Strategic Plan for the Friends of the Wissahickon, 2002-2005," November, 2001.

15. *FOW Newsletter* (Winter 1992-93); "Wealth, Wisdom and Willingness to Work" are Paul W. Meyer's (the Morris Arboretum's Director) prescription for the makeup of a successful board.

16. David Pope, interview by authors, June 28, 2008, telephone interview July 12, 2008.

17. Peter Lapham, "Friends Receive Expansion Grant from William Penn Foundation," *FOW Newsletter*, (2002).

18. Interviews and communications with David Dannenberg, November 20, 2007, June 29 and July 3, 2008, and July 14, 2008. Interviews with Robert C. Wallis, June 12, 2008, and with Edward Stainton, February 12 and June 5, 2008.

19. The authors are particularly indebted to Robert Wallis and Antoinette Seymour, co-chairs of the FOW Deer Committee, for interviews, materials and review of relevant parts of this chapter. The authors are also greatly indebted to information provided by David Pope and Edward Stainton, the first two presidents of the reorganized FOW. Both of these board members were very actively involved in fostering the process of deer management and ensuring a successful outcome.

20. Samuel H. Tucker, telephone interview by Contosta, January 29, 2004.

21. Bryon P. Shissler, Natural Resource Consultants, Inc. to Samuel Tucker, June 1, 1992, FOW Archives.

22. Bryon P. Shissler, Natural Resource Consultants, Inc. to FOW, April 5, 1995, FOW Archives; Deer Management in the Wissahickon (flier), FOW Archives.

23. *FOW Newsletter*, Spring 1996. This debate is also covered in *Philadelphia Inquirer*, September 25, 1996; Bryon P. Shissler, Natural Resource Consultants, Inc., Report.

24. Robert C. Wallis, "Values and Communication Strategies for Achieving Consensus on Suburban/Urban Deer Density Management, *Proceedings of the Conference on the Impact of Deer on the Biodiversity and Economy of the State of Pennsylvania*, September 24-26, 1999; Minutes of the FOW Conservation Committee, October 13, 1992. See also Calvin W. DuBrock, "Managing Metro Deer," *Game News*, September 1994, 16-21.

25. Antoinette Seymour, interview by Franklin, April 15, 2008

26. *Philadelphia Inquirer*, March 6, 2001; *Chestnut Hill Local*, April 29, 1999; FOW Statement to the Planning Committee of the Fairmount Park Committee, April 14, 1998; *Philadelphia Inquirer*, March 19, 1999; *The Volunteer*, Newsletter of the Wissahickon Restoration Volunteers (Spring 2001).

27. Seymour, interview by Franklin, April 15, 2008.

28. *FOW Newsletter*, (Summer, 1998).

29. "Organizations Which Have Formally Supported or Endorsed the Resolution of the Friends of the Wissahickon to Reduce the Deer Herd," list provided to authors by Wallis.

30. Wallis, interview by Contosta, April 21, 2001, interviews by authors, January 28, 2004, and June 12, 2008; Seymour interview by Franklin, April 15, 2008.

31. Stainton, Interviews by authors, February 12 and June 5, 2008.

32. Wallis interview, June 12, 2008.

33. Seymour interview, April 15, 2008.

34. Barry A. Bessler, Chief of Staff, Fairmount Park Commission, FOW Deer Committee Meeting, February, 2008

35. USDA, *APHIS Wildlife Services Activities Summary Report, Deer Management Program,* May 2001; *Philadelphia Inquirer*, April 3, 2001. The number of deer counted has varied depending on the time of the survey and the methods used. In the winter of 2000, an on-the-ground survey by the FPC recorded 193 animals, but another count using an airplane equipped with infrared cameras, also undertaken by the park commission, came up with 295 deer. See *FOW Newsletter*, Spring 2000; USDA, *APHIS Wildlife Services Activities Summary Report, White-tailed Deer Management Program,* May 2002; USDA, *APHIS Wildlife Services Activities Summary Report, White-tailed Deer Management Program,* May, 2003; *Roxborough Review*, April 9, 2003. Wallis, telephone interview by Contosta, August 9, 2004.

36. Ibid.

37. To ensure that Wissahickon Park can maintain numbers of deer characteristic of the forest of the Lenni Lenape, without the large animal predators of the past, money must be raised yearly to pay to organize the cull, the sharpshooter and for those who process the meat. With the continuation of this program, new issues arise and need to be resolved. For example, charity organizations are increasingly demanding small packages of meat for their clients, and local meat processing companies are going out of business or cannot afford the time and effort to prepare large amounts of venison for distribution. However, in a public park, dead deer cannot be simply left to be eaten by other animals or to decay, which would create a public health hazard.

38. Ann Rhoads and Timothy Block, Morris Arboretum of the University of Pennsylvania, Report to the FOW Deer Committee on "exclosure" results.

39. Simone and Jaffe, Landscape Architects (now Simone Collins, Landscape Architects), *Wissahickon Valley Trails Master Plan* Fairmount Park Commission (Philadelphia, 1996), 4-5.

40. Ibid.

41. David Dannenberg, Interviews by authors, November 20, 2007, June 29 and July 3, 2008 and field trip, November 10, 2007. The authors are especially indebted to Dannenberg for providing the story of the Sustainable Trails Initiative and for a chronological summary of the FOW's mountain bike committee activities, along with his reviews of chapter 15 and the provision of extensive materials; David Dannenberg, Louise Johnston and David Pope, Report of the Committee to Review the Current Mountain Biking Policy in the Wissahickon, September 16, 2002; FOW Summary of Mountain Bike Committee Work and Biking Regulations in the Park, Summer 2004; FOW Board Minutes, February 1, 2000; *FOW Newsletter*, Fall 2000.

42. IMBA Trail Solutions, Website: www.imba.com/resources/trail_building/trail_solutions.html

43. Wallace Roberts and Todd (later WRT), *Master Plan Report*, Fairmount Park Commission, (Philadelphia 1983).

44. *Daily News*, June 5, 2001.

45. Mark A. Focht, NLREEP Program Administrator (now Director of the Fairmount Park system under the Philadelphia Department of Parks and Recreation), telephone interviews by authors, May 15, 2003 and January 23, 2004.

46. Fairmount Park Natural Lands Restoration and Education Program, March 4, 1996, FOW Archives; *FOW Newsletter* (Winter, 1997-1998, Winter, 2000, Winter, 2001); FPC, Natural Lands Restoration Master Plan, Volume I, General Observations, 1-3; FOW Board Minutes, February 1, 2000; *FOW Newsletter* (Fall, 2000).

47. Andropogon with Campbell Thomas and Hunt Engineering, Trail Master Plans, Fairmount Park Commission, Natural Lands Restoration and Education Program, April 2001.

48. Focht telephone interviews by authors, May 15, 2003 and January 23, 2004.

49. Ibid.

50. Leon Younger and PROS "A Bridge to the Future, Fairmount Park Strategic Plan, Executive Summary," July, 2004.

51. Ibid.

52. Focht, telephone interviews by authors, May 15, 2003 and January 23, 2004.

53. *National Geographic Traveler*, quoted in "Sustainable Philadelphia Initiative," Pennsylvania Environmental Council, Website: www.pecpa.org/node/96.

54. Ibid

55. *Philadelphia Daily News*, June 5, 2001.

56. Ibid.

57. "A Bridge to the Future: Fairmount Park Strategic Plan," Executive Summary, Younger and Pros, July, 2004.

58. Bettina Yaffe Hoerlin, Board Member, *FOW Newsletter* (Spring, 2006).

59. Philadelphia Parks Alliance, Victory for Our Parks Today, June 19, 2008. Philadelphia Parks Alliance, New Commission on Parks and Recreation, December 2008.

60. Bettina Yaffe Hoerlin, Board Member, *FOW Newsletter* (Spring, 2006).

61. Ibid.

62. Philadelphia Parks Alliance, Victory for Our Parks Today, June 19, 2008

63. "The Nutter Plan" for a Sustainable Philadelphia Environment, Introduction, (Philadelphia, 2007).

64. Ibid.

65. Philadelphia Parks Alliance, City to Convene for Community Forums to Gather Citizen Input to Inform Decisions on Budget Cuts, February 4, 2009.

66. *Philadelphia Daily News* February 27, 2009

67. *Philadelphia Inquirer*, February 1, 2008; Philadelphia Parks Alliance, FPC lease Agreement—Burholme Park & Fox Chase Cancer Center, July 25, 2006.

68. *Philadelphia Daily News*, December 10, 2008.

69. *Philadelphia Inquirer,* December 10 2008

70. Philadelphia Parks Alliance, Developments: Parkland Use & Protection, May 18, 2009.

71. Ibid.

72. *Philadelphia Inquirer*, May 20, 2009

Chapter 16:
Middle Valley Renaissance (1975-2010)

1. "Constructed by the Pennsylvania Department of Highways in the late 1950's as part of a much longer US 309 Expressway, the Fort Washington Expressway is characterized by design flaws that plague older expressways: limited sight distances, short acceleration and deceleration lanes, ... and a lack of shoulders. The first

section of the Fort Washington Expressway, from PA 63 (Welsh Road) in Ambler south to PA 73 (Church Road) in Flourtown, was completed in 1958. Included in this section was the Fort Washington interchange with the Pennsylvania Turnpike (I-276) The remainder of the expressway, from PA 73 south to PA 152 (Limekiln Pike) in Wyncote, was completed in 1960. Near the southern terminus, the 'high-speed' interchange with Easton Road was originally constructed for the unbuilt Ten-Mile Loop Expressway. In 1967, US 309 Expressway was renamed PA 309." Website: www.phillyroads.com/roads/PA-309/

2. David Froehlich, former Executive Director, Wissahickon Valley Watershed Association (WVWA), telephone interview by Contosta, June 19, 2001.

3. *Philadelphia Bulletin*, July 1, 1961.

4. Jamie Stewart and Nereee Aron-Sando, *Wissahickon Worth Preserving* (Ambler, Pa., 2007), 9.

5. *Philadelphia Evening Bulletin*, July 1, 1961, January 24, May 9, and October 24, 1965, March 26, 1976; Froehlich, telephone interview by Contosta, June 19, 2001

6. *Philadelphia Evening Bulletin*, October 14, 1971.

7. Froehlich, telephone interview by Contosta, March 3, 2004.

8. Froehlich, telephone interview by Contosta, June 19, 2001.

9. Randolph Gray, Executive Director, WVWA, interview with authors, May 15, 2008.

10. Paul W. Meyer, Executive Director, The Morris Arboretum, Interview by authors, May 12, 2006.

11. "Curated Natural Habitats" was a term coined by Jerry Lefevre, former Director of Horticulture at Tyler Arboretum, Media, Pa.

12. "Holding up a mirror to the institution" was a phase coined by William M. Klein. See Morris Arboretum, *Firmly Planted*, 23.

13. Mark B. Thompson, Associates LLC, Strategic Master Plan for Chestnut Hill College, June 1996.

14. Dagit Saylor, Architects (later SaylorGregg Architects), Master Plan Reports 2005, 2008.

15. Quote from Greenfield Foundation President Pricilla Luce, in the *Chestnut Hill Local*, February. 23, 2006.

16. *The Beacon*, May 1972 (a publication of Philadelphia Conservationists, Inc.).

17. Steven L. Nelson, Deputy Chief Operating Officer, Montgomery County, quoted in the Whitemarsh Foundation Website: whitemarshfoundation.org/farm.aspx

18. Dena Shur, "Preserving Erdenheim Farm as Open Space," *FOW Newsletter*, Winter, 2007; *The Philadelphia Inquirer*, January 2, 2001; *The Colonial*, January 11-17, 2001; Steven Brown, interview by authors, May 29, 2001; *Whitemarsh Township Residents Association (WTRA) Newsletter* (March 27, 2001); The Hill at Whitemarsh (promotional pamphlet).

19. WRTA to Dear WRTA Member, December 28, 2001; *The Chestnut Hill Local*, February 21, 2002; Kim Shepherd, telephone interview by Contosta, February 19, 2004; *Philadelphia Inquirer*, December 15, 2007.

20. This action by the Whitemarsh Township Planning Commission took place on March 13, 2001. Sean Scully, "Preservation Efforts Tame Retirement Community Concerns," *Philadelphia Business Journal*, February 11, 2005.

21. Richard F. Dye and David F. Merriman, "Tax Increment Financing: A Tool for Local Economic Development," Lincoln Land Institute Website: www.lincolninst.edu

22. Shur, "Preserving Erdenheim Farm," *FOW Newsletter* (Winter, 2007); Jeff Shields, "Philanthropist's legacy: Green space just outside Philadelphia," *Philadelphia Inquirer*, August 31, 2006.

23. On the racial integration of Carson see Contosta, *Philadelphia's Progressive Orphanage,* 189-90.

24. Ibid., 201-2.

25. Criteria for Land Use/Land Development, adopted by the Board of Trustees, Carson Valley School, November 24, 1986, Archives, Carson Valley School. For a discussion of Carson's various plans to develop part or all its campus, see Contosta, Philadelphia's Progressive Orphanage, 166-68 and 209-10.

26. Among the other top Tillinghast courses are Winged Foot, in West Chester County, New York, the San Francisco Golf Club and the Black Course at Bethpage on Long Island. See Richard C. Wolfe et al. eds., *A. W. Tillinghast: Reminiscences of the Links* (Rockville, Md.,1998). Thomas later moved to California and designed the Bellaire Country Club, the Riviera Country Club and several other great golf courses there. Thomas Road, which runs along one side of the Whitemarsh Valley Country Club, celebrates his name.

27. A Brief History, *Sunnybrook Golf Club*, courtesy of Sunnybrook Golf Club.

28. Quarry Facts, Whitemarsh Township Residents Association, May 2001.

29. *WTRA Newsletter* (November, 2001).

30. Robert Ford, assistant manager, Whitemarsh Township, interview by Contosta, March 3, 2004.

31. Simone, Jaffee, Collins, Inc., Landscape Architects (later Simone Collins, Landscape Architects), Whitemarsh Township Quarry Site, Report for Whitemarsh Township, December, 2001.

32. *Philadelphia Inquirer*, August 20, 1953.

33. Eric Brown, Head Ranger, Fort Washington State Park, interview by Contosta, June 19, 2001; "A Recreational Guide for Fort Washington State Park," Pennsylvania Department of Conservation and Natural Resources, 1998.

34. This figure for county park acreage is from the Montgomery County Planning Commission in Norristown, Pa., courtesy of Eric Jarrell.

35. Montgomery County is committed to and aggressively involved in trail planning and development. The Montgomery County Planning Commission and the Department of Parks are the offices that coordinate and implement trail proposals. In 1996, the Board of Commissioners adopted an open space plan, which proposed a trail network totaling approximately 160 miles. This plan included policies for regional trail development. Montgomery County Website: 2.montcopa.org/trails/site and Montgomery County Planning Commission, Website: mc-mncppc.org/.